£ 5.95

H6

CORPORATE FINANCIAL DISCLOSURE IN THE UK AND THE USA

Corporate financial disclosure in the UK and the USA

GEORGE J. BENSTON
Center for Research in Government Policy and Business
Graduate School of Management
University of Rochester

SAXON HOUSE | LEXINGTON BOOKS

Published by
SAXON HOUSE, D.C. Heath Ltd.
Westmead, Farnborough, Hants., England

Jointly with
LEXINGTON BOOKS, D.C. Heath & Co.
Lexington, Mass. USA

ISBN 0 347 01133 0
Library of Congress Catalog Card Number 75-36967
Printed in Great Britain by Butler and Tanner, Frome and London

Contents

Acknowledgements

This study was supported by The Institute of Chartered Accountants in England and Wales and The Earhart Foundation. Neither body directed the scope or organisation of the study or dictated or even attempted to influence the conclusions drawn. Consequently, they cannot be assumed to support or reject the study in whole or in part.

The author is most appreciative of the corrections and suggestions made by the following persons (whose affiliations are mentioned for the purposes of identification only): Harold Edey (London School of Economics), William DeWitt (Arthur Andersen, Rochester, New York), G.H. Fryer (The Stock Exchange, London), Nicholas Gonedes (University of Chicago), Robert Hamilton (University of California, Berkeley), Homer Kripke (New York University Law School), Thomas L. Holton (Peat, Marwick, Mitchell, New York), I.A. Leeson (Whinney Murray, London), D.A. Mallinson (Price Waterhouse, London), J.W. Margetts (Peat, Marwick, Mitchell, London), Bernard Maas (American Stock Exchange), Leonard Schutzman (Arthur Young, New York), J.M. Renshall (Institute of Chartered Accountants in England and Wales), Stephen Zeff (Tulane University).

Of course, they are in no way responsible for any remaining errors, nor should their kind assistance be construed as approval or disapproval of any parts of this study.

The author, alone, is responsible for the study, including errors and absurdities.

1 Usefulness of a comparison of required disclosure in the UK and the US

1.1 Introduction

The securities markets in the UK and the US, in contrast with those in most other countries, are very similar. Almost instantaneous sales and purchases can be made of securities representing claims of thousands of companies. The securities are owned and traded by a large number of individuals and institutions at prices that are made public. In these markets, as in few others, people with little expertise can instruct their brokers to buy or sell securities 'at the market' without having to do much comparative shopping and without much concern about being cheated.

Many people believe that disclosure of financial information is a major reason why the UK and US securities markets are a 'fair game' in which a large part of the public feels free to risk direct ownership of securities. Publicly owned limited liability companies whose securities are traded on the stock exchange (and, in the US, also over the counter) make their financial statements available to the public. In part, this disclosure is voluntary and in part it is mandated by the countries' securities laws and the regulations of the stock exchanges. This study is directed at outlining and comparing the financial disclosure required in the two countries and determining whether and to what extent these requirements benefit the public. The word *required* is emphasised, because it is not disclosure as such that is evaluated, but disclosure required by law and regulation. This comparative analysis should aid practitioners, consumers and government officials in both countries in deciding whether or not to change the requirements and, if change is desired, whether or not to emulate the other.

The UK Companies Acts (first enacted in 1844), which require financial disclosure of corporations, predate the US Securities Acts by almost a century. Although the corporate disclosure requirements of the US Acts were based, in large measure, on the UK Companies Acts, the two systems differ in important respects. The UK has continued a system of specific

1

disclosure of a limited number (relative to US requirements) of specific accounts while the US has created a regulatory agency, the Securities and Exchange Commission (SEC), which promulgates and enforces a large number of rules and regulations.

For a number of years there has been some agitation in the UK to move towards the type of regulatory system established in the US. (The arguments for and against such a move, which are many and varied, are considered in some detail in chapter 5). In contrast, few people in the US have called for a move towards the UK system.[1] Indeed, it is possible that many, perhaps most, people in the US who are aware of the securities markets would find it very difficult to imagine that the markets could operate efficiently and fairly were the federal Securities Acts repealed and the Securities and Exchange Commission dissolved. The over forty-year life of the Acts and of federal regulation of the securities markets spans the working and even the physical life of a large proportion of brokers, analysts, investors, financial writers, and others actively involved in 'the market'. For them, federal disclosure requirements are an accepted, almost unquestioned, aspect of ordinary business life. Those who recall the pre-SEC days may not remember that time with fondness if their memories come primarily from the 1929 stock market crash and the Great Depression. For many of them, the necessity of the federal Securities Acts is too obvious to be questioned. Partly for these reasons, the desirability of US security laws and regulatory institutions has rarely been challenged.

Perhaps because the necessity and desirability of federal regulation of corporate disclosure by the SEC is so generally accepted in the US and/or perhaps because the US financial markets and economy seem so successful, many other countries have thought seriously of emulating the US system. Among systems that require disclosure (as compared to those in which a government agency passes on the 'merits' of securities before they can be offered to the public), the US is at one extreme. The US system is characterised by an active administrative agency (the SEC) that is empowered to promulgate and enforce regulations governing the type and extent of financial disclosure by corporations. At the other extreme are the UK Companies Acts which require specific disclosure of corporations but which are not actively administered by a regulatory agency. The systems of many countries (particularly the English speaking countries) may be characterised as combinations of the US and UK systems, with Canada being closer to the US and Australia closer to the UK.[2] But the UK may be moving in the direction of the US system. Had the lapsed Companies Bill (Bill 52), proposed in December 1973, been enacted, Clause 69 would have empowered the Secretary of State '. . . to

2

prescribe by regulations the matters to be disclosed in accounts, directors' and auditors' reports and annual returns and to make different provisions for different classes of companies.' (Companies Bill 52, p. viii.)

Consequently, it would seem a good time to outline and analyse the corporate financial disclosure requirements of the UK compared to those of the US. The outline is desirable because it would otherwise be very difficult to grasp the extent to which the requirements of the two countries differ. It should also be useful to those who want an overview of the specific disclosure mandated in the US and the UK. The outline is preceded by a brief history and description of the laws and institutions that govern disclosure in the two countries concerned, in order to give the reader some indication of the present situation and how it evolved.

An analysis of required corporate financial disclosure follows the outline of the requirements. Empirical evidence that supports or rejects hypotheses about the effect and usefulness of financial disclosure as practised in the UK and the US is brought to bear whenever possible. This analysis should be useful for public policy decisions on whether and to what extent the UK should move towards the US system and vice versa.

A comparative study of the usefulness of systems in two countries is of limited value, however, if other factors so differ between the countries that one cannot separate their influence from those of the disclosure laws and regulations. Consequently, it is necessary to determine first the extent to which the UK can be compared to the US.

1.2 Similarities of institutions and markets in the UK and the US

A comparative study between countries is useful if those countries are similar in the sense that, were a procedure practised in one country adopted in the other, the results would be like those experienced in the first. While one can never really 'prove' such a contention, there is reason to believe that the UK and the US are two such countries, particularly with respect to accounting and securities markets. (Important differences are considered in section 1.3 below.)

The US and the UK are politically similar, both being representative democracies in which the rule of law is paramount and, economically, both having essentially capitalist economies characterised by private ownership of property. The financial and industrial institutions of both countries also are quite similar. Monopolies and cartels do not characterise most markets. Most of the larger companies and many of the smaller ones are publicly owned by numerous individuals. Banks are neither government owned nor controlled and, in contrast to countries such as France and Germany, they do not dominate the securities markets. The market for corporate shares is rather a public one. Prices at which securities trade are published in the press and a large number of shares are exchanged among a large number of investors daily. While there are differences in particular institutional arrangements, securities traders and investors can and do feel 'at home' in each other's securities markets.

Financial reporting and auditing in the UK and the US is also very similar. The basic accounting and auditing practices in both countries developed from a common base. Several large US public accounting firms were founded by leading UK practitioners. All large firms today have branches and/or affiliates in the two countries. The common language allowed and supported production and use of a common professional literature: consequently, accountants in both countries studied from the same or similar text books. Of course, the professional literature and the practice and education of accountants in the two countries exhibit differences that are important for some questions.[3] But, for the purposes of this investigation, the similarities are, on balance, overwhelming.

The US Securities Act of 1933 and the periodic financial disclosure requirements of the Securities Exchange Act of 1934 were also modelled on the UK Companies Acts. In both countries, disclosure rather than approval or disapproval of a security issue is the basic philosophy of the statutes. In both countries also, the stock exchanges and the public accountants' institutes impose a standard of disclosure on publicly owned companies.

However, the laws and regulations of the two countries are not the same. Since the 1930s, public accounting in the US has developed under the mandated disclosure requirements of the Securities and Exchange Commission. The regulations promulgated and the administrative practices followed by the SEC over the years have shaped accounting practices. In contrast, the UK Companies Acts, while more specific than the US Securities Acts, are not administered by an active regulatory agency that administers the Acts by drawing up, changing, interpreting and enforcing detailed regulations. These differences in two similar environments provide a 'laboratory' in which the effects of the respective regulatory systems can be studied usefully.

1.3 Differences in the institutions and markets in the UK and the US

1.3.1 Institutional differences

Although there are some institutional differences between the UK and the US, few are of consequence for this study. For example, although commercial banks cannot deal in equity securities on their own account in the US, as can their counterparts in the UK, they are active market participants for trust accounts. Another difference, the existence of over the counter markets in the US but not in the UK, is not as important as it might seem at first glance. In the US, securities may be and are sold and traded locally (virtually anywhere), in contrast to UK practice, where almost all publicly sold and traded securities are listed on The (London) Stock Exchange. However, financial disclosure by almost all larger US corporations is essentially controlled by the SEC, whether or not the securities are traded on a stock exchange or over the counter.[4] In the UK, The Stock Exchange's Quotations Department acts much like a regulatory agency, since few prospectuses can be issued or securities sold without its approval. The implications of this difference in administration are examined in chapter 5. Other administrative differences (particularly with respect to periodic reporting) are considered in chapters 4 and 5.

Another difference that should be considered is the relatively greater ownership of shares by individuals in the US than in the UK. Reliable data on the proportion of shares owned by individuals are difficult, perhaps impossible, to obtain, in part because shares are often recorded in a broker's 'street' name. The available data show that, at the end of 1969, some 68·4 per cent of US corporate stock outstanding was held by individuals (and some minor institutional investors), compared to 47·4 per cent held by individuals, executors and trustees in the UK.[5] Also, since American corporations are generally larger than their British counterparts, they obviously have a greater absolute number of owners. In addition, corporations listed at The (London) Stock Exchange tend to be more closely held than US listed corporations. The New York Stock Exchange requires that corporations have at least 2,000 shareholders who hold no less than 100 shares each. The American Stock Exchange requires listed corporations to have at least 1,200 shareholders holding 100 shares or more. In contrast The (London) Stock Exchange requires only that at least 35 per cent of a class of equity shares be in the hands of the public, with no requirement for a minimum number of shareholders.

Perhaps because of this difference in the ownership by individuals of corporate shares, interest in financial disclosure appears to have been greater in the US than in the UK. As a consequence, there is reason to believe that rules governing financial disclosures may tend to be more explicit in the former than in the latter.[6] The implications of this difference are considered further in the conclusions to this study (chapter 5).

The considerable difference in the size of the two countries has no doubt also had some impact on financial disclosure. The UK is much smaller than the US, both relatively and in absolute size. London is not only the central securities market: for most purposes it is the only market. Hence should an issuing house, broker, corporate director, chartered accountant, etc. engage in a fraudulent or even flagrantly misleading or questionable manner, the reputation of the firm or person would be damaged and perhaps destroyed. As a consequence, that firm or person would be unable to engage in future securities transactions or other activities that require fiduciary trust. In addition, the social standing of the individuals concerned would be harmed, perhaps irreparably.

In contrast, the US has a number of major markets. A broker's New York reputation might not be well known in San Francisco or Boston. Nor is the fact of a securities fraud indictment or even conviction necessarily damaging to social position. And if it is, one can always move to another, equally desirable community in another part of the country. This is not to say that one's reputation is not without considerable value in the US nor that a new person is not investigated before he is trusted with a fiduciary responsiblity. But the business and social pressures for conformity with the rules of 'proper' behaviour do not appear to be nearly as strong in the US as they are in the UK.

Similarly, UK accountants are subject to greater peer reviews than are their US colleagues. A UK chartered accountant receives his designation (and his authority to conduct statutory audits) from membership of one of the six recognised accountancy bodies. In addition, members are subject to the rules of the bodies even if they are not engaged in the practice of public accounting. US certified public accountants receive their licences from individual states. Each state determines the educational and personal qualifications and experience required of candidates. While the examination required is the same in each state and is graded centrally (with a few exceptions), the states individually determine when candidates may sit for all or part of the examination and the state authorities may assign final passing or failing grades to marginal papers. Each state also determines the conditions under which a certified public accountant (CPA) licensed in another state may move his practice. Only the states may revoke a CPA's licence or otherwise discipline him/her for inept practices, lack of integrity, breach of fiduciary responsibility, or other conduct that tends to bring dishonour to the profession to the detriment of other CPAs. CPAs need not join the American Institute of Certified Public Accountants (AICPA): about one-third are not members. Hence non-members are not subject to the AICPA's Code of Professional Ethics. Nor are CPAs subject to the SEC's disciplinary authority if they do not audit the records of a client who is subject to the Securities Acts.

The UK accounting profession's greater potential for peer review has implications for the value of explicitly versus implicitly defined accounting standards and mandated financial disclosure. Because US accountants may not have the power of their UK counterparts to control and 'punish' colleagues and resist pressure from clients who would discredit the profession, their need for explicit rules and laws may be greater.[7] This possibility must be recalled when policy recommendations are considered.

1.3.2 Legal differences

The legal environment in the two countries differs primarily in the ability of and incentives for shareholders and others to sue corporate officers, directors and public accountants. This difference is due to (a) some small differences in the interpretation of common law; (b) considerable differences in statutory law; and (c) considerable differences in the ability and propensity of third parties to sue accountants.[8]

Common law   The common law in the US and the UK is essentially the same. The accountant is liable to clients and to third parties for fraud and for gross negligence.[9] Until 1963, the primary benefits rule expressed in *Ultramares* [1931] governed the liability of accountants towards third parties for negligence.[10] The Court held that investors and other third parties could not hold accountants liable for a negligent audit if the report '. . . was primarily for the benefit of the [client] . . . for use in the development of the business, and incidentally or collaterally for the use of those to whom [the client] and his associates might exhibit it thereafter.' (*Ultramares* [1931], p. 446). This rule was applied very narrowly, so as to make the efforts of third party plaintiffs generally unsuccessful in proving that they were the primary beneficiaries of a negligent audit.

The first important change in the application of the primary benefit rule occurred in the UK, as a consequence of the *Hedley Byrne* [1963] decision. Although the House of Lords did not discuss liability for annual accounts (the case involved an accommodation credit report by a bank upon which a third party relied to his damage), the decision makes it clear that an accountant who makes a negligent, though honest, misrepresentation, may be liable for financial damages caused to a person with whom no contract exists. The counsel for the Institute of Chartered Accountants in England and Wales (ICAEW) interpreted this decision as limiting the accountant's liability to persons whom the accountant knew or ought to have known would place reliance on the statements [Council of the ICAEW, 1965]. Counsel stated that, in his opinion:

> . . . a decision by the shareholders collectively taken on the basis of negligently prepared accounts and resulting in improper payments by or financial loss to the company could result in liability. No claim by an individual shareholder, however, would succeed in respect of loss suffered through his own investment decisions made on the strength of misleading company accounts supported by an auditors' report containing negligent misrepresentations . . . (Council of the ICAEW, 1965, para. V8b.)

However, this interpretation is not unanimous in the UK. In particular, Mary Arden argues:

> . . . It would be extremely difficult for an auditor to argue that he undertook no duty of care to shareholders in respect of loss suffered as a result of individual investment decisions taken on the basis of negligently prepared accounts. It is true that he had no particular shareholder, or transaction by a shareholder, in mind when reporting on the accounts. But he undertook a duty of care to the shareholders as a body and must have known that the accounts could be used by shareholders for their personal purposes. In other words it is very possible, although the matter is not free from doubt, that an auditor owes a duty of care to individual shareholders under *Hedley Byrne* when reporting on the annual accounts. (Arden, 1972, p. 26.)

The accountant's liability with respect to prospectuses, however, does not appear to be in doubt. The Institute's counsel states:

> But if the audited accounts comprised in effect part of a document of offer, and the auditors know or ought to have known that the accounts were intended to be so used, they could be liable to third parties for financial loss suffered through reliance on a negligent auditor's report in connection with the offer. (Council of the ICAEW, 1965, para. 8b.)

8

US law is also being extended to include liability of accountants towards third parties. From his survey, R. James Gormley concludes that 'The trend suggests the likelihood either that the primary benefit rule is broadening to coincide with the foreseen person concept of the Second Restatement [American Law Institute, Second Restatement of the Law of Torts, 1965], or that the foreseen person concept is absorbing and superseding the primary benefit rule.' (1974, p. 1211).

Thus, US and UK common law is now interpreted as possibly, perhaps probably, supporting damage suits against accountants for negligence by shareholders, investors, and other third parties who use published financial statements for investment decisions. There seems little doubt that accountants who certify financial statements for inclusion into prospectuses used to sell shares are liable for negligence towards investors.

Statutory law Despite the common law similarities, considerable statutory law differences exist between the statutory treatment of accountants' liability in the two countries. The UK statutes add very little to the common law. The Companies Act 1948 prohibits companies only from indemnifying their auditors against liability as a consequence of any negligence, default, breach of duty or breach of trust (section 205).[11]

In the US, the Securities Act of 1933 and the Securities Exchange Act of 1934 made significant alterations to the common law. As interpreted in the BarChris case [*Escott v. BarChris Construction,* 1968], section 11 of the 1933 Act does away with the requirement of privity of contract between the auditor and the investor as a condition of recovery by the investor. The auditor who has examined and reported upon the financial statements contained in a securities registration (and has consented to their use therein) is also deprived of his most important common law protection in suits by third parties. All an investor need do to maintain a suit against the auditor is prove that the statements contained a material omission or misstatement. For his defence, the auditor must prove 'due diligence', i.e., that after reasonable investigation he had reasonable grounds to believe, and did believe at the time the registration statement became effective (declared by the SEC to be available for public use), that the financial statements were true. It should be emphasised that the auditor's responsibility continues to the time the statements became effective even though this is after completion of the audit and preparation of the report.

Section 11 of the 1933 Act applies only to purchases of securities in offerings. Section 10b of the 1934 Act and SEC rule 10b-5 extends to periodic statements the auditor's liability for making any untrue statement or omission of a material fact. Though the rule was originally adopted to prohibit (in the words of section 10b) 'any manipulative or deceptive device or contrivance . . . in connection with the purchase or sale of any security', it has been interpreted by the courts as applying to auditors. As Gormley (1974) concludes: '. . . auditors whose opinions are used in connection with a sale or purchase of securities are exposed to potential liability in private suits under rule 10b-5 even though they did none of the purchasing or selling and realized no profit in any securities transaction' (p. 1220). He also observes: 'Since 1968 [when the Texas Gulf Sulphur case was decided] the term 'in connection with' has been construed broadly enough so that audit opinions and audited or unaudited financial statements with which auditors became associated may, along with other corporate statements and information, be statements "in connection with" purchase and sales of the corporation's securities by investors, even though . . . not in a prospectus or in a purchase or sale of the corporation's securities' (p. 1221). He concludes, however, that '. . . it is reasonable to require a plaintiff in a rule 10b-5 suit against independent accountants to prove more than ordinary negligence in connection with . . . financial statements, audited or unaudited' (p. 1222).

The US accountant is thus somewhat more vulnerable to suits claiming misrepresentation and negligence in the preparation of periodic statements than is his UK counterpart, and he is considerably more vulnerable than a UK accountant with respect to financial statements included in prospectuses registered with the regulatory agencies. The most important difference in the legal environment between the two countries, however, is the likelihood that aggrieved third parties will sue accountants.

Ability and propensity of third parties to sue accountants It is much easier and more profitable for investors and other third parties to sue accountants for damages in the US than in the UK. In the US a derivative action suit may be filed by aggrieved minority shareholders against the officers and directors. Should the shareholders win, the amounts recovered are paid by the defendants to the corporation, and the plaintiffs and their attorney may be awarded legal costs and attorney's fees (the latter being an important motivation for such suits). In the UK a similar action can be taken under the 'fraud on a minority' exception to the rule in *Foss v. Harbottle*[12] but this exception has been applied very restrictively. Hence the Jenkins Committee (1962) recommended that the Companies Act should give the courts express power 'to authorize proceedings to be brought against a third party in the name of the company by such person or persons and on such terms as the Court may direct.' (Para. 206, p. 76.) But this change has not yet been enacted. In addition, the UK Companies Act 1948 does not support a suit against an issuer of securities for a false prospectus as does the US Securities Act of 1933. And while there is reason to believe that the UK Prevention of Fraud (Investments) Act 1958 would support a suit similar to the rule 10b-5 actions in the US, there have been very few such suits.

In the US the shareholder's ability to succeed in a derivative suit is limited by a number of technical requirements, including a subtle (and some claim often almost unworkable) requirement of proof that the injury be to the corporate entity itself and not to the individual shareholders in their individual capacities. If the latter is found to have been the case, a derivative action will not be allowed. Although this inability to demonstrate the validity of a derivative action suit is not unusual, US investors still have tremendous procedural advantages over their UK counterparts by virtue of the class action suit under Rule 23 of the Federal Rules of Civil Procedure. Even though the scope of these suits has been reduced and the costs of maintaining them increased by recent Supreme Court decisions,[13] they can still be a potent weapon.

Although the shareholders' derivative suit and the class action have a number of technical and often strategically important differences between them, the similarities are much more significant. In each case the purpose of the procedure is to allow a large number of persons with possibly small injuries to be compensated in one action. Without the availability of these procedures, no single injury might promise sufficient recovery to warrant bringing the suit. By aggregating a large number of similarly situated parties in one action, however, the total amount recovered is often quite substantial. Even so, the *pro rata* recovery to any member of the group may often be very small, and the problem remains of motivating someone to initiate such action. Here one of the most striking differences between US and UK legal practices prevails. In the US, if the shareholders are successful in a derivative action suit, the court will award a substantial legal fee to the successful attorney; in a class action suit, the initiating member of the class may arrange, with the approval of the court, for the attorney to recover a contingent fee (that is a specified percentage of any amount recovered in the action).

Even if a class action is allowed in the UK, the practice of 'taxing' unsuccessful litigants for costs and not allowing contingent legal fees is a powerful disincentive to law suits. Thus, while lawsuits are common in the US, it is rare for UK shareholders to sue corporate directors, officers and accountants. In the US, then, a significant part of the total enforcement of the security laws results from private actions, rather than from those initiated by the SEC, since the courts have held that violations of most federal securities laws are admissible as bases for private civil actions. Indeed, the Commission has on occasion specifically mentioned the use of private actions as the preferable mode of enforcement.

Thus US statutory law and the practice of contingent legal fees make suit against a public account much more likely in the US than in the UK.

1.4 Conclusion

Although these two major differences – institutional (primarily with respect to greater peer pressure towards conformity with accepted behaviour in the UK) and legal (with respect to the greater likelihood of legal action against accountants in the US) – somewhat reduce the usefulness of an inter-country comparative study, they do not invalidate it. In some ways the two differences offset each other. While it is much more difficult to sue offending directors, officers and public accountants in the UK than in the US, the size and traditions of the UK substitute informal sanctions for formal legal procedures. These informal sanctions may be more effective than the formal legal actions that can be effected in the US. The considerable similarities in the two countries must also be considered. Thus, while it is necessary to keep the differences in mind, the conclusion is that an inter-country comparison and analysis is still meaningful.

Notes

[1] A notable exception is Henry G. Manne (1974) and earlier work cited therein.
[2] If the Corporation and Securities Industry Bill under consideration in the Australian Parliament is enacted, Australia will move closer to the US system.
[3] See Lee Siedler (1969) for some interesting observations.
[4] Essentially, only intra-state owned corporations and corporations with less than $1 million in assets and 500 or fewer holders of a class of equity securities are not regulated by the SEC.
[5] US data: Securities and Exchange Commission (1972), p. 151; UK data: John Moyle (1971), p. 11. The latest date of available UK data is 1969.

12

[6] See Benston (1975) for an analysis of differences in the explicitness of accounting standards in the US and the UK.

[7] A further discussion is presented in Benston (1975).

[8] The following discussion is taken from Benston (1975a).

[9] The accountant's liability for failure to meet his specific contractual obligations to a client is not considered since it is no different than is anyone's obligation to fulfil a contract. Neither is consideration made on the accountant's liability towards third parties for fraud or gross negligence amounting to constructive fraud, for which accountants in both countries are liable.

[10] See R. James Gormley (1974) for a more complete discussion and for citations that support the description given here. See also Tom Hill (1972) for a discussion of the accountant's liability under the laws and regulations of the US and the UK.

[11] However, a company may indemnify the auditor against liabilities incurred in his defence if judgement is found in his favour (section 205b) and the court may relieve him of liability if it believes that he acted honestly and reasonably and ought fairly to be excused (section 448). Furthermore, Arden (1972, p. 207) believes that a company could agree to indemnify auditors against liability towards parties other than the company.

[12] See A.J. Boyle (1969) for a fuller discussion.

[13] *Eisen v. Carlisle and Jacquelin et al.,* 94 S.Ct. 2140 [1974], and *Zahn v. International Paper,* 94 S.Ct. 505 [1973].

2 Brief history and outline of laws and institutions governing disclosure

2.1 Disclosure laws

2.1.1 UK company law and the City Code

The basic laws that require financial disclosure in the UK are the Companies Acts, 1948 and 1967. These laws require a company with limited liability (with some exceptions) to issue a prospectus upon the public offer for sale of securities, to make an annual return listing information about share capital and members, and to file prescribed documents with the Registrar which the public may inspect, to keep 'proper books of account' and to lay before the members at least annually a director's report, balance sheet, and profit and loss account, together with an independent auditor's report. Other laws and quasi-laws affecting disclosure of financial data (other than The Stock Exchange Rules and the Institutes of Chartered Accountants statements, discussed in sections 2.2 and 2.3 below) are the Prevention of Fraud (Investments) Act 1958 and the City Code on Take-overs and Mergers.[1]

The first Companies Act was the Joint Stock Companies Act of 1844, which allowed incorporation with unlimited liability by registration.[2] The legislation required surprisingly contemporary standards of financial disclosure. Books of account were to be kept and audited, and a 'full and fair' balance sheet was to be prepared, sent to shareholders and filed with the Registrar of Joint Stock Companies. However, an income and expense report was not required nor were the form or contents of the balance sheet or the duties of the auditor specified. General registration with limited liability was introduced in 1855. The Joint Stock Companies Act 1856 abandoned the compulsory accounting and auditing requirements of the 1844 and 1855 Acts for most companies, requirements that were not replaced until 1900.[3]

The general philosophy of the period was that a company's financial affairs were a matter of concern only to its shareholders and their employees, the managers and directors. The Companies Act 1856 contained model sets of articles of incorporation which included provisions for accounts, audits and statements, but companies were not obliged to adopt the articles. Penalties could be imposed on company officers for misfeasance. It was established (around 1895) that auditors were officers of a company within the meaning of the (then current) Companies Act, and as such they could be sued if they failed to observe the duties called for in the articles and if their neglect injured the company. Creditors, it was felt, would look to the reputations and assets of the proprietors of companies with unlimited liability and the designation 'limited' would warn them to investigate carefully the condition of limited liability companies. In addition, there were legal sanctions against fraud. These were strengthened by the Prevention of Frauds Act of 1857, which made it an offence for company directors, officers or managers to falsify or tamper with the books of account or make or circulate a false financial statement with intention to defraud a creditor or investor. (Exceptions to the *laissez-faire* philosophy of the nineteenth century were the audit and reporting requirements imposed on certain types of companies by Parliament. Such companies included railways, and insurance companies, banks and deposit, provident and benefit societies, where a failure would cause losses to the general public.)

The Companies Act 1900 made an annual audit obligatory for all registered companies, although a requirement compelling public filing of statement in the form of balance sheets was not made law until 1904.[4] However, private companies (whose shares are held by no more than fifty members, are not offered to the public, and whose transferability is restricted), introduced in this act, were exempted from the public filing provisions (but not the auditor requirements) on the grounds that their affairs were not a matter of public concern.[5] (This exemption continued until enactment of the Companies Act 1967.)[6] The next significant requirement affecting accounting did not occur until 1928/29, when the Companies Act made presentation of a profit and loss account to shareholders mandatory for the first time. The provisions of this law were also applied to prospectuses (even when the shares were issued through underwriters), for which an auditor's report on three years' profit was required. However, the profit and loss reporting requirements were not specified: in particular, the legislation was silent with respect to the use of secret reserves. Even so, explicit requirements were introduced for disclosure of loans to directors and officers, directors' remuneration, etc.

In general (as Harold Rose (1965) points out), legislation was passed in reaction to specific scandals that created public demands for 'reforms'.

For example, the failure of the Royal British Bank in 1856 was followed by the Prevention of Frauds Act 1857 and the Joint Stock Banking Act 1858. A rash of insurance company failures led to the Life Assurance Companies Act of 1870 and the collapse of the City of Glasgow Bank in 1878 was followed by the Companies Act 1879. Although the Companies Act 1928 requirement for publication of profit and loss statements (consolidated into the Companies Act 1929) was recommended by the Greene Committee in 1926, the Royal Mail case (which in 1931 revealed the use of secret reserves to manipulate income statements) was a key event which resulted in a change in accepted practice that greatly increased the meaning of reported net income.

The Companies Act 1947 (consolidated into the Companies Act 1948) marked the beginning of the 'modern era'.[7] In contrast with most previous Companies Acts, its provisions were concerned more with the needs and rights of stockholders and investors with respect to a management over which they were presumed to have little control than with protection of creditors or reaction to a specific scandal.[8] The Cohen Report, on which the Act was based, stressed the desirability of disclosure for stockholders and society in general and rejected the earlier (predominantly nineteenth century) philosophy that a company's affairs were primarily a matter of contract among shareholders.

Among other important new features, the 1947 Act required consolidation of subsidiaries, disclosure of trading companies' reserves and of directors' interests, and clarified the position of auditors. The Act also restricted the class of companies which were not required to file audited balance sheets and income statements with the Department of Trade and Industry (then the Board of Trade) to private companies with non-corporate members. These companies were required to register a statement in lieu of a prospectus on ceasing to be a private company.

The Companies Act 1967, which supplemented rather than replaced the 1948 Act, followed (by several years) an extensive review by a Committee chaired by Lord Jenkins (Report of the Company Law Committee, 1962). Not all of the recommendations of the Committee were adopted. However, most of the more important suggestions for accounting changes were included in the Companies Act 1967. The most striking of these was the required disclosure of sales (turnover) where the company is a member of a group or when sales (turnover) was in excess of £50,000 (amended in 1971 to £250,000), rents of land, emoluments of chairmen, directors (where turnover was over £7,500), and principal employees, and political and charitable contributions. The Act also abolished the exemption of the 'exempt private companies' who previously were not subject to the annual filing requirements.

At the present time, the Companies Acts 1948 and 1967 are the statutes governing the preparation, audit and publication of accounts. Only the 1948 Act refers to new issues of securities. The annual reporting provisions of the Acts apply to all limited companies whether or not their shares are closely or widely held. Specific items to be disclosed (such as particulars of share capital, reserves, amount of investments by type etc.) are expressly listed. The auditors' duties, qualifications, responsibilities and rights are stated. However, the accounting requirements of the Acts are not limited to the specifically mentioned items. The letter and spirit of Companies Acts is rather that companies shall keep '. . . such books as are necessary to give a true and fair view of the state of the company's affairs and to explain its transactions' (Companies Act 1948, section 146(2)).

The Acts apply to all companies with limited liability, whether widely held or not. In 1975, 598,000 companies not in liquidation were registered.[9] Of these, 15,500 were public companies, about 27 per cent of which were listed on The Stock Exchange. The prospectus requirements[10] of the Companies Act 1948 apply to all securities offered to the public. However, such an offer is usually made in conjunction with obtaining a Stock Exchange listing. While the number is subject to a large amount of variation, currently the securities of some 120 companies are newly listed each year (about 4,150 companies are listed in total). Unlike the situation in the US, prospectuses are not required for rights offerings or other issues that are in all respects similar to securities previously listed. Furthermore, many instruments are considered 'securities' in the US, though not in the UK. For example, interests in petroleum wells, limited partnership interests, investment plans, and a wide variety of other instruments are considered 'securities' in the US and are thus subject to prospectus requirements.

Finally, take-over bids, mergers or acquisitions for stock or cash are subject to the City Code on Take-overs and Mergers (as well as the Rules of The Stock Exchange). These guidelines were promulgated as a result of public concern about the propriety of actions taken by parties to mergers. A panel on take-overs and mergers was formed under the auspices of the principal financial institutions of the City to devise guidelines for take-overs and merger bids. All parties to these bids (as specified in the Code) are required to adhere to the guidelines and to submit their proposals to the panel who can object privately and, if need be, publicly. With respect to reporting and auditing, the Code relies essentially on the existing Stock Exchange regulations (discussed below), although additional disclosures may be requested if the panel thinks they are required.

2.1.2 US state and federal law

In contrast with the history of securities regulation in the UK, US laws were enacted later and are more restrictive. The first securities legislation in the US was passed by the state of Kansas in 1911, followed by twenty-two additional states (primarily southern and western) in the next two years.[11] This legislation was motivated by the 'populist' sentiment in these states. People distrusted the eastern bankers and speculators who, it was felt, were cheating trusting country folk out of their hard earned dollars. Indeed the title for the legislation, 'blue sky laws', comes from the description of promoters as people who 'would sell building lots in the blue sky.' Consequently, the first blue sky laws required registration of securities that would be offered for sale to state residents and gave a state administrator the power to determine whether or not a security should be sold. After World War I the eastern states also passed laws that regulated the sale of securities, though most of these were not as restrictive as the earlier blue sky laws. Today, all states except Connecticut have laws that require registration for stock issues offered exclusively to state residents. All but a few states (most notably, New York) require registration whether or not the securities are subject to the federal Securities Act of 1933.

The state laws vary in their legislation approaches. Three categories may be distinguished: (a) regulation of brokers, dealers and investment advisers; (b) fraud statutes; and (c) registration of securities. Most states' laws include two or three of these objectives. The first two categories are broadly similar to the provisions of the UK Prevention of Fraud (Investments) Act 1958. The provisions for registration of securities may be further categorised into (a) 'merit' regulation and (b) 'disclosure' requirements. Merit regulation is used in some form and to some degree by most states. This legislation empowers a state administrator to deny permission for a security to be offered to state residents if he believes that the potential purchasers might be defrauded or might otherwise lose their investments. Section 306a of the Uniform Securities Act, which has been adopted in whole or part by a majority of states, empowers a state administrator to issue a stop order or not accept a registration statement if he finds that: (a) the offering would constitute a fraud on the purchaser; (b) the underwriting and selling discounts are unreasonable; (c) promoters' profits or participation are unreasonable; or (d) amounts or kinds of options are unreasonable. In other states, administrators can deny registration if they find that: (a) the issuer is in any way dishonest; (b) the issuers' affairs are in unsound condition; or (c) the business of the issuer is not based on sound business principles. Some additional states require their administrators to find that the securities offered for sale are 'fair, just and equitable' and 'not working (constituting) a fraud'.[12] The other states require some form of disclosure of financial information, underwriters' fees and commissions, etc., but do not judge the merits of the securities issued.

Federal legislation was first enacted in 1933 with the passage of the Securities Act. This applies only to securities that are not sold or traded entirely within a state. Like the state statutes, the Securities Act of 1933 governs disclosure upon the offer for sale of securities. Prior to the stock market crash of 1929 and the Great Depression of the early 1930s, agitation to enact a federal law regulating securities was not effective. However, many people, in and out of Congress, associated the 1929 crash with the Depression and believed that the securities industry was, in some way, responsible for the losses borne by investors and the bad state of the economy in general. Although little evidence was presented to show that inadequate and/or misleading disclosure was associated with subsequent losses to investors, the belief in the necessity for and efficacy of merit regulation was strong. A number of bills that sought to establish a federal blue skies law and commission were introduced and strongly supported in Congress. Nevertheless, President Roosevelt rejected merit regulation and introduced a disclosure statute. In his message to Congress, he described the philosophy of the Securities Act of 1933 as follows:

> There is, however, an obligation upon us to insist that every issue of new securities sold in interstate commerce shall be accompanied by full publicity and information, and that no essentially important element attending the issue shall be concealed from the buying public.
> This proposal adds to the ancient rule of *caveat emptor* the further doctrine 'let the seller also beware.' It puts the burden of telling the whole truth on the seller. It should give impetus to honest dealing in securities and thereby bring back public confidence.

Thus the Securities Act of 1933 is characterised as 'a disclosure statute'. It sought to protect investors by requiring that prospectuses be filed which included specified financial data audited by independent public accountants.

The Securities Exchange Act of 1934 required periodic financial statement disclosure of corporations for the first time. Originally, the regulations applied only to corporations whose stock was traded on registered exchanges or who had registered securities under the Securities Act of 1933 and had over $2 million in assets. (The Act also provided for the registration of stock exchanges and securities dealers and brokers.) Unlike the UK, not all publicly traded securities are listed on a stock exchange. A large portion of the stock in publicly held corporations is traded on the over the counter market, which is highly decentralised. Securities of local corporations may be traded only in their areas, while a large number of more well-known over the counter securities are traded regionally or nationally. However, in 1964 the Securities Exchange Act of 1934 was amended to apply to all corporations (where stock is not owned entirely by residents of a single state) that have over $1 million in assets and a single class of equity securities that has over 500 holders – before 1 July 1966, 750 or more holders – (Section 12). Thus the Securities Acts now essentially apply to all but small or intra-state owned corporations. But, unlike the Companies Acts in the UK, the large number of small, privately owned, companies with limited liability is not required to make their accounting reports public.

The Securities Acts of 1933 and 1934 are similar to the UK Companies Acts in calling for disclosure of information in prospectuses of underwriters' commissions and other issuing fees and expenses, contracts with, emoluments to, and interests of management and directors, balance sheets, and profit and loss statements for prior years certified by independent public accountants, etc. The Acts also include provisions that are broadly similar to those outlined in the City Code on Take-overs and Mergers and fraud provisions similar to those contained in the Prevention of Fraud (Investments) Act 1958. However, the US Securities Acts go beyond the provisions of the UK laws in many respects, most notably in the greater detail required (see chapter 3) and in requiring quarterly earnings reports and monthly reporting by companies of 'significant' events.

Aside from their wider scope, the US Securities Acts differ importantly from the Companies Acts in three interrelated regards. First, the primary purpose of the Securities Acts is to provide information for investors in contrast with the basic stewardship approach of the Companies Acts. (Chapter 3 illustrates this difference.) Second, the Securities Exchange Act of 1934 created a commission, the Securities and Exchange Commission (SEC), to administer the securities laws actively. Unlike the Companies Acts, which require disclosure of specific items and additional disclosure as required to give a 'true and fair view', the US statutes state that the financial statements shall be '. . . in such detail and in such form as the Commission (SEC) shall prescribe.' Third, the disclosure requirements drawn up by the SEC greatly exceed those contained in the Companies Acts. (The extent of the detail required is also outlined in chapter 3.) These three associated conditions (discussed further in chapters 4 and 5) have resulted in disclosure far more extensive and expensive (for government and corporations) than that required in the UK.

The Securities Act of 1933 also applies to a much wider range of instruments and securities issues than does the Companies Act 1948. Firstly, the term 'securities' has been held to apply to a very wide range of ownership instruments. A 'security' is defined in Section 2(1) to mean:

> . . . any note, stock, treasury stock, bond, debenture, evidence of indebtedness, certificate of interest or participation in any profit-sharing agreement, collateral-trust certificate, preorganisation certificate or subscription, transferable share, investment contract, voting-trust certificate, certificate of deposit for a security, fractional undivided interest in oil, gas, or other mineral rights, or, in general, any interest or instrument commonly known as a 'security', or any certificate of interest or participation in, temporary or interim certificate for, receipt for, guarantee of, or warrant or right to subscribe to or purchase, any of the foregoing.

In addition, a considerable number of rulings and body of case law has extended the definition. Secondly, the prospectus requirements apply to all issues of securities, whether or not an identical security was previously registered.[13] During the fiscal year 1973, 3,744 registration statements were filed with the SEC and 3,285 became effective (some of which were filed in the previous year).[14] Of the 3,744 registration statements filed, 1,309 were by companies filing with the Commission for the first time. Many of these issues were secondary offerings, exchanges for securities, and other transactions not considered security sales but which would require a prospectus in the UK. The number of securities that fall into these categories is not given. However, an indication of their magnitude may be seen by considering that 43 per cent of the dollar amount of effective registrations were securities offered for cash to the general public by corporations. An unknown proportion of these were identical to securities already traded. Thus a large proportion of the prospectuses registered would not have been required under similar circumstances in the UK.

However, the coverage of the Securities Exchange Act of 1934 with respect to companies subject to the law is not as great as that of the Companies Acts, since smaller companies with limited liability (those with less than $1 million in assets and 500 holders of a class of equity) are not required to register with the SEC or to file periodic statements. In 1973, some 10,000 companies filed about 50,000 reports (annual, quarterly and current) with the SEC, a number far less than the 500,000 plus filed with the Department of Trade.

Finally, the Securities Acts make it rather easy to sue accountants and others who sign financial statements. The litigant need not prove that he was misled or even saw the allegedly misleading financial statement. The accountant must rather demonstrate either that the statement is not misleading and that he could not reasonably have known that the figures presented were fraudulently prepared, or that the litigant in fact suffered no damage.[15]

2.2 Administration of the laws

2.2.1 UK Department of Trade (DT)

The financial statements prepared in accordance with the Companies Acts are filed with the Registrar of Companies, where they are open to public inspection. Administration of the Acts is the responsibility of the Department of Trade (DT), formerly the Board of Trade and the Department of Trade and Industry. It has the power to instigate investigations, appoint inspectors, require corporate officers to produce books, documents and themselves as requested by the inspectors, and bring proceedings in the name and on behalf of shareholders.[16] The Acts also give the DT (and the Director of Public Prosecutions and Lord Advocate) the power to make summary judgements on all matters punishable by fines.

Flexibility in administering the Acts is provided by giving the DT the power to adapt the disclosure provisions to the circumstances of individual companies (Companies Act 1948, section 149).[17] The 1948 Act also gives the DT the power to 'alter or add to the requirements of this Act as to matters stated in a company's balance sheet, profit and loss account and group accounts . . .' (section 454[1]). However, the section goes on to state that: 'No regulation shall be made under sub-section [1] of the section so as to render more onerous the requirements therein referred to . . .'

Despite the power given to the DT, it functions primarily as a repository for company reports and only secondarily as an enforcement agency, rather than as a regulatory agency (in the US sense). Although from time to time it (and its predecessors, the Board of Trade and the Department of Trade and Industry) issues statutory instruments which clarify or extend the Companies Acts, it has not issued regulations and extensive interpretations of the Act (unlike the Securities and Exchange Commission in the US). Nor does it routinely examine the reports filed with it or systematically verify that all limited companies have filed reports as required by law.[18] Rather, as the Jenkins Committee reported (with approval): '. . . except where fraud or misfeasance is in question and damage has been caused, they do not ordinarily proceed to prosecution unless requests to the company to comply with the Act have been made and failed' (paragraph 505).

In addition, the police fraud squad may conduct an investigation leading to prosecution under the Prevention of Fraud (Investments) Act 1958. In general, though, the 4,150 listed companies whose shares are publicly traded are 'supervised' by The Stock Exchange, since its rules are more extensive than those imposed by the Companies Acts and since it may deny listing approval if it finds a prospectus inadequate.

2.2.2   US Securities and Exchange Commission (SEC)

The Securities and Exchange Commission (SEC), which administers the Securities Act of 1933, the Securities Exchange Act of 1934 and four other laws that regulate public utilities, trust indentures, investment companies and investment advisers, is an independent agency functioning as a quasi-judicial, quasi-legislative and administrative body. The Commission consists of five members, appointed by the President (who also designates the chairman), each serving a staggered five-year term. The Commission is served by a professional staff of lawyers, accountants, engineers, security analysts, and examiners, who in turn are supported by clerical and other personnel. In the fiscal year ending 30 June 1973, the SEC spent about $30·3 million (of which 73 per cent was collected in fees) and employed some 1,556 people in the Washington headquarters, regional offices in nine cities and branch offices in eight other cities.

In contrast with the UK Companies Acts, the US Securities Acts require corporations to report directly to the SEC and only indirectly to shareholders. The Securities Act of 1933 requires that registration statements be filed with the SEC and that most of the data be contained in a prospectus to be given to potential purchasers of securities in advance of a solicitation. The Securities Exchange Act of 1934 requires that annual and other reports [10-K, 10-Q, 8-K, etc.] be filed with the SEC where they may be inspected by the public. However, the SEC's regulations (14A and 14C) with respect to the proxy requirements of the Act (section 14a) require companies to send annual reports, including financial statements, to stockholders in advance of meetings. The regulations also extend the SEC's control over the contents of financial statements sent to stockholders. Rule 14a-3 (as amended from 1 March 1967) states that a company must note and explain any material differences between the statements presented to shareholders and those filed with the SEC. Although the SEC does not specify the form of the reports made by management to security holders, Rule 14a-3 effectively puts the contents of the statements under the control of the SEC.[19]

It is important to emphasise that the SEC is much more than a repository for prospectuses and periodic reports. It serves (as does the DT to a limited extent) as an enforcement agency with respect to the laws. It undertakes investigations, administrative proceedings, civil cases and injunction actions. Cases that require criminal prosecution are referred to the Justice Department.[20]

Of greater importance with respect to disclosure, the Securities Acts delegate extensive rule-making power and responsibility to the Commission. Sections 19a of the 1933 Act and 13b of the 1934 Act give the SEC the power to prescribe

> . . . the items or details to be shown in the balance sheet and the earnings statement, and the methods to be followed in the preparation of reports, in the appraisal or valuation of assets and liabilities, in the determination of depreciation and depletion, in the differentiation of recurring and nonrecurring income, in the differentiation of investment and operating income, and in the preparation, where the Commission deems it necessary or desirable, of separate and/or consolidated balance sheets or income accounts . . .

In general, the SEC has not used this power extensively, but has rather followed the generally accepted practices followed by the accounting profession. However, although it has not been an active force for change (until recently), the SEC has actively prevented experimentation and departures from 'generally accepted accounting principles'. Although disclosure rather than approval is the philosophy of the Securities Acts, the SEC has taken the position that:

> . . . where financial statements filed . . . are prepared in accordance

with accounting principles for which there is no substantial authoritative support, such financial statements will be presumed to be misleading or inaccurate *despite disclosures* contained in the certificate of the accountant or in footnotes to the statements provided the matters involved are material. (SEC Accounting Series Release No. 4, 1938, italics added.)

The SEC prepares forms that list the specific items that registrants must disclose. Specific forms are provided for corporations in particular circumstances, such as mining corporations in the promotional stage, closed-end investment corporations, oil and gas interests, certain real estate companies, etc. Until 1940, the accounting regulations that governed reporting were contained in the instructions for the forms. In 1940, the SEC published Regulation S-X, which contains the regulations that pertain to all financial statements. Regulation S-X has been rewritten several times since then, most recently in 1972. The SEC also publishes statements which contain additional regulations, opinions and suggestions. For the period up to October 1975, these Accounting Series Releases number 178, of which some 77 may be considered currently relevant. Rulings in court cases and the SEC's official decisions in administrative proceedings also govern disclosure.

The SEC has done more than promulgate regulations and rules governing the form and content of financial reports and then receive and make these reports available to the public. Although the Securities Acts and the SEC's annual and other reports proclaim the statutes 'disclosure laws', and although the SEC requires that each prospectus contain on its face, in block letters, the warning 'these securities have not been approved or disapproved by the Securities and Exchange Commission nor has the Commission passed upon the accuracy or adequacy of this prospectus. Any representation to the contrary is a criminal offense', the staff of the agency may effectively block registrations which they believe to be misleading, incomplete or inaccurate. They may issue a deficiency letter or 'Memorandum of Comments' with an implied threat that they will issue a stop order to prevent the registration from becoming effective if the registrant does not comply with their views. Since securities cannot be sold until a registration is effective (i.e. accepted by the SEC), the SEC acts much like the Quotations Department of The (London) Stock Exchange, with the exception that it is much larger, more formal and slower. (The effects of the administrative differences between the US and UK are considered more extensively in chapter 5.)

This difference in administration coupled with other factors increases considerably the cost of securities regulation in the US as compared with the UK. The other factors include the much wider scope of the prospectus requirements of the Securities Act of 1933 and the US legal system and provisions of the Act which make suit against accountants and others who participate in a registration very much easier. Another factor is the role of The Stock Exchange and issuing houses in 'screening' prospectuses. These are discussed next.

2.3   Stock Exchange regulations and issuing house supervision

2.3.1   The UK

Stock Exchange regulations are particularly important since there is no over the counter market in the UK.[21] Hence, with a few exceptions, quotations are available only for securities admitted for Stock Exchange trading, making virtually all public companies subject to the Exchange's rules and supervision. Thus in the UK The Stock Exchange is the primary regulatory agency for public companies, particularly with respect to prospectuses, since its rules are more extensive than those of the Companies Act 1948.

In many important respects, The Stock Exchange's disclosure requirements have been greater than those of the Companies Acts and were imposed before the Acts made them applicable to all limited companies. The Stock Exchange's rules also reflect the philosophy of their times. Until 1914 The Stock Exchange's listing requirements were minimal.[22] The basic rule was *caveat emptor.* To obtain a quotation a company had only to satisfy The Stock Exchange Committee that the issue was of marketable magnitude with respect to number of shareholders and lack of impediments to settlement. World War I brought a temporary closing of The Stock Exchange and Treasury requirements that all bargains be marked and recorded. Even though some rules for admission to the lists (imposed to meet Treasury regulations) were continued after the war, the first disclosure requirements were not adopted until 1930. Formulation and adoption of these requirements was stimulated by the legislative activity of 1928 and 1929, the Hatry crash (in which stock certificates were forged), and the 1928/29 boom in which, according to the MacMillan Committee, (1931, p. 166) capital issues sold in 1928 showed a loss of at least 47 per cent by 31 May 1931.

The 1930 rules required prospectuses to reproduce a copy of the last audited accounts and auditors' report, together with any notes required to be published by an Act of Parliament relating to the company. In 1945 The Stock Exchange required annual accounts to include consolidated figures and in 1948 this requirement was extended to prospectuses. This provision was not enacted for companies generally until the Companies Act 1947, which was consolidated into the Companies Act 1948.

The next major change occurred virtually at the same time as the passage of the Companies Act 1947. The Stock Exchange rules and regulations adopted in May 1947 were substantially the same as the requirements of the 1948 consolidating Act's 4th Schedule (which now is the governing statute). In May 1954 a section calling for disclosure of directors' emoluments was added to the rules and regulations. Annual reporting of sales turnover, analysed geographically, was added in 1965. (The Companies Act 1967 extended a somewhat similar requirement to all limited companies.) However, The Stock Exchange's requirement of semi-annual reports, adopted in 1965, was not included in the Companies Act 1967. Although previously a company was subject only to The Stock Exchange rules in force at the time it was first listed or issued additional shares, The Stock Exchange now requires companies to abide by changes in the listing agreement made after the date of signing.

Because The Stock Exchange emphasises requirements for listing rather than trading, its rules with regard to prospectuses in particular are more extensive than those of the Companies Act 1948. Until March 1973, The Stock Exchange required audited financial statements for ten years. The requirement now agrees with the five-year provision of the Companies Act 1948. However, The Stock Exchange usually insists on statements that relate to five years of *meaningful* operations. The Stock Exchange's Quotations Department reviews and approves (or disapproves) the figures presented and, in so doing, is not restricted to a mechanical checking of the 'rules'. Their approach is rather to require all information that appears necessary for investors to make an informed judgement about the shares they are asked to purchase. In this regard, The Stock Exchange relies on the requirements of the issuing house[23] and sponsoring broker (who both have their reputations to protect) and the professional accounting bodies.

The role of the issuing houses and brokers who sponsor a new listing is important since the Prevention of Fraud (Investments) Act 1958 makes direct sales of securities by someone other than a recognised Stock Exchange dealer or issuing house very difficult. In addition, the compactness and personal relationships that characterise the UK securities market make the reputation of issuing houses an important factor in the success of an issue. Consequently, The Stock Exchange (and government authorities) rely on the issuing houses to check carefully the background and history of a company they sponsor. The issuing houses also usually require disclosure and auditing requirements of companies that go beyond the law or The Stock Exchange's rules. For example, prospectuses often include forecasts of sales turnover and profits (which are allowed but not required by The Stock Exchange). When a company has been audited by a small or medium-sized firm of chartered accountants, it is also usual for a well-known firm of chartered accountants to be appointed additionally as reporting accountants to sign the report jointly with the auditor.[24] This practice is not followed in the US, although it is not unusual for a company 'going public' to engage a national or large regional firm of CPAs where it previously used the services of a small firm that did not have experience with SEC filings.

Since the prospectus prepared by the issuing house must be printed on no more than two newspaper pages, the document is not long by US standards. Additional data is filed with the Quotations Department and may be inspected by the public at the offices of the company's lawyer or other adviser acting on the issue, usually in the City of London. Essentially, though, potential security holders are presented with a brief, summarised statement of past history, present status and prospects, and, in effect, rely on The Stock Exchange's review and on the integrity and judgement of the issuing house and the accountants who sign the report.

2.3.2 The US

Because state legislation required disclosure of only a limited amount of financial information upon offers for sale of securities and generally did not require periodic reports, it is often assumed that disclosure as it is known today was not widespread until passage of the federal Securities Acts. However, such is not the case. The principal stock exchanges – the New York and American – required audited statements of listed companies. While the extent of disclosure was not as great as that which evolved under the SEC, the items given were, for the most part, as extensive as those now required by the Companies Acts. For example, an examination of data published by New York Stock Exchange (NYSE) listed companies in *Moody's Manuals* (Benston, 1969b, p. 519), revealed that, in 1926, all provided balance sheets and income statements, of which 82 per cent indicated audits by certified public accountants. All the balance sheets separated current from non-current assets and liabilities. On the income statements, all reported net income, 55 per cent revealed sales (turnover), 45 per cent the cost of goods sold and 71 per cent depreciation. By 1933 (before passage of the Securities Exchange Act 1934 appeared possible), these percentages had risen to 62 per cent for sales (turnover), 53 per cent for cost of goods sold, and 93 per cent for depreciation, and 94 per cent of the companies indicated audits by CPAs. Given that the New York Stock Exchange accounted for 70 per cent of security transactions on all exchanges and that the American Stock Exchange (and possibly the others) had disclosure rules similar to those in force at the New York Stock Exchange, it is fair to conclude that disclosure in the United States, on the whole, did not await legislative action. In this regard, it is important to restate the fact that periodic disclosure requirements were not applied to over the counter companies until after 1964.

One might ask why federal legislation was imposed despite the fact that most stock exchange listed companies published standard, audited financial statements. One reason may be the agitation throughout the 1920s by such writers and economists as William Z. Ripley (1927) who accused publicly-owned corporations of giving the public dishonest and deceptive financial reports. Stephen A. Zeff reports that a 1926 article by Ripley resulted in widespread consternation, marked by a decline in the stock market and one of President Coolidge's rare reported utterances [Zeff, 1972, pp. 119–20]. As a result of the Depression, hearings were held by the US Senate in 1933 and 1934 on the allegations made by Ripley and others. A survey of the seventeen volumes of the 1934 hearings which preceded the imposition of periodic disclosure requirements revealed only two instances of alleged dishonest and deceptive reporting (Benston, 1969a, pp. 52–3). Furthermore, prior to 1934 there were very few cases on record in which companies or accountants were charged with issuing fraudulent financial statements (Benston, 1969a, pp. 54–5). Thus, while some fraudulent or misleading financial statements may have been prepared prior to the imposition of legal standards in 1934, there is little evidence of such practice.

In part because of agitation for change in the 1920s and in part because more widespread ownership of securities created a demand for data that appeared more reliable, the NYSE increased its interest in disclosure in 1926, with the appointment of a full-time executive assistant (J.M.B. Hoxsey).[25] In 1930, the NYSE began a cooperative venture (headed by George O. May) with the American Institute of Certified Public Accountants (AICPA, then the American Institute of Accountants), to formalise acceptable accounting and auditing policies and practices. In 1932, the Committee outlined five 'principles' on which audited statements should be based. (In 1934 a sixth was added and the 'principles' were adopted by AICPA.) In 1933, the NYSE adopted the requirement (already followed by almost all companies) that applications for listing be accompanied by an auditor's certificate and applicants agree to send annual audited financial statements to their shareholders.

Since the advent of federal disclosure requirements, the stock exchanges have played a minor role with respect to annual statements and prospectuses. Instead they have concentrated on day-to-day and even hour-to-hour disclosure by corporations of events that may be of material significance to investors (as does The (London) Stock Exchange). Their emphasis has been on assuring investors that these events are publicly announced so that 'insiders' do not have the opportunity of benefiting from the news before others.

The issuing houses (investment bankers, brokers, etc.) also play a considerably less important role in the US than in the UK with respect to financial disclosure. The SEC's regulations on prospectuses are not only extensive, but also restrictive. At present, sales (turnover) or profit forecasts[26] and current values of assets[27] cannot be included in the prospectus or related material, since the SEC is very sensitive to the appearance of 'puffing' by issuers of securities. Indeed, the SEC's conservative approach and the legal liability should a prospectus appear over-optimistic is so pervasive that prospectuses are almost always very detailed, rather pessimistic documents. To avoid delays and litigation, the efforts of the issuing houses (with respect to disclosure) are directed largely towards meeting the requirements of the SEC's regulations and avoiding any language in the prospectus upon which a law-suit might be based.

2.4 Professional accounting associations

2.4.1 The UK: The Institute of Chartered Accountants in England and Wales (ICAEW)[28]

The role of the professional accounting bodies has become stronger since the recent (June 1972) adoption by The Stock Exchange of the following provision: 'The Council supports the accountancy bodies in the formulation of their Accounting Standards, and expects reports to be prepared in conformity with those standards. Any significant departure therefrom must be disclosed and explained.' (The Stock Exchange (1974), chapter 3, para. 6, p. 63.) While The Stock Exchange (and the Companies Acts) previously relied expressly on the auditor's judgement of what constituted a 'true and fair view' of the state of a company's affairs, The Stock Exchange now explicitly supports the ICAEW's (and the other accounting bodies') rule-making power.

Although, with minor exceptions, public accountants must be members of one of the accountancy bodies whose members are recognised as possessing qualifications in auditing by the Companies Act 1948, the accountancy bodies themselves have not been nearly as active in rule-making as have their counterparts in the US. Before 1942 (when the Taxation and Financial Relations Committee of the ICAEW was founded), pronouncements on accounting and auditing concepts and procedures were not made.[29] Between 1942 and 1953 the Council of the English Institute approved fifteen 'Recommendations on Accounting Principles'. These recommendations (which were not binding on the members of the Institute) dealt with such subjects as income tax charges, disclosure of reserves, consolidated accounts, the content of balance sheets and income and expense statements, depreciation, valuation of stock in trade, accounting for changing price levels and accounting reports for prospectuses. From 1953 to 1969, fourteen additional recommendations were issued, of which four replaced earlier ones. Topics covered included two on which the Council of the English Institute disagreed with the position taken by the Research and Publications Committee of the Institute of Chartered Accountants of Scotland – accounting for investment grants and the treatment of unrealised capital gains by investment trusts.

The recommendations published were, as their title indicates, only recommendations. It was not mandatory that chartered accountants follow them. Rather, as the usual introductory paragraph to the recommendations states: 'Whilst it is recognized that the form in which accounts are submitted to shareholders is [subject to compliance with the Companies Act] a matter within the discretion of directors, it is hoped that the Recommendations will be helpful to members in advising, in appropriate cases, as to what is regarded as the best practice.'

The English Institute's position with respect to auditing was similar. As Zeff (1972) puts it, before 1960 the English Institute's Council '. . . felt that official guidance on auditing would be an improper intrusion into the sphere of the auditor's professional judgement' (p. 26). However, this approach changed somewhat during the 1960s. Since 1961, the Council has issued nineteen statements on auditing procedures.

In 1969 the ICAEW's approach to pronouncements on accounting practices also changed. Partly as a result of several highly publicised events that led financial journalists to 'wonder' how different accountants could report different profit amounts for what appeared to be the same event, and partly because it was moving in that direction anyway (though perhaps rather slowly in the opinion of some), the ICAEW in association with the other accountancy bodies formed an Accounting Standards Steering Committee (ASSC) in 1970.

In contrast to the usual introduction to the recommendations, the 'explanatory foreword' to the Statements of Standard Accounting Practice prepared by the ASSC and issued by the ICAEW states that:

> The Council expects members of the Institute who assume responsibilities in respect of financial accounts to observe accounting standards.
>
> Where this responsibility is evidenced by the association of their names with such accounts in the capacity of directors or other officers the onus will be on them to ensure that the existence and purpose of standards are fully understood by non-member directors and other officers. They should also use their best endeavours to ensure that standards are observed or, if they are not observed, that significant departures from them are disclosed and explained in the accounts. The effect of such departures should, if material, be disclosed unless this would be impracticable or misleading in the context of giving a true and fair view.
>
> Where members act as auditors or reporting accountants the onus will be on them not only to ensure disclosure of significant departures but also, to the extent that their concurrence is stated or implied, to justify them.
>
> The Council, through its Professional Standards Committee, may inquire into apparent failures by members of the Institute to observe accounting standards or to disclose departures therefrom. (1975, paras. 3–6.)

However, paragraph 8 states that: 'Accounting standards are not intended to be a comprehensive code of rigid rules.' The following paragraph then qualifies the paragraphs quoted above, and paragraph 10 concludes: 'In judging exceptional or borderline cases it will be important to have regard to the spirit of accounting standards as well as to their precise terms, and to bear in mind the overriding requirement to give a true and fair view.'

By the end of January 1975 the ICAEW had issued fifteen exposure drafts which cover such topics as accounting for mergers and acquisitions, extraordinary items, stocks and work in progress, value added tax, deferred taxation, inflation, the contents of a required funds statement, accounting for research and development, and accounting for depreciation. Two discussion papers – inflation and accounts, and corporation tax under the imputation system – were also published. Ten of the fifteen exposure drafts were converted into Statements of Standard Accounting Practice: 'Accounting for the Results of Associated Companies'; 'Disclosure of Accounting Policies'; 'Earnings per Share'; 'The Accounting Treatment of Government Grants'; 'Accounting for VAT'; 'Extraordinary Items and Prior Year Adjustments'; 'Accounting for Changes in the Purchasing Power of Money';[30] 'The Treatment of Taxation Under the Imputation System in the Accounts of Companies'; 'Stock and Work in Progress'; and 'Statements of Source and Application of Funds'.

2.4.2 The US: The American Institute of Certified Public Accountants (AICPA)

The role of the AICPA in the US is broadly similar to that of the present position of the Institutes of Chartered Accountants (England and Wales, Scotland and Ireland) in the UK. In one important respect, however, the influence of the UK institutes is greater, since an accountant must obtain and maintain membership of an Institute in order to use the title 'chartered accountant'.[31] In the US membership of the AICPA is voluntary, since the CPA certificate is granted by the individual states. (About two-thirds of US CPAs and virtually all partners of large firms are members.) Nevertheless, the creation of the SEC In 1934, with the power to make and enforce accounting rules, gave the AICPA (the then American Institute of Accountants) considerable derivative *de facto* power over accounting and auditing procedures. Rather than develop its rules by itself, the SEC has until recently relied heavily on the AICPA's own 'self-regulation'.[32] Thus the AICPA, as the principal non-government authoritative body, in effect has had considerable power to prescribe accounting disclosure and measurement. Recently, however, the AICPA's powers have been delegated in large measure to the Financial Accounting Standards Board (FASB), whose pronouncements are now considered by the SEC as authoritative (Accounting Series Release No. 150, 1973).

Although creation of the SEC, with its power to prescribe accounting practices and disclosure, no doubt acted as a considerable spur to the AICPA, the Institute's concern predated the passage of the Securities Acts.[33] In 1917, the Institute endorsed an influential memorandum, 'Approved Methods for the Preparation of Balance Sheet Statements'. In

1929, this memorandum, rewritten and entitled 'Verification of Financial Statements', was approved by the Council of the Institute and endorsed by the Federal Reserve Board. As the discussion above indicated, a series of discussions and exchange of letters with the New York Stock Exchange in the late 1920s and early 1930s led to the formal adoption of a memorandum of six rules or principles in 1934. However, there is no doubt that the existence of the SEC and the policy of its chief accountant that it was preferable for the AICPA to promulgate its own accounting rules and principles was instrumental in the greater activity of US accounting institutes compared with those of the UK.

Over the years the AICPA has adopted a fairly long series of accounting releases and pronouncements. The Committee on Accounting Procedure, created in 1936 and enlarged in 1938, issued fifty-one Accounting Research Bulletins (ARBs) until it was disbanded in 1959. As is the case with the ICA's 'Recommendations on Accounting Principles', the ARBs suggest rather than demand specific practices and, on occasion, allow that several alternative methods are acceptable. However, unlike the ICA's recommendations, the AICPA's ARBs generally had the force of the SEC behind them. Also, as was not the case with the ICA, the SEC could veto or change an opinion. One example of this is the Committee on Accounting Procedure's failure, because of SEC opposition, to issue an ARB in 1950 that accepted upward revaluation of assets in a quasi-reorganisation, despite its unanimous approval by the Committee (Zeff, 1972, p. 156–7).

In 1959 the Accounting Principles Board (APB) was established because of dissatisfaction with the 'progress' of the Committee on Accounting Procedure. Unlike its predecessor, the APB commissioned research projects that were supposed to lead to pronouncements. However, less than half the pronouncements were preceded by published studies. Before its replacement in 1973 by the Financial Accounting Standards Board (FASB), the APB issued thirty-one opinions and four statements. The major opinions covered topics such as investment credit, funds statements, leases, reporting the results of operations, income tax allocation, convertible debt, earnings per share, business combinations, intangible assets, investments in common stock, accounting changes, and interest on receivables and payables. These opinions were not always universally accepted. Opinion No. 2, on investment credit accounting, was rejected by some of the eight major firms and the SEC, and was partially rescinded by Opinion No. 4.

In the main, the thrust of the APBs was to eliminate or at least reduce alternative accounting methods for what appeared to be the same transaction. This approach was dictated, in large measure, by the criticism the profession received from the financial press, lawsuits against CPA firms and pressure from SEC Chairman Manuel Cohen. Nevertheless, the criticism continued, directed largely at the accounting practices of conglomerates and other firms who grew by mergers and acquisitions, and of land development and real estate companies. In addition, the number of lawsuits filed against accountants with accompanying news stories increased. In part because of these pressures, the APB was scrapped in 1973 in favour of a new body, the Financial Accounting Standards Board (FASB), which is autonomous and independent of the AICPA and endowed with a large budget and the determination to reduce the area of choice among alternative accounting practices. In its first three years (up to and including 1975), the FASB has issued nine Statements of Financial Accounting Standards ('Disclosure of Foreign Currency Translation Information'; 'Accounting for Research and Development Costs'; 'Reporting Accounting Changes in Interim Financial Statements'; 'Reporting Gains and Losses from Extinguishment of Debt,; 'Accounting for Contingencies'; 'Classification of Short-Term Obligations Expected to be Refinanced'; 'Accounting and Reporting by Development Stage Companies'; 'Accounting for the Translation of Foreign Currency Transactions and Foreign Currency Statements'; and 'Accounting for Income Tax – Oil and Gas Producing Companies') and six interpretations (three on APB Opinions 20, 21 and 8 and three on FASB Statement No. 2, 'Accounting for Research and Development Costs'). In addition, two exposure drafts are outstanding ('Financial Reporting in Units of General Purchasing Power'; and 'Accounting for Leases').

Furthermore, the adoption of Rule 203 of the restated Code of Professional Ethics approved by the AICPA membership in 1972 requires that 'A member shall not express an opinion that financial statements are presented in conformity with generally accepted accounting principles if such statements contain any departure from an Opinion of the Accounting Principles Board which has a material effect on the statements taken as a whole.'[34] An exception is allowed if the member believes that the statements would otherwise be misleading, in which event the departure and its effects must be disclosed: but the onus is on the accountant to justify the deviation from the opinions. The SEC's requirement that published statements either conform to SEC filings or state the reason and effects of non-conformity similarly imposes uniformity of accounting methods on financial statements. In many respects, the current situation in the US with respect to a move towards uniformity is similar to that in the UK: the FASB is similar to the ASSC (aside from its budget and its independence from the AICPA); the AICPA requires general observance by accountants of its pronouncements, as does the ICAEW; and the SEC, along with the American and New York Stock Exchanges, requires that certifying accountants rarely depart from the generally accepted accounting principles formulated by the AICPA, the FASB and the Commission's regulations. A major difference exists, however, in the way the different bodies view and administer their rules and regulations. In particular, the existence of the SEC and the legal situation in the US (discussed in section 1.2) and perhaps the much larger size and consequent diversity of the US, has led the accounting profession towards greater uniformity than obtains in the UK.

2.5 Overall conclusions

2.5.1 The UK

The Companies Acts and The Stock Exchange rules, which govern financial disclosure in the UK, evolved from three somewhat overlapping basic forces. One was specific major scandals and/or business failures that resulted in an apparent public demand for laws that would prevent or at least anticipate the perceived situation. A number of the earlier Companies Acts were so motivated. A second force for extending disclosure is greater public interest in company accounts as a result of more widespread public ownership of companies. The Stock Exchange's increasing disclosure requirements since World War II are influenced by this factor. Finally, the belief that disclosure is desirable for the general economic and social needs of the nation resulted in some specific disclosure requirements of the Companies Act 1967, such as the sections calling for disclosure of charitable and political contributions, exports and sales turnover by country.

It is important to note that while the Companies Acts 1948 and 1967 and The Stock Exchange rules prescribe disclosure of specific items, the form of disclosure and the definition of what constitutes a 'true and fair view' of a company's state of affairs as reflected by its balance sheet and profit and loss accounts (other than is required by the Acts) is not specified. Rather it is the responsibility of the directors, auditors and (with regard to a prospectus) the issuing houses and managing brokers to present financial statements that are 'true and fair'. In this regard, the ICAEW recommended a series of auditing and reporting practices. However, the principal factor that 'regulates' the quality of financial statements is the integrity of chartered accountants, the issuing houses, brokers and The Stock Exchange.

2.5.2 The US

State regulation of publicly owned corporations in the US preceded federal legislation by some twenty-two years. The early state 'blue skies' laws, first enacted in 1911, were 'merit' statutes which required the approval of a state commissioner before securities could be offered to state residents. Federal legislation was not passed until 1933. Before this time, however, almost all companies listed on the major stock exchanges published balance sheets and profit and loss statements prepared from audited accounts certified by independent public accountants. One reason for the greater disclosure in the US than in the UK before enactment of the Securities Exchange Act of 1934 was probably the greater involvement in the stock market of the US public.

Federal legislation was modelled on the UK Companies Acts with one very important exception: a regulatory agency, the SEC, was created with the power to prescribe accounting and auditing methods and draw up and administer specific disclosure rules and forms. Before securities can be offered to the public (with some exceptions), the SEC must accept the issue for registration. No such provision is made in the Companies Acts. As a consequence, disclosure in the US is much more explicit, of much greater scope and detail, and much more uniform and restrictive than that in the UK. Although the Securities Acts are called 'disclosure statutes', the SEC has increasingly taken an active role in deciding the manner and extent of disclosure. Its administrative procedures are also more cumbersome, time- and resource-consuming than those followed by The (London) Stock Exchange.

The legal system in the US (discussed briefly in section 1.2) has also played an important role in the extent and cost of disclosure, as has liability under the Securities Acts. Consequently, there is much greater emphasis in the US on presenting prospectuses and financial reports that meet the letter of the law and give few grounds for suit, even at the expense of not communicating valuable information to investors. While slavishly following the SEC's regulations is not a complete defence against adverse legal actions, it still helps. As a result, the scope for exercise of professional judgement by independent accountants is more limited in the US than in the UK.

Whether or not the US system provides more gross benefits to the public than the UK system and whether, net of costs, one system is preferable to the other is the concern of chapters 4 and 5. In the next chapter, a detailed (though not complete) outline of the financial disclosure required in each country is therefore presented to give the reader an overview and comparison of the situation in the two countries.

Notes

[1] Additional legislation (i.e., the Protection of Depositors Act of 1963) regulates specific types of companies.

[2] For a more complete history, see H.C. Edey and Prot Panitpakdi (1956). See also H.C. Edey (1956) and Harold Rose (1965), pp. 20–23.

[3] Various Acts before 1900 (including the Companies Act 1856) imposed accounting and auditing requirements on banking and insurance companies and deposit, provident and benefit societies.

[4] Since the Act did not state that the statement must be current, some companies filed the same balance sheet each year.

[5] The Companies Act 1948 continued this exemption from filing annual reports only for 'exempt private companies', defined (broadly) as private companies with no corporate shareholders.

[6] All private companies are still exempt from filing prospectuses.

[7] As with previous acts, the Companies Act 1948 consolidated the Companies Act 1947 and the previous consolidating act (Companies Act 1929).

[8] However, the eighth schedule, paragraph 27, may reflect a delayed reaction to the Royal Mail case.

[9] Source of figures: Economic Statistics Division of Companies.

[10] The financial documents and data required to be given or made available to prospective purchasers of securities are indicated in the 'prospectus requirements' referred to. Other aspects of the formal requirements of the Companies Act, 1948, the Securities Act of 1933 and The (London) Stock Exchange are not considered.

[11] For a more extended description of state regulations of securities, see James S. Mofsky (1971) and *Commerce Clearing House Blue Sky Law Reporter* (current).

[12] See Mofsky (1971), p. 27, note 3.

[13] Since 1971, secondary offerings and conversions of shares for convertible securities and warrants of large 'seasoned companies' who qualify to use Form S-16 can incorporate financial statements previously filed by reference (see pp. 76–7).

[14] Source of figures: Securities and Exchange Commission, 39th

Annual Report, 1973 (1974), pp. 163–5.

[15] Under Section 11 of the 1933 Act, the accountant is liable only as an expert and, therefore, only for the portions of the registration statement within his expertise.

[16] The last provision was added by the Companies Act 1967 (Section 37(1)).

[17] 1948: refers to the Companies Act, 1948.

[18] In 1971, inspectors (10 of whom were previous appointees) were appointed for 24 companies, 517 charges for failure to forward annual returns were filed, 15 charges for failure to keep proper books and 13 for fraudulent trading (Department of Trade and Industry, 1972).

[19] Kellogg and Poloway (1971) note that 'The SEC's position under Rule 14a-3 is so strong that it can and has forced companies to revise and re-mail financial statements contained in stockholders' reports.' (Para. 3154, p. 467.)

[20] In 1973, 27 administrative proceedings related to disclosure cases were instituted, 145 injunctions were ordered, 654 defendants enjoined and 49 cases referred to the Justice Department for a variety of causes. (Securities and Exchange Commission, 39th Annual Report, 1973 (1974), p. 170.)

[21] Some trading is made directly among financial institutions, bypassing The Stock Exchange completely.

[22] Much of the following history is taken from A.F.B. Cooke (1954).

[23] An issuing house in the UK is analogous to an underwriter or investment banker in the US. It provides the services required for a company to issue shares to the public, including underwriting the issue, if desired.

[24] There are no requirements in The Stock Exchange rules or the Companies Acts for the expression of opinion by reporting accountants in a prospectus as to the truth and fairness of the financial information given in their reports. However, the reporting accountants are directly responsible for the information given in their reports, and the practice is now developing of expressing an opinion thereon.

[25] This narrative is based on the account given by Zeff (1972, pp. 119–26).

[26] On 2 February 1973 the SEC indicated that it would permit some registrants to include economic forecasts in prospectuses and reports, subject to regulations [Release Nos. 5362 and 9984]. These regulations have not, as yet, been issued.

[27] In a recent case (*Gerstle v. Gamble-Skogmo*) the SEC asserted that current market values must be disclosed in the textual material of a proxy

statement dealing with a merger where the data are necessary for shareholders to make an 'informed' judgement.

[28] This section emphasises the activities of the English Institute (ICAEW) to conserve space. The other accountancy bodies – the Institute of Chartered Accountants of Scotland, the Institute of Chartered Accountants in Ireland, the Association of Certified Accountants and the Institute of Cost and Management Accountants – who are associated with the English Institute in the Accounting Standards Steering Committee, are also of considerable importance. See Zeff (1972, pp. 1–90) for details.

[29] See Zeff (1972, pp. 7–49) for an extended discussion of the development of accounting principles and pronouncements.

[30] The provisions of this SSAP (No. 7) are not binding.

[31] Membership of a specific institute limits, somewhat, the designation that an accountant may append to his name in the area of another institute's jurisdiction. Members of the Institute of Certified Accountants may also engage in public practice.

[32] See the quotation from the Accounting Series Release No. 4, 1938,pp. 2–17 cited on pp. 24–5.

[33] See Zeff (1972, pp. 110–268) for a full history of the role of the AICPA in the development of accounting methods.

[34] The rule also applied to opinions of the Financial Accounting Standards Board.

3 Requirements for specific financial disclosure – a comparative outline

3.1 Introduction and overview

Disclosure requirements in the UK and the US differ primarily in two regards: (a) US requirements are more detailed and specific and allow less scope for judgement by companies and auditors; and (b) an administrative agency, the SEC, monitors the disclosure requirements in the US, which leads to costs and perhaps benefits that are not present in the UK. The first of these regards is considered in the present chapter, the second in the following chapters.

3.1.1 The UK

In the UK all companies with limited liability are required by the Companies Acts to appoint an auditor and prepare annual audited accounts. A few special requirements apply to specific types of enterprises, such as insurance and deposit taking companies. Stock Exchange listed companies are also required by the terms of their listing agreements to disclose additional material. In practice in the UK, all information disclosed by publicly owned companies is presented to all stockholders, debenture holders and others entitled to attend the annual meeting in the form of periodic reports. In the US, reports made to the SEC are not sent to stockholders, although they are available to them at the SEC's offices or by subscription to a copying service (Leasco). However, the SEC is moving in the direction of requiring that information presented to it also be sent to all security holders.

Four statements are required by current UK legislation: a directors' report, auditors' report, profit and loss account and balance sheet. Although the directors' report is not reported or commented upon by the auditors, they almost always review the document to ensure that it does not contain misleading or contradictory statements. If the directors do not make the appropriate corrections, the auditors may qualify their report.

In addition, as in the US, a funds statement is required in accordance with SSAP 10 (July 1975).

Neither the Companies Acts nor The Stock Exchange rules prescribe a format for the reports. Rather the statutory rule provides that: 'Every balance sheet of a company shall give a true and fair view of the state of affairs of a company as at the end of its financial year, and every profit and loss account of a company shall give a true and fair view of the profit and loss of the company for the financial year.' (Companies Act 1948: 149(1)). Although the phrase 'a true and fair view' is basic to the disclosure requirements of the Acts, it is not defined explicitly, nor is there recent case law that provides a definition. However, it is generally understood to require accounts that present a layman's definition of 'a true and fair view' of specific circumstances, within the constraint that financial statements are not expected to report completely current realisable or other definitions of economic values.

Nevertheless, the Companies Acts (and, to a much lesser extent, The Stock Exchange rules and ICAEW pronouncements) require disclosure of specific items, outlined below. The Companies Act 1967, Schedule 2 (which replaced the 8th Schedule of the Companies Act 1948) specifies the financial information that must be presented. Sections of the 1948 Act, particularly those relating to group accounts, are also important. With respect to prospectuses for listed companies, The Stock Exchange's requirements are most important.

Finally, general price level adjustments (not specific adjustments to current market prices) are strongly suggested, though not required, by SSAP 7, 'Accounting for Changes in the Purchasing Power of Money'. The index number adjustment procedures suggested there are being followed by a number of publicly held companies.

3.1.2   The US

In the US, the Securities Exchange Act of 1934 is the principal statute governing periodic disclosure. Virtually all larger companies with more than 500 shareholders and 1 million dollars of assets (and some other issuers of instruments defined as securities plus stock exchange members, brokers and dealers) must file reports with the SEC. An initial report is made and annual, quarterly and other special reports update the information recorded in this.

The instructions and rulings governing the reports required by the SEC (Rappaport, 1972 and Kellogg and Poloway, 1971) contains 1,217 and 929 pages of descriptive and instructional material directly related to the accounting requirements of the Securities Acts and Regulation S-X. Nevertheless, practising accountants generally find it inadequate and not sufficiently up to date. Consequently, they subscribe to one or more services that updates the SEC's regulations and rulings and reports on current cases. The large CPA firms also maintain their own 'services' and files. Thus the outline that follows cannot be read as anything more than a very brief and necessarily incomplete description of US disclosure requirements. For reasons of length, the requirements described are those for the majority of companies: excluded are the specialised forms and instructions prescribed for banks and insurance companies, utilities and others who report to federal agencies, real estate companies, mining companies, exchange members, brokers and dealers, etc.

The form and content of the financial statements is governed primarily by the SEC's Regulation S-X. Since the SEC requires that financial statements be prepared in accordance with generally accepted accounting principles (GAAP) and supported by authoritative pronouncements where they deviate from or are not covered by the SEC's rules, regulations and releases, the opinions of the AICPA and the FASB are also important determinants of the content of financial statements. The stock exchanges' rules, in general, are less extensive that Regulation S-X.

General price level accounting is still at the decision stage in the US. An FASB Exposure Draft published in December 1974 reviews the procedures, but no decision has been reached by the FASB or the SEC as to what form, if any, price level adjustments should take. Therefore, at present, only a few US corporations publish such numbers in their financial reports.

3.1.3 The effect of auditing and legal differences on reports

Some differences in auditing practices should be mentioned here. In the US, the AICPA's 'Statement on Auditing Standards' and the SEC's guidelines effectively mandate specific practices. In contrast, auditors in the UK are less constrained. They are expected to use their professional judgement in determining the extent to which audit procedures are necessary to support their opinions as required by the Companies Acts.[1] In both countries, the standards are essentially those accepted by the profession, though in the US an important role is also played by the SEC and the courts. Specific differences between the countries include the following. Independence is defined specifically in the US, where an auditor signing a report for the SEC is precluded from ownership of *any* stock in or book-keeping work for the company audited. In the UK, the auditor may hold a financial interest in or provide record-keeping and tax services for a client, but may not use privileged information to deal in the client's securities. The UK auditor is not required to confirm receivables and observe the procedures for inventory verification physically, as he must in the US. However, these practices are common in the UK and, if the items are material, may be required to justify the auditor's opinion on the reports. A change in the application of an accounting principle having a material effect is mentioned in the auditor's report in the US, but in the UK need not be mentioned if there is sufficient disclosure in the accounts. In both countries, though, a divergence between the client's statements and a 'generally accepted accounting principle' (in the US) or a 'standard accounting practice' (in the UK) is explained in the auditor's report. If sufficiently material, the divergence could result in an adverse or qualified opinion.

Some differences in legal practices which influence reporting should also be mentioned. The capital accounts, in particular, are affected. No par shares and treasury shares (with the exception of some redeemable preference shares) are not permitted in the UK. The Companies Acts also require that any surplus over par value be credited to a non-distributable share premium account. However, this account may be charged with preliminary expenses, commission paid or discount allowed on a debenture issue, premium paid on a redemption of preference shares or debentures or for paying up fully paid up shares to be issued as bonus shares. In the US equity related amounts would usually be charged against retained earnings and non-equity accounts would be charged or credited to income immediately or over time. More important legal differences are the liability of auditors to clients, security holders and third parties (discussed in section 1.2), and the auditors' liability for unaudited financial statements. The latter is a specific instance of the much greater legal liability of auditors in the US. In the UK, auditors are generally not responsible for statements to which they did not append an audit report, particularly if they make a specific disclaimer. In the US the situation is, at best, unclear. Auditors may be liable for statements if they are in any way 'associated' with them, whether this association is explicit or not. In general, the provisions of the Securities Laws, allowance of contingent legal fees, and class and derivative action suits in the US increases the auditor's concern for legal action. This concern tends to increase his reliance on rules laid down by official and semi-official agencies as a defence against lawsuits that question his professional expertise and judgement in potentially ambiguous situations.

3.1.4 Outline of disclosure requirements

The balance of this section is devoted to an outline of the specific items required by each country to be disclosed by companies,[2] which will give the reader an overview of the similarities and differences between UK and US reporting requirements. But it is not sufficiently complete to be used as a check list. Particularly with respect to US requirements, such a list would require an entire book. Reference to the laws, regulations and accounting institute pronouncements are therefore given to enable the reader to find and review the exact wording and context of the requirements.

In the outline, UK requirements are presented first because US requirements are generally inclusive and more extensive than those of the UK. The similar US requirements are then compared to UK specifications and additional requirements are listed.

Annual reporting requirements are presented first. Both countries require annual balance sheets (see section 3.2) and profit and loss accounts (section 3.3). Some information presented in the US in these statements is given in the directors' report in the UK. For comparative purposes, directors' report items are listed with the other balance sheet and profit and loss account items. Group (consolidated) accounting applies to the statements required in both countries (section 3.4). In the US, the SEC also requires statements of stockholders' equity and sources and applications of funds (working capital), and, since 1975, a similar statement is also required in the UK (section 3.5).

US companies must report figures for the current and previous year.[3] In the UK, comparative figures are mandated and companies must explain why material items that appear in the previous report do not appear in the current report. (This practice is usually followed in the US.) Both countries also require explanation of significant accounting principles followed, particularly with respect to stock (inventory), investments, fixed assets, consolidations, and significant departures from pronouncements (other than recommendations) of the Institutes of Chartered (or Certified Public) Accountants. Audited annual reports in the UK must be issued within eight months of the end of the financial period in question.[4] The Stock Exchange requires listed companies to report within six months. In the US, the SEC requires the annual report (form 10-K) to be filed with it within ninety days of the end of the fiscal year.

Interim statement requirements are discussed in section 3.6. The (London) Stock Exchange (but not the Companies Acts) requires semi-annual reports which must be presented not more than six months from the date of the notice convening the annual general meeting. Since 28 October 1970 the SEC requires quarterly reports (form 10-Q), which need not be certified.[5] These must be filed within forty-five days after the end of each fiscal quarter (except the fourth quarter). In both countries, the interim statements are fairly brief. In addition to the interim financial statements, the SEC requires a monthly 'current report' (form 8-K), on which specified significant events must be reported if they occur. This report must be filed within 10 days after the end of a month, but may be amended. Finally, the stock exchanges of both countries require immediate notification of events that may affect security prices, and in the US the major stock exchanges require publication of quarterly earnings statements.

Prospectus requirements for new stock issues (section 3.7) are outlined after the periodic reporting requirements because they include and extend the provision for annual reporting. As is the case for the periodic reports, the US requirements are more extensive than those prevailing in the UK. In addition, the contents of prospectuses are generally scrutinised more formally by the SEC than by the Quotations Department of The (London) Stock Exchange. As a partial consequence, the time required for processing is greater in the US than in the UK.

In the penultimate section (3.8) the SEC's requirements for an 'initial report' for new companies registering securities with the SEC for the first time are outlined. If no securities were previously registered with the SEC, the information filed in a registration statement under the Securities Exchange Act of 1934 (form 10) is similar to that required for a prospectus issued under the Securities Act of 1933. Additional issues of securities must also be registered under the Securities Exchange Act of 1934, but much less information is required (form 8-A). The final section (3.9) outlines the disclosure requirements related to take-overs and mergers.

The references given in the outline in square brackets refer to the following:

UK: all references are to the Companies Act 1967, 2nd Schedule, unless otherwise noted. Other references are:

    1967 – Companies Act 1967, other than 2nd Schedule
    1948 – Companies Act 1948
    SE – Stock Exchange, *Admission of Securities to Listing* ('Yellow Book'), as amended, February 1974
    SSAP – Statement of Standard Accounting Practice (up to and including SSAP 10)

Thus [1967, 2(c), 3(e)] refers to paragraphs 2(c) and 3(e) of the 2nd Schedule, Companies Act 1967.

US: references are to rule numbers of Regulation S-X (as amended up to and including ASR 178, October 1975), unless otherwise noted as follows:

    10-K etc. – SEC form 10-K

    ARB – Accounting Research Bulletin

    APB – Accounting Principles Board Opinion

    FASBS – Financial Accounting Standards Board Statement

Thus [5-02.38] refers to rule 5-02.38 of Regulation S-X and [APB5] refers to Accounting Principles Board Opinion 5.

Since reporting requirements are constantly changing (particularly in the US) the reader is advised to check the provisions of additional releases.

3.2 Balance sheet – annual

3.2.1 Introduction

In practice, the balance sheet presented by UK companies is quite similar to that presented in the US. The primary differences are the considerably greater detail and supplementary schedules of investments, fixed assets, etc. required by the SEC and the imposition of increasingly standardised procedures by the AICPA. Another important difference is the non-acceptance by the SEC of revaluation of assets.[6]

3.2.2 Share capital and reserves

Overall, the disclosure requirements in the UK and US are similar.

The UK Accounts must give the information required by statute and be in a form appropriate to the business so as to show a true and fair view.[2,4(1)]. The following items are specified:

C1   authorised and issued share capital, summarised [2]; new issues are given in directors' report [1967:16(1)(b)]

C2   share premium and discount [2(c), 3(e)]

C3   redeemable preference shares, giving particulars [2(a)]

C4   shares in company held by subsidiaries [15(3)]

C5   options on unissued shares, giving particulars [11(2)]

C6 arrears of cumulative dividends, amounts and periods [11(3)]
C7 share capital on which interest has been paid out of capital and rate of interest, unless shown in profit and loss statement [2(b)]. (This practice is obsolete; it applied mainly to the original construction of railways, canals, etc.)
C8 reserves:
   (a) aggregate or classified under headings appropriate to the company's business [4(1), 6(a)]
   (b) reserves shall not include amounts required to reduce assets to their 'true' value to provide for known liabilities or to offset tax charge fluctuations [27(1)(b)]
   (c) sources of any increase or decrease in aggregate and classified reserves, unless shown in profit and loss statement[7]
C9 capital redemption reserve fund [1948:58(1)d]
C10 undistributed earnings of unconsolidated associated companies where the investing company's interest is long term and not less than 20 per cent of the equity voting rights are owned [SSAP 1]

In addition, The Stock Exchange's listing agreement calls for the following in the annual Report of the Directors:

C11 interests and change of interests of each director in the share capital of the company, distinguishing between beneficial and non-beneficial interests [SE: ch. 2, 9(e)]
C12 interest in a substantial part of the share capital of persons other than directors [SE: ch. 2, 9(f)]

The US In general, all of the information required by the Companies Acts is required by Regulation S-X with the exception of item C7.[7] Regulation S-X also asks for information on:

C13 warrants or rights outstanding, in detail [3–16(p), 12–15 (schedule XIV)]
C14 shares subscribed but unissued (subscriptions receivable deducted) [5–02.38]
C15 dividends, distribution preferences, participation rights, call or conversion dates and prices, sinking fund requirements and unusual voting rights of each security outstanding [3–16(f)]
C16 restrictions which limit the availability of retained earnings for dividends [3–16(h)]
C17 effects on retained earnings for ten years subsequent to a reorganisation of capital [5–02.39]
C18 number of holders of equity securities of the registrant [10-K, item 7]

C19 options granted to management to purchase securities from the registrant or its subsidiaries [10-K, item 14, 3–16(n)]

3.2.3 Liabilities and provisions

US requirements are considerably more extensive and specific than those of the UK. In addition, where the Companies Acts call for information that might result in excessively long lists, provision is made for summary statements. However, practice in the UK often exceeds the legal requirements. For example, current liabilities are reported separately from long term liabilities, although this separation is not mandated:

The UK

L1 debentures of the company held for the company by a nominee, trustee or subsidiary [10, 15(3)]

L2 debentures of the company which may be reissued [2(d)]

L3 particulars of charges on assets to secure liabilities of the company or of another person, and whether any liabilities are secured by assets other than by operation of law [11(4), 9]

L4 bank loans and overdrafts [1967:8(1)(d)]

L5 long term (over five years) borrowings, in aggregate [8(1)(d)]; new issues are given in the Directors' Report [1967, 16(1)(b)]

L6 medium term borrowings are distinguished, if relevant and practical [SE: R, A.25]

L7 details of repayment terms and rates of interest on borrowings other than bank loans are called for, unless this would result in an excessively long list, in which event a general indication is permitted [8(4)(30)]

L8 intra-group borrowings [15(2), 16(1)]

L9 contingent liabilities [11(5)]

L10 deferred taxation, amounts set aside, basis of computation, and (by way of a note) amounts transferred from such provision for another purpose [7A, 11(10), 11(8A)]

L11 future capital expenditures, stating where practical the estimated amounts, if material, respectively contracted but not provided for and authorised by the directors but not contracted for [11(6)]

L12 movements on provisions (other than provisions for depreciation, renewals and diminution in value of assets), unless immaterial or shown in profit and loss account [7]

L13 amount of recommended dividends [11(5)] (dividends proposed or declared and not yet payable should be included in current liabilities), with specified provisions made for advanced payment of corporate tax [SSAP 8]

L14 issues of debentures (reported in the Directors' Report)
[1967:16(1)(b)]

The US With the exception of L1, L6 and the last part of L11, all of
the items required in the UK are required by Regulation S-X. However,
Regulation S-X calls for disclosure of considerably more detail with
respect to these items than do the Companies Acts.[8] In particular:

L2 reacquired evidence of indebtedness must be deducted from the
appropriate liability caption [3–13]

L4 compensating balances (demand (current amount), time or certificate
of deposit) arrangements related to loans or lending agreements must
be disclosed in a footnote if constituting over 15 per cent of liquid
assets [5–02.1, 5–02.18] (reference to UK requirement L4 – 5.02.25,
5–02.34)

L5 (a) each obligation must be described as to general character
(including rate of interest and maturity date), contingencies
relating to payment of principal or interest, priorities, basis of
conversion, details on sinking fund requirements, and the
aggregate amounts of maturities and sinking fund requirements
for all issues each year for five years [5–02.29, 5–02.32]

(b) unused commitments, amount and terms (including commit-
ment fees and conditions under which the commitments may be
withdrawn) [5–02.29]

(c) bonds, mortgages and similar debt is shown separately from
other long-term debt [5–02.29, 5–02.32]

(d) there is no general provision for aggregate amounts or a general
statement describing the obligations; a supporting schedule
giving details of bonds, mortgages and similar debt must be
filed [12–10 (schedule 9)]

(e) commercial paper and other short term debt must be classified
as current unless the borrower has and intends to use a non-
cancellable binding agreement to refinance the debt and the
refinancing would extend the maturity beyond a year [5–02.25,
FASBS 6]

L7 (a) for *each* category of aggregate short term borrowings, including
bank loans [5–02.25]:
(i) average interest rate paid
(ii) general terms, including formal provisions for maturity
extensions

(b) for aggregate short term borrowings [5–02.25]:
  (i) maximum amount outstanding at any month end
  (ii) average amount outstanding during the year and weighted average interest rate paid
(c) unused lines of credit, amount and terms (including conditions under which the lines may be withdrawn [5–02.25]

L8 intra-group borrowing:
(a) provisions and amounts owed to affiliates that are eliminated and not eliminated on consolidation must be given in detail [5–02.31]
(b) a supporting schedule giving details of non-current indebtedness to affiliates and other persons must be filed [12–11 (schedule 10)]
(c) current accounts and notes payable to parents, subsidiaries, other affiliates and persons accounted for by the equity method must be given [5–02.25]

L9 contingent liabilities (mentioned on balance sheet, details given in notes) [5–02.34] (see also [FASBS 5]):
(a) a schedule – 'Guarantees of Securities of Other Issuers' – is required [3–16(i); 12–12 (schedule XI)]
(b) firm purchase commitments for acquisition of permanent or long term investments and property, whether or not by lease. [3–16(i)]
(c) leases (non-cancellable) in excess of 1 per cent of consolidated revenue, not recorded as liabilities: detailed information must disclosed, including: [3–16(q)]
  (i) future lease commitments for each of the five succeeding years; each of the next three five-year periods; and the remainder as a single amount
  (ii) non-capitalised financing leases, the present value of: minimum lease commitments in the aggregate and by major categories of assets; and the present value of rentals to be received from existing non-cancellable subleases; interest rate information (the weighted average interest rate and range of interest rates or specific rates) must also be given
  (iii) non-capitalised financing leases, the impact on net income were all such leases capitalised and amortised
  (iv) additional information on contingent rental payments; terms of renewal or purchase options, escalation clauses, etc.; guarantees made or obligations assumed; and

51

restrictions on paying dividends, incurring additional debt, further leasing
- (d) material pending legal proceedings is reported in Form 10-K [10-K, item 5; also in Form 8-K (monthly)]
- (e) indemnification arrangements for directors and officers [10-K, item 9]

The AICPA also requires the following additional information:[9]
- (f) leases:
  - (i) lessors should disclose significant amounts invested in leasing activities, details of future maturities of rentals receivable if the company is predominantly in leasing and uses the financing method of accounting, and principal accounting method used [APB7]
  - (ii) lessors should treat a lease as equivalent to a sale under specified conditions, in which case revenue should be recognised on a present value basis against which the cost of the property and estimated future costs are charged [APB 27]
  - (iii) lessees should disclose the significant provisions of capitalised leases and the principal details of material sale and leaseback arrangements. Material gains and losses from sales of property subject to such arrangements should be amortised over the life of the lease [APB 5]
- (g) amount of unused letters of credit [ARB50]
- (h) amount of assets pledged as security for loans and other commitments [ARB50]
- (i) contingent liabilities generally: for each there should be given an appraisal of the outlook and estimate of the amount involved or a statement that no estimate can be made, and, if it is available, an opinion of management or counsel as to the ultimate outcome [ARB50]

L12 all movements in reserves (with a few exceptions) must go through profit and loss statement [5–03]

L14 all significant changes are called for [3–16(k)]

Regulation S-X requires that additional items be disclosed, including:

L15 amounts payable to each of the following separated into current and long term [5–02.25, 5–02.32]:
- (a) banks for borrowing
- (b) holders of commercial paper
- (c) trade creditors

(d) parents and subsidiaries

(e) other affiliates and other persons the investments in which are accounted for by the equity method

(f) underwriters, promoters, directors, officers, employees and principal holders of equity securities

L16 amounts eliminated and not eliminated on consolidation for current accounts payable and notes payable, accrued liabilities, other current liabilities and each type of long-term debt [5-02.25, .26, .27, .32]

L17 amount of default in debt or breach in covenant (in practice this is also disclosed in the UK) [3-16(e)]

L18 deferred credits (including deferred income taxes stated separately, see L10), current and long term [5-02.35]

L19 accrued liabilities, individually, for:

(a) payrolls [5-02.26]

(b) taxes [5-02.26]

(c) interest [5-02.26]

(d) other material items [5-02.26]

L20 any current liability in excess of 5 per cent of total current liabilities must be stated [5-02.27]

L21 pension and retirement plans – liability for unfunded portions must be estimated, described and disclosed [3-16(g)]; (the SEC's rule conflicts with APB 8, which concludes that information about unfunded past service costs is not essential)

L22 any item not properly classified elsewhere which is in excess of 5 per cent of total liabilities must be stated [5-02.33]

3.2.4 Assets

The laws and regulations of the UK and the US call for a separation of assets into current (where conversion into or use in lieu of cash is within one year or the company's operation cycle, whichever is longer), fixed or neither. As is the case for liabilities, US regulations require considerably more detail than UK law. The other major difference relates to reappraisal of assets, allowed in the UK but not accepted by the SEC.

The UK In addition to the general requirement that accounts must give the information required by statute and be in a form appropriate to the business, valuation alternatives and requirements are also specified:

Valuations:

A1 fixed assets may be recorded at cost less depreciation (both shown) [5(1)] or revalued as appropriate [5(2)(b), 5(3)], in which case details must be given [5(4)] including names or qualifications of valuers

[11(6A)] and methods used [4(3)]; revaluation of other than property accounts is unusual

A2 quoted investments, aggregate market value when different from stated value, and stock market value if lower, by note if not otherwise shown [11(8)], distinguishing between UK and foreign quotations [11(28)]

A3 unquoted investments, giving either the directors' estimate or particulars of the investing companies' share of income and undistributed profits and the amounts written off, since date of acquisition [5(2)(c)]

A4 current assets, if not reduced to realisable value (where less than book value); the directors must disclose this fact by note, if it is not otherwise shown [11(7)]

A5 stocks and work in progress must be stated at cost or net realisable value, whichever is lower: the accounting policies followed in arriving at the amounts should be set out in a note [SSAP 9], though [11(8B)] requires only that the policies followed be disclosed. Long term contracts work in progress should be stated at cost plus attributable profit, less attributable losses, with the amount of progress payments received or receivable stated separately [SSAP 9]; LIFO accounting is not practised

A6 government grants relating to fixed assets should be credited to revenue over the expected useful life of the asset by reducing the cost of the asset or treating the grant as a deferred credit [SSAP 4]

A7 basis of conversion of foreign currencies, disclosed by way of note, etc., if not otherwise shown [11(9)]

Specific Accounts

A8 movements on fixed assets (other than investments), for each group in aggregate, showing the amount acquired and disposed of or abandoned during the period [11(6B)]

A9 land, showing separately freehold land, land held on long lease and land held on short lease [11(6C)]

A10 goodwill, patents, and trademarks, in aggregate [8(1)(b), 8(2)]

A11 equities, in general: the accounting for investments in equities must be revealed [SSAP 2] and the name, etc., given of investments not accounted for by the equity method of which 20 per cent or more of the stock is held [SSAP 1]

A12 quoted investments, in aggregate [8(1)(a)], separated into securities admitted to quotation in Great Britain and elsewhere [8(3), 28]

A13 unquoted investments, in aggregate [8(1)(a)]; where not valued by

54

the directors [5(2)(c)], cost and aggregate amount written off since acquisition must be given [5(1), 5(3)]

A14 unquoted equity investments in aggregate, where directors' valuation is not given, showing the income for the year, investing company's share of undistributed profits less losses since investments were acquired, and the manner in which losses were dealt with in the company's accounts [5A];

A15 shares in fellow subsidiaries, in aggregate [15(2), 16(1)]

A16 for each investment representing 10 per cent of any class of equity capital or 10 per cent of book value of an investing company's assets: name, country of incorporation and registration. The Stock Exchange requires for each investment representing more than 20 per cent of equity capital held by the company and its subsidiaries: name, principal country of *operations,* particulars of issued share and loan capital and total amount of reserves, and percentage of each class of share and loan capital attributable to the company's interest [SE: ch. 2, 9(d)]. If the list is excessively long or if disclosure may be harmful to the company, simplifying procedures can be used [1967:3(4) (5), 4(4) (5)]

A17 amounts owing from subsidiaries and other group indebtedness, amount of debentures shown separately [15(2), 16]

A18 loans to officers of the company (including those repaid during the year) by the company or subsidiary or by a third party on the guarantee of the company or subsidiary, except loans made in the ordinary course of business (loans to directors are not permitted) [1948:197(1)]

A19 loans to employees or trustees of employees or salaried directors for the purpose of purchasing fully-paid shares in the company or its holding company [8(1)(c)]

A20 expenditures not yet written off, as follows:
    (a)   preliminary (organisational) expenses [3(a)]
    (b)   expenses incurred on any issue of share capital or debentures [3(b)]
    (c)   commissions paid in respect of shares or debentures [3(c)]
    (d)   discount on debentures [3(d)]
    (e)   discount on shares issued [3(e)]

The US

Valuations:
As noted above, there are some important differences in the valuation

rules, the SEC being more restrictive than the Companies Acts. The SEC has also admonished registrants to disclose 'unusual risks and uncertainties', particularly with respect to loans and loss reserves of financial institutions, marketable securities, deferral of fuel costs by public utilities, cost or raw materials where the price is still under negotiation and the status of major projects that have a documented effect on results [ASR 166, December 1974]:

A1 since fixed assets must be valued at cost less associated depreciation, depletion or amortisation, revaluations are not allowed

A2 market quotations only [12–02]

A3 no provision

A4 required for investments by ARB 43–3

A5 similar to UK rules with respect to disclosure of procedures, except that disclosure of whichever is lower of cost or net realisable value is not required and LIFO may be used (in which event the excess of replacement over book value must be given [5–02.6]). If the inventory method is changed (e.g., from LIFO to FIFO), the effect of the change (if material) in the current years and, in the summary of operations, in the previous three years, must be reported [ASR 159 and 169, Release 34–11079, 3–07]

A6 investment credit is treated similarly [APB 2, APB 4]: however the flow-through method is equally acceptable

A7 disposition of unrealised gain or loss must also be given [3–16 (b), FASBS 1].

Specific accounts:
The SEC requires greater detailed disclosure. The following outline contains these additional requirements, keyed to the UK requirements where possible:

A8/9 property, plant and equipment:

(a) location and character of principal plants, mines and properties (required for initial statement, Form 10, and updated annually in Form 10-K) [Form 10, Item 3; Form 10-K, item 3]

(b) grouping of fixed assets and accumulated depreciation by major class (e.g., land, buildings, machinery and equipment, leaseholds) or functional groupings (e.g., revenue producing equipment, industry categories) [5–02.14(a), 15]. In the UK, assets are to be grouped as required to disclose their general nature[2]

(c) schedule of changes (balance beginning, additions, retirements, other changes, balance end) of each classification [12–06 (schedule V)]. In the UK, aggregate changes of asset groups are required [11(6B)]

(d) schedule of changes in depreciation, depletion and amortisation of each classification [12-07 (schedule VI)]. In the UK, aggregate changes of asset groups are required [11(6B)]

(e) description of depreciation methods used for each class and adjustments made to accumulated depreciation; disposition of gains or losses on retirement, etc., of assets; and accounting treatment for maintenance, repairs, renewals and betterments [3-16(m)]. In the UK, SSAP 2 requires disclosure of material accounting policies

(f) amount of interest cost capitalised in each period for which an income statement is presented, reason for the interest capitalisation policy, and effects on net income for each period of capitalising compared with expensing interest, as a note to the financial statement [3-16]

A10 intangible assets: rather than the aggregate required by the Companies Act 1967, Regulation S-X requires a separate statement of the amounts, accumulated depreciation or amortisation, and whether the assets were written off or not amortised for each major class of patents, trade marks, franchises, goodwill, etc. [5-02.16, 5-02.17, 3-16 (m)]. In addition, schedules are required showing the amounts and changes of:

(a) intangible assets, pre-operating expenses and similar deferrals [12-08 (schedule VII)]

(b) accumulated depreciation and amortisation of intangible assets [12-09 (schedule VIII)]

A11-14 investments, reported much as indicated by A10-A14 except that for:

(a) securities:

(i) marketable securities; a schedule must be filed for each, giving security, name of issuer, number of shares or other units, balance sheet value, and market value if the aggregate cost or market value constitutes 10 per cent or more of total assets [12-02 (schedule I)]

(ii) other security investments: same requirements

(iii) if the cost or market value of total securities (i) and (ii) exceeds 15 per cent of total assets, the schedule must be filed [12-02 (schedule I)]

(b) investment in affiliates:

(i) the equity method must be used or the difference explained if more than 20 per cent of the stock is held; details must be given if the equity method is not used for more than 20 per cent of stock held (same as SSAP 1) or if the equity method is used for less than 20 per cent of stock held [APB 18]

  (ii) supplementary schedules must be filed showing amounts and changes of each security, dividends or interest received, and equity in profit and loss unless neither the sum of securities nor indebtedness of affiliates exceeds 5 per cent of total assets or there have been no material changes in the information required to be reported since that last previously reported [12–04 (schedule III)]

  (c) other investments: any items in excess of 5 per cent of total assets must be stated separately, by class of investments [5–02.13]

A15–17 shown separately, receivable from

  (a) parents and subsidiaries [5–02.3]

  (b) other affiliates and persons accounted for by equity method [5–02.11]; non-current amounts must be detailed in a supplementary schedule [12–05 (schedule 4)]

  (c) the amounts included in (a) and (b) which are respectively eliminated and not eliminated in the related consolidated balance sheet must be shown on the registrant's balance sheet [5–02.11]

A18–19 loans to and amounts receivable from each person among the directors, employees, promoters, underwriters, and principal holders of equity (as well as officers), from whom an aggregate indebtedness of more than $20,000 or 1 per cent of total assets, whichever is the lesser, is owed, excluding amounts receivable from ordinary business transactions; a schedule must be filed showing the name of each debtor, the balance at the beginning of the period, additions, amounts collected, amounts written off, and balance as of the close of the period (amounts arising in the ordinary course of business may be excluded) [12–03 (schedule II)]

A20 expenditures not yet written off, as above [5–02.21,. 5–02.22, 5-02.23] plus:

  (a) deferred research and development expenses [5–02.20]

  (b) prepaid expenses [5–02.8, .19]

  (c) other items: separately if material, otherwise in aggregate [5–02.19]

In addition, Regulation S-X requires that additional items be disclosed, including:

A21 each pension and other special fund [5-02.18]
A22 receivables (in addition to A15), current and non-current separately, from:
- (a) trade customers [5-02.3]
- (b) others [5-02.3]
- (c) if notes receivable exceed 10 per cent of aggregate notes and accounts receivable, they must be shown separately [5-02.3]
- (d) defence and other long term contracts: amounts billed but not yet paid under retainage provisions, by year; amounts representing recognition of sales value of performance that is not billed or billable; and amounts subject to uncertainty [5-02.3]
A23 valuation and qualifying reserves and accounts:
- (a) allowance for doubtful accounts, balance and analysis of changes, is shown in a schedule [12-13 (schedule XII)]
- (b) unearned discounts, finance charges and interest included in receivables are shown separately and deducted from the applicable receivable [5-02.5]
- (c) (discount or premium on note where face value is materially different from its market value at date of transaction is called for in APB 21)
A24 cash and cash items, separated into:
- (a) cash on hand and unrestricted demand deposits (current accounts) [5-02.1]
- (b) restricted demand deposits held as compensating balances against short term borrowing arrangements: the arrangements must be described [5-02.1]
- (c) deposits held as compensating balances against long term borrowing arrangements [5-02.18]
- (d) time deposits and certificates of deposit (excluding amounts included in (b) and (c)) [5-02.1]
- (e) funds subject to repayment on call or immediately after balance sheet data [5-02.1]
- (f) other funds subject to withdrawal or usage restrictions [5-02.1]
A25 inventories (stocks):
- (a) major classes, such as finished goods; inventoried costs relating to long term contracts; work in progress; raw materials; supplies
- (b) basis for determining amounts shall be stated (i.e., cost,

59

market, amounts of general and administrative expense charged to inventory, etc.)

(c) if LIFO, excess of replacement cost over LIFO shall be stated

(d) defence or long term contracts: details as to amount of manufacturing or production costs and any related deferral costs; claims subject to uncertainty; and amount of progress payments netted against inventory [5-02.6]

A26 any other item in excess of 5 per cent of total assets [5-02.18]

3.3 Profit and loss account and appropriations (including directors' report) – annual

3.3.1 Introduction

As with the balance sheet, the detail required in profit and loss accounts and appropriations by the Companies Acts and The Stock Exchange is less than that required by the SEC. These differences are outlined below as they were above, UK requirements given first because US requirements include and extend them in most instances. (The fact that relatively more is required of balance sheets than of income statements in the US may surprise some readers, however.)

Three structural differences should be noted. First, a number of items given in the US profit and loss accounts are given in the UK Directors' Report. For comparative convenience, the Directors' Report items are included here with profit and loss account items. Secondly, in the US *all* items of profit and loss given recognition during the period (except retroactive adjustments) must be included in the income statement for the period [5-03]. In the UK, some items may go through the reserves.[10] Thirdly, the SEC specifies the order in which items should be listed on the income statement. (Until recently, the 'single step' form was not accepted.) The SEC also specifies items, such as 'income or loss before income tax expense' [5-03.14], 'minority interest' [5-03.16], 'equity in earnings of unconsolidated enterprises' [5-03.17], 'income or loss before extraordinary items' [5-03.18], and 'net income or loss' [5-03.21]. In the UK, the form of the statement is similar, but is not prescribed nor are the item subtotals specified. However, calculation of earnings per share is called for both in the US [5-03.22, APB 15] and the UK [SSAP 3], although US rules are more specific. Finally, dividends per share are called for in the US [11-02.4] but not in the UK.

In addition to the information outlined below, the SEC's annual form

60

10-K calls for a 'summary of operations' for each of the last five fiscal years (or the life of the registrant and its predecessors, if this is less) and any additional years which may be necessary to keep the summary from being misleading [10-K, item 2]. However, registrants may elect to present five complete annual statements of earnings in lieu of a summary. This requirement, added in 1970, makes the annual report almost as comprehensive as the prospectus. An outline of the summary of earnings is deferred until prospectus requirements are discussed in section 3.7.

3.3.2 Income

Disclosure of items I1 to I4 is required in the UK and the US, with some exceptions. I1b and I1c (geographical analysis of turnover and exports) are not called for in the US; however, other detailed information is specified. I4 (rent) is not specifically mentioned in the US except for subleases on financing leases. Some additional items (I5, I6, I7) are specified.

The UK

I1 turnover (sales), unless the company is neither a holding company nor subsidiary and the amount does not exceed £250,000; the method by which turnover is arrived at is not prescribed, but must be stated [13A (amended 1971)]; the basis of recognising profits on instalment and deferred sales, etc. must be stated [SSAP 2]; VAT is deducted [SSAP 5]

In the directors' report:

(a) the proportions in which turnover (and profits) is divided amongst substantially different classes of business on a group basis [1967:17]

(b) geographical analysis of turnover and of the contribution to trading results of those trading operations carried on by the company (or group) outside the UK [SE: ch. 2, 9(b)]

(c) exports [1967:20]

I2 investment income, distinguishing between income from quoted and unquoted investments [2, 12 (1)(g)]

I3 associated companies (50 per cent or less owned), share of profits if companies are essentially joint ventures or long term interests (ownership of equity not less than 20 per cent) reported in group accounts as profits before tax, taxation, extraordinary items, net profit retained by associated companies, other items [SSAP 1]

I4 rent income from land, after deduction of ground rents, rates and other outgoings, if a substantial part of revenue [2, 12(1)(g)]

The US   The differences and sources of items I1 to I4 are the following:

I1   sales (turnover): items (b) and (c) are not required. Sales are defined as net of discounts and returns [5–03.1A]. (Reference to reporting basis of reporting profits on instalment sales, etc. is 3–16(1).)

The rule for disclosing amounts derived from lines of business and products is explicit:

(d)   lines of business – if a product or service (line of business) contributes 10 per cent or more to the gross turnover (sales), or if there is pre-tax income exclusive of losses or a loss greater than 10 per cent of the pre-tax income from a line of business, the amount of turnover expenses and net income attributable to it must be given, if possible. For corporations with turnover below $50 million the percentage specified is 15 rather than 10. Also, no more than ten separate lines of business need be reported and the breakdown need not be certified by the auditor [10-K, item 1(c)]

(e)   a description of the principal products and services rendered and changes in products, services, markets, competitive conditions, and methods of distribution since the beginning of the year are also required [10-K, item 1]

(f)   sales to unconsolidated subsidiaries and 50 per cent owned persons (companies) [5–03.1A]

(g)   sales to others [5–03.1a]

(h)   excise taxes, if included in sales and revenues and equal to 10 per cent or more of the total (including the taxes) [5–03.1A]

I2   investment income: a greater breakdown is required than by the Companies Acts, namely as follows:

(a)   dividends from securities of affiliates; marketable securities; and other securities (dividends received from subsidiaries and from investments accounted for by the equity method are excluded) [5–03.7]

(b)   interest on securities from categories as in (a); interest from equity method companies reported parenthetically or in a note [5–03.8]

(c)   profits on securities, net of losses; method of determining cost presented in a note [5–03.9, 5–03.12]

I3   associated companies: share of profits reported separately as equity in the earnings of unconsolidated persons and 50 per cent or less owned persons, net of tax, indicating dividends received thereon

[5–03.17] in detailed income and expense items given below (see I5, E10, E11); equity in the net profit or loss of affiliates is also reported in a supplementary schedule [12–04, (schedule 3)]

I4 rented income from non-capitalised financing leases (see L9c(ii) and (iii) [3–16(q)]

The following two items, not specifically mentioned in the UK laws and regulations, are required in the US:[11]

I5 other revenues (e.g., royalties, rents, sales of services and products), stating separately amounts from unconsolidated affiliates and 50 per cent owned persons (companies); and others [5–03.1c]

I6 miscellaneous other income (net of disclosed expenses), stating separately any material amounts and the nature of the transactions out of which they arose [5–03.10]

3.3.3 Expenses

Items E1 and E2, required in the UK, are not specifically required in the US. These deal with hire (rental) of plant and machinery, auditors' remuneration, political and charitable contributions. (Political contributions are illegal under US federal statutes.) Items E3 to E9 are required in both countries, with some differences. The balance of the items listed for the US are required only by that country.

The UK

E1 auditors' remuneration including expenses [2, 13]

E2 political and charitable contributions, separately if greater than £50 and giving name of recipient if political contribution is greater than £50 (in directors' report) [1967:19]. (N.B. political contributions for federal elections are illegal in the US.)

E3 hire of plant and machinery, amounts charged to revenue, if material [2,12(1) (gb)]

E4 directors' emoluments, stating separately
   (a) aggregate emoluments including expense allowances charged to UK tax, pension contributions, and estimated money value of benefits in kind [1948:196]
   (b) aggregate pensions for past and present directors, excluding pensions from schemes maintained by contributions (reported in E4a) [1948:196]
   (c) aggregate compensation paid to directors past and present for

loss of office [1948:196]

(d) prior year adjustments [1948:196]

(e) number of directors, bracketed in groups rising by £2,500, according to their compensation (exempting directors whose duties are mainly outside the UK), if aggregate remuneration exceeds £15,000 [1967, 6(1) and SI 2044 (1971)]

(f) number of directors who have waived rights to receive emoluments and amounts thereof, if aggregate exceeds £15,000 [1967: 7(1)]; particulars in directors' reports [SE: ch. 2, 9(1)]

(g) chairman's emoluments, including contributions paid under any pension scheme and those of highest paid director if greater, if aggregate exceeds £15,000 [1967: 6]

The Stock Exchange also requires information on:

(h) particulars of any contract subsisting during or at the end of the financial year in which a director is or was materially interested or which was significant in relation to the company's business [SE: ch. 2, 9(h)]

E5 employees:

(a) number paid whose compensation (excluding pension contributions) is £10,000 a year or more (and whose duties are mainly in the UK) bracketed in groups rising by £2,500 [1967:8]

(b) average number of employees per week, if 100 or more (in directors' report) [1967: 18]

(c) aggregate remuneration, if 100 employers or more (in directors' report) [1967: 18]

E6 depreciation, renewals or diminution in value of fixed assets charged to revenue [12(1)(a)]

(a) amounts charged by way of provision for renewal of assets shown separately [12(3)]

(b) state if depreciation calculated other than by reference to balance sheet amounts [12(4)]

(c) if other than by a depreciation charge or provision for renewals, the method used or the fact that no provision has been made must be stated (by note, if not otherwise shown) [14(2)]

E7 interest payable, showing separately

(a) interest on bank loans and overdrafts and loans wholly repayable within five years, and

(b) interest on all other loans [12(1)(b)]

E8 taxation, distinguishing between

(a) UK corporate tax (before and after double tax relief) and basis for computation [12(1)(c)]

(b) UK income tax and basis of computation

(c) overseas tax [12(1)(c)]

(d) deferred taxation due to material difference between book and tax depreciation and amortisation must either be provided for or disclosed, together with the reasons why a provision was not needed [SE: ch. 3, 19 (c)]

(e) any special circumstances affecting liability to taxation for a certain period or succeeding periods [14(3A)]

E9 extraordinary, exceptional and prior year items (if material):

(a) charge or credit arising in consequence of the occurrence of an event in a preceding period, if not reported under another heading [12A]

(b) transactions of a sort not usually undertaken by the company or by circumstances of an exceptional or non-recurrent nature [14(6)(a)]

(c) any change in the basis of accounting [14(6)(b)]

(d) less applicable tax [SSAP 6]

(e) shown on statement after net income from operations net of taxation [SSAP 6]

(f) prior year adjustments should be accounted for by restating prior years; the effect should be disclosed, where practicable, by showing separately in the restatement of the prior year the amount involved [SSAP 6].

The US Items E3 to E9, required in the UK, are also required in the US, with the following exceptions:

E3 rent (gross) if over 1 per cent of consolidated revenues [3–16(q), 12–16]. Separate disclosure is required of:

(a) total rent expenses, less sublease rental separately disclosed

(b) total minimum and contingent rentals

(c) rentals on non-capitalised financing leases, including portions applicable to minimum and contingent rentals

(d) impact on net income, were all non-capitalised financing leases capitalised and amortised

E4, 5 directors' and officers' remuneration is asked for in the aggregate and for each director where remuneration is over $40,000 and for each of the three highest offices where remuneration is over $40,000 [10-K, item 13]; the interest of management and others in material transactions is also called for [10-K, item 15]

E6 depreciation on individual or groups of assets is detailed in supplementary schedules for tangible assets [12-07] and intangible assets [12-09]. (Also required in 'Supplementary Income Statement Information', schedule [12-16].)

E7 interest and amortisation of debt discount, stating separately:
   (a) interest on bonds, mortgages and similar debts [5.03.11]
   (b) amortisation of debt discount and expenses (or premium) [5-03.11]
   (c) other interests [5-03.11]
   (d) if interest is capitalised, the effect on net income had the interest been charged to expenses (in a footnote) [3-16]
   (e) (gain or loss on extinguishment of debt is recognised as an extraordinary item, net of its related tax effect [APB 30 as amended by FASBS 4]

E8 income tax expense regulations differ somewhat because of circumstances peculiar to each country; in particular, a reconciliation must be presented between the effective and the statutory federal income tax rate [5-30.15, 3-16(o), APB 11]

E9 extraordinary items:
   (a), (b), (d), (e) [5-03.19]
   (c) cumulative effects of changes in accounting principles also required [5-03.20]

The AICPA also requires:

   (f) disclosure of prior year adjustments, the effect on retained earnings at the beginning of the year and the effect on income of each year [APB 9]
   (g) discontinued operations of a segment of a business: income or loss from operations and applicable tax shown separately from continuing operations [APB 30]
   (h) disposal of a segment of a business, details [APB 30]
   (i) see E7(e)

Items E10 to E22 are peculiar to US regulations:

E10 cost of tangible goods sold, stating separately:
   (a) purchase from unconsolidated affiliates and 50 per cent owned persons (companies); and others, where practical [5-03.2A]
   (b) amount of opening and closing inventories used in the computation and the basis for determining such amounts [5-03.2A]

(c) accrued net losses on firm purchase commitments for inventory [ARB 43-4.17]

E11 costs and expenses applicable to other revenues (see I6 above [5-03.2C])

E12 other operating costs and expenses, stating material amounts not included elsewhere [5-03.3]

E13 selling, general and administrative expenses, stating separately any unusual amounts [5-03.4]

E14 provision for doubtful accounts and notes [5-03.5]

E15 pension costs, describing the essential provisions, and accounting and funding policies of the plan(s), including groups covered, provision for the period, amounts of back service liability, etc. [3-16(g)]

E16 minority interest in income of consolidated subsidiaries [5-03.16] (given in practice in UK)

E17 bonus, profit sharing and other similar plans in which only directors, officers or key employees may participate, showing amounts charged to expenses and describing the essential provisions and participants [3-16(j)]

E18 other general expenses not normally classified under item E13, stating material amounts separately [5-03.6]

E19 maintenance and repairs, in supplementary schedule [12-16]

E20 taxes other than income tax, in supplementary schedule [12-16]

E21 royalties, in supplementary schedule [12-16]

E22 advertising costs, in supplementary schedule [12-16]

E23 research and development costs, in supplementary schedule [12-16]; the amount incurred disclosed in a note [FASBS 2, ASR 178]

E24 Foreign currency translation – disclosure is required and methods specified [FASBS 1, FASBS 8]

3.3.4 Appropriations

Particular types of appropriations are mentioned in UK law, while the US regulations generally merely state all changes should be shown.

The UK

AP1 amounts provided for share and loan redemption [12(1)(d)]

AP2 transfers to or from reserves [12(1)(c)]

AP3 transfers to provisions (other than depreciation) and withdrawals therefrom for another purpose [12(1)(f)]

AP4 aggregate dividends paid and proposed [12(1)(h)]

The Stock Exchange requires details of arrangements for waiver of dividends payable for the financial year and for future waivers [SE: ch. 2, 9(j)].

The US Regulation S-X calls for a 'Statement of Other Stockholders' Equity' in which balances and an analysis of changes in each class of stockholders' equity are given [11–02]. Balances and changes in 'Valuation and Other Qualifying Accounts and Reserves' are given in a supplementary schedule [12–13].

3.4 Group (consolidated) accounts

The requirements of the Companies Acts and Regulation S-X are quite similar with respect to group accounts of the holding company (parent) and its subsidiaries. The only major difference is that exclusion of subsidiaries because their inclusion would be insignificant, misleading or harmful to the company is at the discretion of the directors in the UK (subject to the consent of the DT) and at the discretion of the SEC in the US.

The UK
G1　group accounts not required where:
- (a)　the company is a wholly owned subsidiary of a UK company [1948:150(2)(a)]
- (b)　consolidation is impractical or of no real value to members of the company because of insignificant amounts involved [1948: 150(2)(b)(i)]
- (c)　the result would be misleading or harmful to company (with permission of DT) [1948:150(2)(b)(ii)]
- (d)　the business of holding company and subsidiary is not meaningfully a single undertaking (with permission of DT) [1948:150(2)(b)(iii)]

G2　alternative forms and groupings of accounts (other than consolidated accounts) are permissible if the directors believe this to be preferable [1948:151(21)]

G3　if subsidiaries are omitted (in directors' report):
- (a)　explanation by directors [15(4)(a)]
- (b)　net aggregate amount attributed to the holding company of profits less losses of subsidiaries included and not included in the accounts for the current and previous years [15(4)(b)(c)]

(c)   qualifications in audit reports of omitted subsidiaries [15(4)(d)]
G4   financial years should be co-terminous or differences and reasons disclosed (in directors' report) [15(6),22]
G5   the balance sheet of the parent company is required to be presented in addition to the consolidated balance sheet [1948: 150]

The US US requirements [Article 4] are similar, with the following exceptions:

G1   the SEC appears reluctant to allow exclusions based on G1(b) or (c) [4–02]
G3   unconsolidated subsidiaries: the SEC requires complete financial statements for significant unconsolidated subsidiaries [Form S-1, item 31, C-6]
G4   a subsidiary *cannot* be consolidated if the difference in year end is greater than 93 days (otherwise same as UK) [4–02]. (However, in retroactive 'pooling of interests', the financial statements of the constituents can be combined despite differences in dates)
G5   parent company profit and loss statement and statement of changes in financial position are also required [10K, instruction 1]

Regulation S-X also requires disclosure of material changes compared to the previous filing of the companies included in and excluded from consolidated statements and changes in the accounting periods and manner of treatment of companies consolidated [4–04].

3.5   Changes in financial position (source and application of funds) – annual

For years beginning after 31 December 1970 the SEC requires a statement detailing the source and application of changes in working capital (funds) [11A–01]. The statement prescribes that (1) sources include, as a minimum, (a) net income, plus or minus specific items which did not require the expenditure or receipt of funds; (b) sale of non-current assets; (c) issuance of long term debt; and (d) issuance of capital stock; and (2) disposition of funds include (a) purchase of non-current assets; (b) redemption or repayment of long term debt; or (c) capital stock; and (d) dividends. In addition, APB19 calls for the net changes in each element of working capital, outlays for purchases of consolidated subsidiaries, summarised by major categories of assets obtained and obligations assumed, and conversion of long term debt or preferred stock to common stock.

A similar statement is required by SSAP 10 (1975) in the UK showing (a) net income, plus or minus specific items which did not require the expenditure or receipt of funds; (b) dividends paid; (c) funds raised by increasing or decreasing loan capital and share capital; and (d) increase or decrease in working capital sub-divided into its components and movements in net liquid funds.

3.6 Interim reports

3.6.1 Semi-annual and quarterly

The UK The Stock Exchange requires semi-annual statements in which the following must be disclosed, as a minimum, by a company which is not a holding company for the current and corresponding previous period [all references are to Schedule VII, Part C, 2]:

IN1 turnover [a]

IN2 UK and, where material, overseas taxation [c]

IN3 if material, the effect on net profit (IN4) of special credits (including transfers from reserves) and/or debits [d]

IN4 profit or loss after all charges including taxation [b]

IN5 rates of dividend(s) paid and proposed and amount absorbed thereby [e]

IN6 earnings per share [f]

IN7 any supplementary information which, in the opinion of the directors, is necessary for a reasonable appreciation of the results of the period or of other material changes in the aggregate of the balance on profit and loss account and other reserves[h]

Holding companies are required to disclose the above for the group and, in addition:

IN8 amounts of group profits attributable to members of the holding company, i.e., after deduction of outside interests [Part C, 1(d)]

The US Quarterly reports have been required by the SEC since 1970. (Before that semi-annual reports were required.) As in the UK, comparative figures are asked for.

All of the items listed above (except IN8) are required by the SEC's form 10-Q, although the calculation of these items is specified concretely in the US, compared with the general requirement in the UK, and is as follows (all references are to form 10-Q):

IN1 turnover: net sales reported separately from operating revenues unless the lesser amount is 10 per cent or less of the total [A1, 2]

IN2 taxation: provisions for deferred taxes and methods used in the allocation to interim periods of the income tax effects of operating loss carry-backs, carry-forwards or other tax credits must be disclosed and explained [A6]

IN3 special credits and/or debits: extraordinary items (material amounts of an unusual or non-recurring nature which qualify as extraordinary items) and the applicable income tax must be given [A9]. (APB 30 requires that both the criteria of unusual nature and infrequency of occurrence shall be met to classify an event or transaction as an extraordinary item)

IN4 net income (or loss) [A10]

IN5 dividends per share [A12]

IN6 earnings per share [A11], including earnings and dividends applicable to common stock and number of shares used in the computation, and method of computation [H(g)]

IN7 supplementary information:
  (a) in addition to the general requirement, mention must be made of material retroactive prior period adjustments and seasonal factors, unusual increases or decreases in sales, and other situations that may make the interim results not indicative of the entire year [H(i)]. The date of any change and reasons for making it must be disclosed. A letter from the registrant's accounting on the change is required [H(f)]
  (b) acquisition or disposal of business or assets by the registrant or any of its subsidiaries must be disclosed and the relevant prior statements adjusted [H(d) (e)]
  (c) the effect of a change in the inventory valuation method (i.e., FIFO to LIFO), made in other than the first quarter should be reported as if it were made in the first quarter [APB 28, FASB Statement 3, H(f)]
  (d) a narrative analysis of results of operations [I] (applicable to reports filed for periods after 25 December 1975)

IN8 minority interests [A7]

Additional required profit and loss accounts include the following:

IN9 interest expense [A4(d)]

IN10 total costs and expenses (including interest) [A4].(Captions listed but not required are cost of goods sold, operating expenses, selling, general and administration expenses, other deductions net)

IN11 short term debt

IN12 long term debt, showing separately the portion due within one year

IN13 deferred credits

IN14 minority interests

IN15 a complete and detailed accounting of the equity section of the balance sheet is also called for, including an analysis of changes in retained earnings [Part B]

IN16 securities sold during the period that were not registered under the Securities Act of 1933, details [Part C]

The following are applicable to reports for periods after 25 December 1975:

IN17 balance sheets, comparative for the quarter and year to date, major captions as set forth in Regulation S-X except for inventories, which must be broken down into raw materials, work in process and finished goods (if applicable) [H(a)]

IN18 source and application of funds, comparative for year to date, only, condensed [H(a)]

The SEC amended Regulation S-X, effective for reports filed for periods beginning after 25 December 1975 [ASR 177] requires disclosure of quarterly income statement data in a footnote to the annual financial statements. Registrants with income (before extraordinary items and the cumulative effect of accounting changes) of $250,000 or less for each of the last three years and assets of less than $200 million at its most recent year-end are exempt. The footnote must include the following: net sales, gross profit, income before extraordinary items and cumulative effect of a change in accounting, per-share data based upon such income, and net income for each quarter within the two most recent fiscal years and any subsequent fiscal period for which an income statement is presented. In addition, the note must include a description of the effect of any disposals of a segment of a business and extraordinary, unusual or infrequently occurring items recognised in each quarter, as well as the aggregate effect and nature of year-end or other adjustments which are material to the results of that quarter. Such disclosure is required in the financial statements included in annual reports to shareholders, as well as in filings with the SEC.

The required note as a part of the audited financial statements may be designated as 'unaudited'. However, even though the note need not be audited, independent accountants will be associated with such quarterly financial data, and the Commission has concurrently proposed a list of procedures it would expect independent accountants to follow in reviewing such data.

3.6.2 Monthly reports

The UK No provision. However, The Stock Exchange calls for immediate reporting of some of the following information which is required by the SEC in the 8-K report (references are to items in the listing agreement, 'Yellow Book', ch. 2):
(1) changes in directorate [4c]
(2) material acquisition or realisation of assets [4a]
(3) capital structure changes [2c]
(4) other information necessary for a proper appraisal [4g]

The Companies Act 1967 also calls for the reporting of changes in securities, where any stockholder's interest in the shares of the company increases from less than to 10 per cent or more or decreases from 10 per cent [1967: 33, 4e]

The US Monthly reports are called for only in the US. The SEC's form 8-K (current report) requires information on the following events, should they have occurred during any one month [the numbers refer to item numbers of form 8-K]:

(1) changes in control of the registrant
(2) acquisition or disposition of a significant amount of assets other than in the normal course of business; if the book value or purchase price exceeds 10 per cent of the registrant's consolidated assets or involves gross revenues on net income greater than 10 per cent of the registrant's consolidated gross revenues or net income, the following financial statements (as described above in sections 3.2 and 3.3, less the supporting schedules) must be filed [item 2, instruction 4 (ASR 155, April 1974)]:
    (a) balance sheet reasonably close to the date of acquisition (if not certified, the certified balance sheet at the close of the preceding fiscal year must also be filed)
    (b) income and surplus statements for each of the last three full

fiscal years and for the period up to the date of the balance sheet: the statements must be certified up to the date of the certified balance sheet

(3) material legal proceedings
(4) changes in registered securities
(5) changes in collateral for registered securities
(6) material defaults upon senior securities
(7) material increases in amounts of outstanding securities
(8) material decreases in amounts of outstanding securities
(9) granting or extension of options to purchase securities of the registrant or its subsidiaries
(10) extraordinary item charges and credits, other material charges and credits to income of an unusual nature, material provisions for loss, and restatements of capital share accounts
(11) matters submitted to vote of security holders
(12) changes in the registrant's certifying accountant
(13) other materially important events

It should be noted that foreign companies (other than North American companies) are exempt from the SEC's requirement for the filing of form 8-K current reports. In lieu thereof, such companies must file form 6-K reports which require that the company supply only such information as it is required to make public in the country of its domicile or in which it is incorporated or organised; or as it is required to file with a foreign stock exchange on which the securities are traded and which is made public by the exchange; or as it distributes to its security holders.

3.6.3 Stock Exchange requirements for immediate reporting

The stock exchanges of both countries require listed companies to report immediately any event that may affect the price of the companies' securities. In addition, the SEC requires monthly reporting of transactions of persons referred to as 'insiders', (i.e. officers, directors and principal users of equity securities). Recent court cases in the US have further restricted the use by insiders of information before it is disclosed to others. Legislation has been proposed in the UK to make insider dealing illegal.

3.7 New issues – prospectus and other requirements

3.7.1 Introduction

The UK The Companies Act 1948 states that 'it shall not be lawful to issue any form of application for shares or debentures of a company unless the form is issued with a prospectus which complies with the requirements of this section.' [Companies Act 1948:38].[12] Sections 37 to 55 require (in general) disclosures of the parties responsible for the prospectus and define their liability for it, list basic procedures that are designed to protect investors' funds in the event that the issue does not carry or a listing on a stock exchange is not secured as promised, and limit the amount of commissions that can be paid. These requirements are supplemented by the 4th Schedule which specifies the matters to be contained in a prospectus.

Three important exemptions from the provisions of the 4th Schedule are allowed:

(1) companies whose shares or debentures are not offered to the public – these are exempt from all the prospectus provisions of the Act;
(2) issues of shares or debentures to existing share members or debenture holders; and
(3) issues of 'shares or debentures that are or are to be in all respects uniform with shares or debentures previously issued and for the time being dealt in or quoted on a prescribed stock exchange' [1948:38(5) (6)].

Thus the prospectus requirements of the Act apply only to companies who issue new securities to the public. Since virtually all public securities issues are admitted to listing on The Stock Exchange, the Exchange's more extensive requirements govern. Thus the Exchange's Quotations Department is, effectively, the regulatory agency.

The US The Securities Act of 1933 governs disclosure with respect to new issues, except principally for securities of governmental units and agencies and those of certain common carriers (such as interstate railroads), banks, securities deemed not offered to the public (as when an entire issue is privately placed with an insurance company), and securities offered solely to residents of an individual state (intra-state issue).[13] In addition, the SEC subjects to somewhat less rigorous registration requirements issues that do not exceed $500,000 (Regulation A offerings) and securities of 'substantial, seasoned' corporations. Unlike the situation in the UK, many securities are not traded on stock exchanges. These over the counter securities are traded by dealers who make markets in them as well as in listed securities. As was discussed in section 2.1.2, state 'blue sky' laws as well as the Securities Act of 1933 govern the issuance of securities. However, the requirements of the Securities Act of 1933 with respect to financial disclosure are, in general, more extensive than those of the states. The federal Act is also generally more extensive than the listing requirements of the stock exchanges. The following discussion therefore concentrates on the disclosure regulations promulgated and enforced by the SEC.

The Securities Act of 1933 requires that issuers of securities file registration statements in accordance with Section 7 of the Act. Schedule A of Section 7 specifies the required information and documents for most corporations. (Section B, which is not discussed here, deals with issues of foreign governments and their political subdivisions.) However, the SEC is authorised to omit or add information requirements as necessary to provide disclosure adequate for the protection of investors. Hence it has promulgated several 'forms' (actually sets of instructions and requirements) which govern the contents of prospectuses much as does Schedule 2 of The (London) Stock Exchange's 'Yellow Book'. Sixteen such forms which require financial statements (and four which do not) have been issued for use in specifed situations. The discussion here, however, will be limited to the general form S-1, used by most corporations.

However, explicit mention should be made of two forms, S-7 and S-16, which may be used by larger, 'seasoned' corporations. Use of forms S-7 or S-16 is limited to corporations who (a) have a class of equity securities registered pursuant to section 12b or 12s (if a US corporation) of the 1934 Act; (b) have been subject to and have complied in all respects, including timeliness, with the requirements of sections 13 and 14 of the 1934 Act for a period of at least three fiscal years prior to filing forms S-7 or S-16; (c) have a majority of the existing Board of Directors who were directors for the three fiscal years prior to filing; (d) have not (and subsidiaries have not) defaulted in the payment of any dividend or sinking fund instalment on preferred stock, or in the payment of interest, principal or sinking fund instalments on any indebtedness for borrowed money, or rentals on long term leases, during the past ten years; (e) have earned at least the amount of dividends paid (including the fair market value of stock dividends) in each of the past five years (stock dividends must have been charged to retained earnings at the aggregate market value of the stock issued); and (f) have net income after taxes (including consolidated subsidiaries), but before extraordinary items net of tax effect, of at least $500,000 p.a. for each of the past five years.

Form S-7 can be used only for stock issued for cash. The financial statements required are very similar to those required for form S-1 (described in detail below). A notable exception is a summary of earnings, which is not required (see F1b(ii) below), but five years of income statements are required compared with three years for form S-1. Thus, with respect to financial statement requirements, form S-7 cannot be said to be a simplified form.

Form S-16 (adopted in January 1971) is restricted to (a) outstanding securities offered for the amount of any person other than the issuer, if securities of the same class are listed and registered on a national exchange or quoted on the automated system of a national securities association; (b) securities offered upon conversion of outstanding convertible securities with no commission or other remuneration paid; or (c) securities offered upon the exercise of outstanding transferable warrants, with no commission, etc., paid. It is truly a simplified form, since the registrant can incorporate the financial statements or prospectuses filed under the 1933 and 1934 Acts by reference. The written consent of the auditor who certified the referenced statements is required. Also, a description of any material adverse changes in the registrant's affairs that occurred since the date of the last certified statement is called for. Form S-16 thus reduces the financial statements requirements of 'large seasoned companies' much as does the third provision of the Companies Act 1948, as stated above.

3.7.2 Outline of prospectus requirements – introduction

The (London) Stock Exchange's prospectus requirements are given in Schedule 2 of the 'Yellow Book' (Admission of Securities to Listing), as amended in May 1975. These differ somewhat depending on whether a listing is sought for securities of a company no part of whose capital is already listed (Part A) or some part of whose capital is already listed (Part B).[14] Although the items are numbered differently in each part, most of them are exactly the same. The requirements differ primarily in calling for financial statements only for companies new to the Exchange (Part A). Reference to the 'Yellow Book' and to the Companies Act 1948 are given in brackets; A and B refer to Part A and Part B of Schedule 2 of the 'Yellow Book'; 1948 refers to the Companies Act 1948. An asterisk also indicates that the item is required by the Companies Act 1948.

The US requirements are those required for form S-1 (as amended by ASR 159, effective as from 30 September 1974),[15] which has two parts. Part I lists information required in the prospectus (given to the public); Part II lists information not required in the prospectus (but required in the registration statement filed with the SEC and available to the public). Descriptions, financial statements and some stewardship information are contained in Part I. Other descriptions and stewardship data are found in

Part II. It is not clear what governs the distinction between Parts I and II.

The following outline of UK prospectus requirements is organised according to the type of information required, and does not accord with the order usually presented in prospectuses or in the regulations. Five classifications are distinguished:

G   – general information about the securities issued, the company and its subsidiaries (section 3.7.3)
S   – stewardship information (section 3.7.4)
F   – financial reports and figures (section 3.7.5)
PA – post audit information (section 3.7.6)
PR – prospects (section 3.7.7)

In the US, supporting documents must also be filed with the SEC as exhibits. The requirement is identified by [Exhibit 1, 2] etc.

3.7.3 General information about the securities issued, the company and its subsidiaries

The UK

G1   share capital:
    (a)* authorised share capital, voting rights, designation and amount issued or agreed to be issued, paid up, etc. [A4(a), B5; 1948:1,17]
    (b)   a statement that no material additional issues of securities (other than *pro rata*) will be made within one year and, where 10 per cent or more of the voting capital remains unissued, that no issue will be made which would effectively alter control of the company without prior approval of the company in a general meeting [A4(b) (c), 11 B6]
G2   loan capital, rights conferred and particulars of security, if any [A13, B7]
G3   loan capital of company and subsidiaries, outstanding or created but unissued, and all mortgages and charges [A5(a)]
G4* previous securities issued or alteration of share capital, prospective or within the preceding two years for company or subsidiaries for part B companies, since last published audited accounts); if issued for cash, the price, term of payment, amount and how proceeds were or are to be applied [A19, 22, 23, 27(a), B13, 14, 15, 16; 1948:6, 8, 9, 10]

G5 general nature of the business, including (very brief) particulars of factories and main buildings operated, principal products and approximate number of employees [A14, 15(b)]

G6 relative importance of two or more materially different activities with regard to profits or losses, assets employed, etc., including geographical analysis of trading outside the UK [A14]

G7 identification and particulars about consolidated subsidiaries and material investments, including proportion of capital held and nature of business [A15(a)]

The US

G1 particulars of the securities and capital structure (including opinion of counsel on the legality of issues in certain circumstances) and offering price [5, 13] [Exhibit 3, 4, 6, 8, 9, 10]; however, no specific limitations are imposed on future issues of securities, as is required in the UK. But additional security issues over 50,000 in the US are subject to the SEC's registration requirements

G2, G3 mortgages and rates disclosed in financial statements [14, 15]

G4 sales of securities otherwise than for case [4]; use of proceeds [3]; accounting for proceeds [30 (not in prospectus)]

G5, G6 description of the business and its development during the past five years and future business to be done [9], including: (a) competitive conditions pertaining to industries and products; (b) particulars, if a material part of the business is dependent on a single or a few customers; (c) principal products produced and services rendered, including markets, methods of distribution and changes therein; (d) backlogs, amount and other details, if material; (e) sources and availability of essential raw materials; (f) importance to business of material patents, franchises, etc.; (g) estimated amount spent during last two years on research and development, indicating which activities were company- and which customer-sponsored, describing substantial new products and number of employees engaged in research and new product development; (h) number of persons employed; and [i] extent to which the business is seasonal. (The instructions for this item contain many other specific disclosure requirements.) The New York and American Stock Exchanges require that the following additional information be given to them: annual output for last five years; operations conducted, merchandising methods, recent growth and development of the industry and of the company and the place it occupies in its field; details about employee relations (including dates and duration of material work stoppages due to labour disagreements in the last three years) and stockholders' relations, etc.

Specific additional information required includes:

G7 name of parent company and basis of control[8] and list of subsidiaries

G8 recent sales of unregistered securities [26 (not in prospectus)]

G9 franchises or concessions held by registrant and subsidiaries [28 (not in prospectus)]

3.7.4 Stewardship information

The UK

Directors:

S1* directors' names, addresses and descriptions (including nationality) [A6, B4(a); 1948:3]

S2 powers of directors, particulars [A12]

S3 interests of each director in the share capital [A27(b); B20(a)]

S4 directors' service contracts and emoluments, particulars [A28(a) (b), B21]

S5* full particulars of interests, direct or indirect, of every director related to assets dealt with (owned, leased, disposed of, etc.) by the company or its subsidiaries within the preceding two years [A29(a), B22(a); 1948:16]

S6 full particulars of significant contracts in which a director is materially interested [A29(b), B22(b)]

Other principals, officers, promoters, expenses, etc.:

S7* auditors' names and qualifications [A9, B4(d); 1948:15]

S8 secretary's name and qualifications; names of bankers, brokers, solicitors, registrars and trustees, if any [A7, 8, B4(b) (c); 1948:15]

S9* name and other particulars of any promoter and the amounts of any consideration given in the past two years or proposed to be given [A31; 1948:13]

S10 interest of any parties other than directors in a substantial part of the capital [A27(c), B20(c)]

S11* capital under option – price, duration, consideration for which option was or will be granted, name of grantor and other particulars

[A24, B17; 1948:7]

S12 expenses of issue (including preliminary expenses for new company), amount and to whom paid or payable [A25, B18; 1948:12]

S13* particulars of commissions, discounts, brokerages, or other special terms granted in connection with a capital issue [A26, B19; 1948:11]

The US

S1 directors' (current and prospective) ages, offices held, family relationships with other directors or executive officers; names, ages, family relationships, etc., of executive officers and their principal occupations during the past five years also required [16]

S2/3 not specifically mentioned (the amount and percentage of each class of equity securities beneficially owned directly or indirectly by directors as a group must be disclosed [19(b)])

S4 remuneration paid by the affiliated group during the last fiscal year (a) to each director and to each of the three highest paid officers of the registrant who received more than $40,000 (including names); and (b) to all directors and officers as a group [17(a)]; also pension or retirement benefits proposed to be paid under an existing plan to the named directors and officers [17(b), Exhibit 11]

S5/6 disclosure required of interests in material transactions of directors, officers and principal holders of securities and their associates within the past three years [20, Exhibit 13]: also any arrangement or understanding between a director and person who selected him [16]

S7/8 not specifically mentioned, but usually given at least to the stock exchanges where listed or to be listed

S9 information about promoters required for past *five* years [11]

S10 particulars required of owners (directly or beneficially) of more than 10 per cent of any class of securities; registrant must give names [19]

S11 same [18, Exhibit 5]

S12 same, but not in prospectus [23]

S13 underwriting discounts and commissions are reported in the prospectus [1, 2]; sales of securities to special parties are not [25, Exhibit 1]

The following additional disclosure is required, but not in the prospectus:

S13 arrangements limiting, restricting, or stabilising the market for securities being offered [22]

S14 relationship with registrant of experts named in the registration statement [24]

S15 indemnification arrangements for officers and directors [29 (not in prospectus), Exhibit 12]

3.7.5 Financial reports and figures

The UK

F1 profit and loss statements:
- (a)* periods: (i) each of *five* preceding years (or for period from incorporation of company if less); (ii) if the last statement is for a period ending more than three months earlier than its date of publication, no accounts should have been made up since that date [A20(a); 1948:19(1)(a)]
- (b) contents [reference: ch. 3, para. 2a of 'Yellow Book']:
    - sales to third parties, specifying method by which such sales are arrived at
    - cost of goods sold
    - other income (e.g., investment income and rents)
    - share of profits of associated companies
    - profit before taxation and extraordinary items
    - taxation on profits (UK, overseas and share of associated companies, including basis on which overseas currencies and taxation have been dealt with)
    - minority interests
    - extraordinary items (less taxation attributable thereto)
    - profit attributable to shareholders
    - amount absorbed by preferential dividends
    - profit attributable to equity
    - amount absorbed by dividends on equity, together with the rate of dividend on each class of shares and details of any waivers of dividends
    - increase in retained profits for the year as shown in the balance sheet
- (c) trend of profits, explanation included in the body of the prospectus, dealing in particular with the effects of changes in financing, acquisition of subsidiaries, etc. [ch. 3, para. 9 of 'Yellow Book']
- (d) holding companies should segregate their interests in the profits and losses of their subsidiaries from those of minority shareholders [A20(b)]

F2* balance sheets at the beginning and end of each accounting period to be reported on (required since 1 October 1973) [A20(d) (e); 1948: 19(1)(a) end only]

F3* dating of financial reports: if the last reports are for a period ending on a date earlier than three months before publication of the prospectus, a statement to this effect must be made [A20(a); 1948: 19(1)]

F4 auditors should make such adjustments and report on any other matters which appear relevant for the purpose of their report [A20(f)]

F5 statement of contingent or actual liabilities, particularly with respect to litigation or claims of material importance [A30, B23], income tax [A33, B24], and estate tax [A34, B25]

F6* material contracts entered into other than in the ordinary course of business within past two years: parties, dates, consideration and other particulars unless the Quotations Committee determines that such disclosure might be detrimental to the company's competitive position [A35, note 3; B27, note 2; 1948:14]

F7* rate of dividend and amount absorbed by each class of shares or waived during preceding five years [A20(c); 1948:19(1)(b)]

The US

F1 profit and loss statements
    (a) periods: each of the *three* fiscal years preceding the date of the latest balance sheet filed and for the period between the close of the latest of such fiscal years and the date of the latest balance sheet filed. These statements should be certified up to the date of the latest certified balance sheet [21, instruction 2]. Regulation S-X applies to these statements
    (b) contents:
        (i) same as for annual statements (see section 3.3) summary of earnings [6] (similar to UK): a five-year summary (in column form) is required for each of the last five fiscal years of the registrant and for any period between the end of the latest such year and the date of the latest balance sheet furnished. Rappaport [1972] states that 'The summary of earnings is, without a doubt, the most important single financial statement in a prospectus prepared for filing with the SEC' (p. 10–2)
            This need not be certified. However, it would be certified

'. . . where one accountant has performed sufficient work to make it appropriate for him to permit use of his name in connection with a summary earnings table . . .' [ASR 62]. The summary of earnings would also be certified where it is furnished in sufficient detail to make it unnecessary to furnish an earnings statement.

   (ii) items required [specifically mentioned in instructions 1, 4, 6 and 7]:

      (1) include those required in the UK (F1b), with the exception of other income (item 3); items 4, 7 and 13 are not explicitly listed but would be given where applicable);

      (2) additional disclosure required includes: interest expenses; income from continuing operations; discontinued operations, less applicable tax; income or loss before extraordinary items; extraordinary items, less applicable tax; and cumulative effects of changes in accounting principles;

      (3) retroactive adjustments affecting the comparability of results should be included;

      (4) difference between the actual and estimated amounts of extraordinary items, charges or credits must be explained;

      (5) basis of computing earnings per share shall be stated and described

  (iii) additional information required:

      (1) additional years are required if necessary to keep the summary from being misleading [6, instruction 1];

      (2) the instructions also state: 'In connection with such summary, whenever necessary, reflect information or explanation of material significance to investors in appraising the results shown, or refer to such information or explanation set forth elsewhere in the prospectus' [6, headnote]. Because it is often not clear what is sufficient to meet this requirement, Rappaport [1972] states that '. . . it is fair to say that the number of deficiencies cited by the SEC in relation to such summaries exceeds those relating to all other financial statements combined.' (p. 10-3).

 (c) textual analyses – Guide 22. 'Summary of Earnings', as amended with effect from 30 September 1974 (ASR 159) (and Guide 1 'Summary of Operations' with respect to the 1934 Act) discusses and describes in considerable detail the textual analysis desired by the Commission

(d) holding company regulations apply to balance sheet as well as profit and loss statements and are more detailed and complex, namely as follows:

  (i) individual (unconsolidated) statements of the registrant may be omitted if consolidated statements are filed and if the registrant is primarily an operating company and all subsidiaries are totally owned, or the registrant's assets and earnings dominate (as defined in the instructions) the group. (The basis for the omission must be stated.) If the prescribed tests are not met, individual statements must be presented for the registrant, for the registrant and its consolidated subsidiaries, or both, as appropriate. *This provision of the regulations may be quite expensive to the registrant if the required records must be constructed* [21, instruction 3]

  (ii) unconsolidated majority owned subsidiaries, 50 per cent owned companies and companies accounted for by the equity method (unless not significant) must file statements as if they were registrants [21, instruction 6, 7, 8]

  (iii) affiliates, securities of which constitute or are to constitute a substantial portion of the collateral securing any class of securities being registered – same as (2) [21, instruction 9]

(e) debt issues ratio of earnings to fixed charges (i) in tabular form for each year as statements; (ii) most recent year, *pro forma* giving effect of changes proposed; (iii) earnings before fixed charges and taxes and after eliminating undistributed income of unconsolidated subsidiaries and 50 per cent or less owned persons; (iv) fixed charges include amortisation of debt discount, expense and premium and portion of rentals equivalent to interest, and preferred stock dividend requirements of consolidated subsidiaries [instruction 5]

F2 balance sheet: only one balance sheet as of a date within 90 days prior to filing date need be filed (or within six months if certain conditions are met, generally available for large, 'seasoned' companies); it need not be certified, in which event a certified balance sheet as of a date within one year must be filed [21, instruction 1]. Regulation S-X applies, including supplementary schedules

F3 (a) dates: registration statements *must* be filed within 90 days of the date of the statements; should the SEC staff raise questions that require changes, then each amendment creates a new filing date unless the amendment is filed with the consent of the Commission which is usually given unless the statements are considered obsolete or otherwise misleading [21, instruction 1(a), Release No. 33–4936, 9 December 1968]

(b) the balance sheet may be of a date six months before the filing date if the registrant (i) files annual statements with the SEC; (ii) has total assets greater than $5,000,000; and (iii) has no long term debt in default [21, instruction 1(a)]

F4 adjustments: the SEC's requirements are much more specific, particularly with respect to the following:

(a) reorganisation during the period for which profit and loss statements are required:

(i) the effect of a reorganisation that resulted in substantial changes in balance sheet accounts must be explained in a note or supporting schedule [21, instruction 10(a)]

(ii) if the registrant is about to emerge from a reorganisation, the effect on the balance sheet must be given [21, instruction 10(b)]

(b) if the registrant has purchased a business in the period for which income statements are presented, the separate statements of the business acquired may be required if the business is of major significance to the registrant as defined [21, instruction 11(a)]

(c) if the registrant has acquired after the date of the most recent balance sheet filed either by purchase or pooling or is about to acquire a business or an investment in a business to be accounted for by the equity method, the statements of the business and appropriate *pro formas* (five years for a pooling and one year for a purchase) will be required if the business is significant [21, instruction 12]

F5 contingent liabilities: legal action specifically mentioned [12]; otherwise included in financial statements

F6 material contracts [Exhibit 13]

F7 dividends: five years required in summary of earnings (see F1b(ii)) [6, instruction 4]

The SEC requires additional information, including the following:

F8 statements of source and application of funds must be furnished for each profit and loss statement period [21, instruction A2]

F9 analyses of retained earnings and other additional capital accounts must be furnished for each year for which an income statement is required [S-X, 5–02.39(d)]

86

F10 survey of selected accounts for the seven-year period preceding the earliest profit and loss statement (the survey may be omitted from the prospectus): an analysis and description of the following accounts (whether or not presently carried on the books) is required for each person (company) for whom a balance sheet is filed. It need not be certified. The survey may be omitted for any company for which equivalent information for the period has been filed with the SEC pursuant to the 1933 and 1934 Acts:

(a) revaluation of property, if material: details for each year [21, instruction 15]
(b) capital shares, material restatements or issue of shares where credit went to accounts other than capital share accounts [21, instruction 16]
(c) debt discount and expenses written off earlier than required under any periodic amortisation plan: details [21, instruction 17]
(d) premiums and discount and expenses on securities retired: details [21, instruction 18]
(e) other material changes in surplus: details [21, instruction 19]
(f) predecessor, if material: entries made respectively in the books of the predecessor or successor and changes effected in the transfer of assets from the predecessor [21, instruction 20]

3.7.6 Post-audit information

The UK

PA1* acquisition (completed, agreed to or proposed) of assets or shares of a company which will become a subsidiary:
(a) an accountant's report of:
    (i) profits and losses attributable to the interests acquired, for the past five years, if available [A21(a), B14(a)(i); 1948:20, 21]
    (ii) last audited balance sheets of the acquired business, if available [A21(b), B14(a)(ii); 1948:20, 21]
    (iii) other relevant matters [A21(c), B14(a)(iii)]
(b) the following additional information is required only for companies some of whose securities are already listed (Part B):
    (i) statement of any change in the financial and trading position [B14(b)]
    (ii) statement of the general nature of the business and fixed assets acquired [B14(c)]

(iii) aggregate value of the consideration for the acquisition and how it was satisfied [B14(d)]

(iv) any changes in the emoluments of directors [B14(e)]

(c) the requirements are relaxed if the acquisition is not material, if shareholders were already issued with adequate information or if the acquired company has listed securities, in which event the information is already publicly available [B14]

PA2 borrowings (other than loan capital) and contingent liabilities of the company and its subsidiaries as at the latest date reasonably practical [A5(b), B10]

The US

PA1 acquisitions:

(a) approximately the same as UK [21, instruction 11(a) (b) and 12(a) (b), Exhibit 2]

(b) no special provision is made for companies some of whose securities are already listed: the statements required are the same as if the acquired company were a registrant [21, instruction 12(a)]

(c) no relaxation of requirements is made except that financial statements need not be filed for acquisitions of totally held subsidiaries [21, instruction 12(c)]

PA2 all material post-audit events that affect the financial statements filed through the date the registration became effective must be reported[16] [1933 Act, section 11]. As a consequence, the auditor must keep in touch with the client's affairs beyond the time of audit and preparation of the statements. Recommended procedures for determining whether subsequent events should be disclosed are given in the AICPA's Statement on Auditing Procedure No. 47 (September 1971)

3.7.7 Prospects

The UK

PR1 material information about the financial and trading prospects of the company or group, particularly those unlikely to be known or anticipated by the general public [A17(a); B11(a)]

PR2 profit forecast, if presented, must include: (a) principal assumptions on which the directors based the forecast, (b) accountant's statement about the accounting bases and calculations, (c) issuing house or sponsoring broker's report [A17(a) (b) and B11(a) (b)]

PR3 for fixed income securities, profits cover for dividend/interest and net tangible assets [A17(c) and B11(c)]

PR4 any waiver of future dividends [A17(d) and B11(d)]

PR5 opinion of directors on the sufficiency of working capital or provisions for additional working capital [A18, B12]

The US

PR1 use of proceeds [3]; description of business [9] – emphasis is on present business and past events, particularly negative events such as bankruptcies, reorganisation, etc.

PR2 forecasts not permitted (though in February 1973 the SEC announced that it will probably permit forecasts under certain conditions in the future)

PR3 required: ratio of fixed charges for long term debt and/or preferred stock to earnings for all periods covered by the summary of earnings and a *pro forma* ratio for the latest year of the summary and for the interim periods (if any). Specific instructions apply; see also Accounting Series Release 119 and 122 (1971)

PR4 not specifically mentioned

PR5 sufficiency of working capital: offering will not be allowed if inadequate [Accounting Series Release 115 (1970)]

3.8 Initial report

An 'initial report', as such, is not required in the UK as it is in the US. The Securities Exchange Act 1934 and the SEC's regulations specify an initial report filed in accordance with form 10 and which is 'updated' annually by form 10-K. In the UK, much of the non-financial 'initial information' called for by form 10 is recorded in registers that are available for inspection by security holders and the Department of Trade and Industry. For listed companies, similar information is required by The Stock Exchange and would be made available to the public in an introductory statement publicised by the company or in a prospectus.

The following financial information is required for form 10 [references are to form 10]:

IR1 general information about and description of the organisation, development, and business done and about to be done by the corporation and affiliated group in the past five years; this item calls for a separation of sales, expenses and net income by 'lines of business' (I1d, section 3.31) [item 1]

IR2   summary of operations of each of the past five years (or more if necessary to keep the summary from being misleading) (see F1b(ii), section 3.7.5) [item 2]

IR3   location and character of principal plants, mines and properties [item 3]

IR4   list of parent companies and subsidiaries [item 4]

IR5   information about officers and directors:
- (a) list of directors and executive officers [item 6]
- (b) voting securities held by principal holders and equity securities owned by management [item 5]
- (c) remuneration of each director who received more than $40,000 from the affiliated group in the last year, each of the three highest paid officers who received more than that amount, and the aggregate remuneration of all directors and officers [item 7]
- (d) interest of management and others in material transactions [item 9]
- (e) indemnification arrangements for directors and officers [item 17]
- (f) management options to purchase securities [item 8]

IR6   material pending legal proceedings [item 10]

IR7   description, etc., of securities outstanding and sold recently [items 12, 13, 14, 15, 16]

IR8   financial statements and exhibits (for each of three years and the period up to registration) [item 18]:
- (a) balance sheet (most recent only)
- (b) income statement
- (c) changes of financial position (funds statement)
- (d) stockholders' equity accounts

Note: If the company has had a recent registration (prospectus) under the Securities Act of 1933, it is possible for it to file a so-called 'short form' registration statement on form 10 or form 8-A under the Securities Exchange Act of 1934 as the 'initial report' under the Exchange Act.

3.9 Acquisitions, realisations, mergers and take-overs

The UK

The principal reporting requirements for acquisitions, realisations and

90

mergers (business combinations) are found in chapters 4 and 5 of The Stock Exchange's *Admission of Securities to Listing* ('Yellow Book'), supplemented by *The City Code on Take-overs and Mergers*. The Stock Exchange's rules specify four classes of situations that require differing degrees of notice and publication of information. The City Code states guidelines governing take-overs and mergers.

The four situations and responses delineated by The Stock Exchange are as follows [references are to the 'Yellow Book']:

Class 1 If sufficiently material to call for an announcement to the Quotations Department and the press and a circular sent to shareholders; applies generally where the value of the assets acquired or disposed of, net profits, consideration given or received, or equity capital issued are 15 per cent or more of comparable figures of the acquiring or disposing company. The required announcement must include information on: [ch. 4, para. 5(c) and 6(a) to (g)][17]

AM1 the working capital of the companies
AM2 assets acquired and disposed of
AM3 a description of the trade carried on
AM4 value of the consideration and means of payment
AM5 net profits attributable to the relevant assets
AM6 the benefits expected to accrue
AM7 service contracts with proposed directors of the company

The circular includes information as required for a prospectus (see section 3.7).

Class 2 if sufficiently important to require an announcement to the Quotations Department and the press; applies where the relevant figures are between 5 per cent and 15 per cent. The required announcement must include items AM2 to AM7 above.

Class 3 no announcement required if the consideration is satisfied in cash or unquoted securities: applies where the value of the assets acquired or disposed of and the profits attributable to those assets are less than 5 per cent of those of the acquiring or disposing company. If an announcement is made, it would be misleading not to state the value of the consideration or indicate the size of the transaction.

Class 4 a transaction that involves the interests of directors or substantial shareholders (past or present) requires notification to the Quotations Department. The Stock Exchange Council will normally require that a circular be sent to shareholders and that their prior approval of the transaction be sought in general meeting. The requirements for the circular are those that apply to a prospectus (see section 3.7), plus any additional matters particular to the transaction.

The City Code on Take-overs and Mergers (amended June 1974) states guidelines and provides a series of rules to govern take-overs and mergers. With respect to the disclosure of financial information, the Code includes the following general principle: 'Shareholders shall have in their possession sufficient evidence, facts and opinions upon which an adequate judgement and decision can be reached and shall have sufficient time to make an assessment and decision. No relevant information shall be withheld from them.' (p. 10, para. 3.) Only three specific items related to financial information are mentioned:

AM8 profit forecasts, including a clear statement of the commercial assumption on which the directors have based their forecasts; the auditors or consulting accountants must examine the accounting basis and calculations for the forecasts and any other financial adviser mentioned must report on the forecasts (rule 16)

AM9 asset valuations supported by the opinion of a named independent professional expert and the basis of valuation (rule 16 and practice notes 4 and 6)

AM10 directors' interests (rule 17 and practice note 1) and particulars of service contracts (rule 19)

AM11 shareholdings of the offeror and related parties to the offer (and vice versa)

The first two items (AM8 and AM9) are not required by the Code. The rules apply only if they are included in the documents.

The US

Except for securities listed on the major exchanges, the situations under which information must be provided to shareholders and the public upon an acquisition are not defined as directly or as specifically in the US as in The (London) Stock Exchange rules. Individual state laws and the listing agreements of the stock exchanges govern the situation in which a vote of the stockholders is required. In general, state laws require stockholder approval for a merger, sale of substantially all of a company's assets or issuance of capital shares. At this point the SEC's Regulations 14A and 14C apply to all registrants under the Securities Exchange Act of 1934. Regulation 14A specifies the information that must be given in a proxy situation (outlined in part below): Regulation 14C (adopted in December 1965) specifies that most of the information required for proxy situations be sent to stockholders from whom proxies are not solicited. Thus, if a stockholders' meeting is held, the SEC's regulations prevail. In addition, if a merger or acquisition of assets is accompanied by an issuance of securities (as with a tender offer), the prospectus requirements of the Securities Act of 1933 (discussed in section 3.7) also apply.

Notification is required by the stock exchanges and the SEC. The New York and American Stock Exchange listing agreements require companies to notify the Exchange promptly if '. . . it or any company controlled by it shall dispose of any property or any stock interest in any of the subsidiaries or controlled companies . . .' that materially affect its financial position [item I.3]. Moreover, the policies of these two exchanges provide that approval of stockholders will be required (pursuant to a proxy solicitation conforming to the proxy rules of the Securities and Exchange Commission) as a prerequisite to approval of applications to list additional shares to be issued as sole or partial consideration for an acquisition of the stock or assets of another company in the following circumstances:

(a) if any director, officer or substantial stockholder of the listed company has an interest, directly or indirectly, in the company or assets to be acquired or in the consideration to be paid in the transaction;

(b) where the present or potential issuance of common stock or securities convertible into common stock could result in an increase in outstanding common shares approximating 20 per cent or more; or

(c) where the present or potential issuance of common stock and any other consideration has a combined fair value approximating 20 per cent or more of the market value of the outstanding common shares.

The SEC's monthly report (8-K), filed within ten days of the end of a month, calls for financial statements and other information on the acquisition or disposition of assets and changes in securities (see section 3.6.2).

Most of the specific information required in the UK (and more) is required by the SEC with the exception of AM8 and AM9 listed above.[18] At present, forecasts and asset valuation other than historical cost are not permitted by the SEC.[19] However, the SEC requires the following specific additional information for mergers, consolidations, acquisitions, dissolution and similar matters [all references are to Schedule 14A of Regulation 14A]:

AM11 'certified financial statements of the issuer and its subsidiaries as would currently be required in an original application for registration of securities of the issuer under the Act. All schedules other than the schedules of supplementary profit and loss information may be omitted' [15]

AM12 brief description of business, underlying methods of production, markets, methods of distribution, sources and supply of new materials, location and description of plants and important physical properties, in addition to AM2 (trade carried on) [item 14(b) (1) (2)]

AM13 particulars of dividends in arrears, defaults in principal or interest in securities, etc. [14(b) (3)]

AM14 existing and *pro forma* capitalisation (in tabular form) [14(b) (4)]

AM15 five-year summary of earnings, underlying per share net earnings, dividends and book value, in column form [14(b) (5)]

AM16 *pro forma* combined five-year summary of earnings, if pooled, otherwise most recent year as in AM15 [14(b) (6)]

AM17 interim current and prior earnings as required by AM15 and AM16 'to the extent material for the exercise of prudent judgement in regard to the matter to be acted upon' [14(b) (7)]

AM18 stock price, high and low for each period within last two years [14(c)]

Notes

[1] Of course, US auditors also exercise professional judgement.

[2] See General Education Trust of the Institute of Chartered Accountants in England and Wales (1969) and Thomas D. Hubbard (1973) for an outline of UK Companies Acts requirements and US AICPA and SEC requirements.

[3] The SEC also requires a five-year summary of earnings. The Companies Act 1948 does not require an auditor's opinion on the previous year's figures. The Stock Exchange recommends that a table of ten years' relevant figures be given.

[4]   The law (Companies Act 1948, para. 148) requires submission of accounts to shareholders at a meeting no later than nine months after the year ends (twelve months for companies having interests abroad). Since three weeks' notice must be given, in practice only about eight months after the end of the year is allowed.

[5]   The SEC has involved auditors with quarterly reports by requiring inclusion of quarterly details in annual reports (ASR 177) though the change was opposed by the AICPA (Exposure Draft, 15 April 1975).

[6]   However, textual disclosure is permitted where the information is material to a particular issue, following the *Gerstle v. Gamble-Skogmo* case.

[7]   References to Regulation S-X are: C1 – 5–02.38, 12–14 (schedule XIII), 10-K, item 6 in narrative section rather than in auditor's report; C2 – 5–02.39, 3–15, 11–02; C3 – 3–16(f), 5–02.38, 12–14 (schedule XIII); C4 – disclosed in consolidated statements; C5 – 3–16(n), ARB 43–13B15; C6 – 3–16(f); C8 – 5–02.36, 12–13 (schedule XII), 3–09; C9 – 5–02.36; C10 – 5–02.39; C11 – 10-K, item 11 (if over 10 per cent and in total); and C12 – Form 10-K, item 11. Regulation S-X, however, calls for more detail than is required by the Companies Acts, such as an analysis of balances and changes of *each* equity category.

[8]   References to Regulation S-X of the UK items not listed below are: L3 – 3–16(c), 3–16(i), L10 – 3–16(o), 5–02.35, ASR 149; L11 – 3–16(i); and L13 – 5–02.27.

[9]   APB 31 was extended by SEC Accounting Series Release (ASR) 147 (October 1973). ASR 149 made mandatory L9c2, L9c3 and F3d, which were only suggested in APB 31.

[10] SSAP 6 (para. 13) requires that 'The profit and loss account for the year should show a profit or loss after extraordinary items, reflecting all profits and losses recognised in the accounts of the year other than prior year adjustments as defined in Part 2 and unrealised surpluses on revaluation of fixed assets, which should be credited direct to reserves.'

[11] The SEC has also suggested that companies disclose the amount of inventory profits reflected in income during periods of rising prices [Accounting Series Release 151, January 1974].

[12] The Companies Act 1967 does not mention new issues and prospectuses.

[13] See section 3 of the Securities Act of 1933 for a complete listing.

[14] Other rules apply to securities of a government, local authority or statutory body (Part C) and to securities of a company whose activities include to a material extent exploration for natural resources (Part D).

[15] ASR 155 (April 1974) makes a considerable number of changes in

prospectus requirements.

[16] Section 11 of the Securities Act of 1933 states: 'In case any part of the registration statement, when such part became effective, contained an untrue statement of material fact or omitted to state a material fact required to be stated therein or necessary to make the statements therein not misleading, any person acquiring such security . . . may . . . sue . . . every accountant . . . who . . . certified any part of the registration statement . . .' A recent court decision (*Escott et al. v. BarChris Construction Corp. et al.,* 283 F. Supp. 643 [SDNY 1968]) emphasises this requirement and the penalties for not heeding it.

[17] Although there is no indication that the disclosure requirements for class 2 situations apply also to class 1 situations, in practice they do.

[18] Reference (to Schedule 14A of Regulation 14A) for the other UK information requirements are: AM1 – included in financial statements required by item 15; AM2 – item 14(b); AM3 – item 14(b); AM4, AM5 – included in financial statements required by item 15 with respect to an acquisition, merger or consolidation; AM6, AM7, AM10 – not explicitly called for, but required under the general requirement for disclosure of all material information.

[19] Forecasts will apparently be permitted, as discussed above. The SEC's *amicus curiae* brief in *Gerstle v. Gamble-Skogmo* would seem to require disclosure of the market value of assets where these valuations are material to the merger or acquisition, etc.

4 Benefit–cost analysis of required financial disclosure

4.1 Introduction

In general, financial disclosure requirements are imposed on companies because the benefits to the public are believed to exceed the costs, however distributed. Among the benefits usually mentioned are (a) the prevention or reduction of fraud and misrepresentation; (b) fairness to non-insiders; (c) lower transaction and information costs to investors; and (d) more efficient allocation of the investors' resources among companies. To these ends, governments require companies to disclose financial information in prospectuses whenever they solicit the public for funds, and periodically to their stockholders and other interested parties. In this chapter, the benefits and costs associated with the disclosure laws and regulations imposed in the UK and the US are set out explicitly and measured to the extent feasible to determine whether the goals of legislation are met and whether they are served better by the different regulations of either of the two countries.

The arguments that support government required disclosure are delineated first, in section 4.2. The emphasis here is on the benefits that are presumed to derive from it, gross of costs. If required disclosure adds nothing to what otherwise would occur in the absence of government laws and regulations (including lower processing, distribution, etc., costs), then the additional costs of required disclosure need not be considered. Once the presumed benefits are delineated, operationally, evidence that supports or rejects the presumptions is presented. This evidence leads one to doubt, though not entirely discount, the value to the public (defined more explicitly below) of government required disclosure.

The costs of required disclosure are discussed in section 4.3. Direct, indirect and opportunity costs are distinguished. Unfortunately, there is little available data from which an exact comparison between the costs of required versus voluntary disclosure can be made. Nevertheless, the analysis does give some indication of the relative cost of required disclosure.

4.2 Benefits deriving from government regulated financial disclosure

4.2.1 Required disclosure of private companies in a free society

In a democracy, it is assumed that government ought not to interfere with nor attempt to regulate people's freedoms, including their right to property, unless this interference is sufficiently for the benefit of 'the public good'. The definition of 'the public good' is more a matter of ethics than of science. For some, the public good is enhanced when an action or policy improves some people's well-being (utility) while not reducing the well-being of others or compensating them for any loss in well-being (a move towards Pareto optimality). Others might view the public good as a situation where the total material production of society is increased, net of the costs of achieving the increase, even though some persons in society are worse off as a result. Thus, if the benefits from information exceed the costs of its production, etc., the public good would be enhanced whether or not the people who receive the benefits are other than those who pay the costs. Some others might believe that the public good is enhanced if resources are re-allocated to more needful people. Thus even though the total costs of producing information exceeded the total benefits derived therefrom, the public good would be enhanced if less affluent or outside investors benefited at the expense of wealthy investors or insiders.

In any event, given the presupposition of a free society, it is necessary that the benefits (however defined) from required disclosure be specified before government imposes costs and restrictions on companies. These benefits do not appear to be obvious, although the costs are. By requiring and regulating financial disclosure of companies, government abridges private rights. Indeed, there is reason to believe that government required financial disclosure expropriates the wealth of shareholders for the benefit of others. Shareholders must pay for the production and distribution of financial information. But they must provide this information, at no charge, to competitors of their corporation and to government agencies, who may use the information to the detriment of their corporation. Non-shareholders are also furnished information at no charge. Though one could argue that a transfer of wealth is beneficial, there is no obvious reason to believe that competitors, government agencies or non-shareholders are 'deserving deprived groups', compared with shareholders.

It is important to note that, in the absence of disclosure statutes, individuals would be able to choose whether or not to invest in companies that provided any quantity and quality of financial information. In general, one would assume that the information provided would be that which people would freely demand and be willing to pay for. It might seem that shareholders would not want financial data disclosed because the information might benefit competitors, government agencies and non-shareholders. However, the interests of shareholders may be advanced more than reduced by the publication of financial statements. General publication may be less expensive than an alternative method of communicating information to shareholders. Shareholders may also consider general publication beneficial *because* a larger group than themselves can review the information critically, and so serve to audit and motivate the performance of managers. Publication of financial statements might also be desired to enhance the marketability of shares and raise new capital, if non-shareholders would otherwise be reluctant to purchase shares in the corporation. All these considerations enter into the decision as to whether and what financial information should be published by a corporation. Why, then, should government interfere with this apparently private matter?

Six reasons may be adduced for government required financial disclosure: (1) the obligation of government to provide for the enforcement of contracts; (2) a concept of fairness in dealings among people; (3) protection of non-shareholders who are affected by companies; (4) improved efficiency of resource allocation; (5) improved administration of government and the public's and the employees' 'right to know'; and (6) political considerations. Each of these is discussed in turn as it relates to disclosure of financial information by companies. The arguments supporting these reasons are given in the next section. Such evidence as is available is presented in the following sections.

Contract enforcement   Government accepts or is given the responsibility of providing for the enforcement of contracts among private parties, in part because this procedure is believed to be more efficient than private enforcement and in part because government has a monopoly in the legal use of force and, consequently, must accept responsibility to enforce private agreements. A contract assumes a 'meeting of minds' of the individuals who enter into it. Should they agree that one party need not tell the other anything or even that they may lie, the contract would be valid since both parties understand and are presumed to accept these conditions. Unless stated explicitly, however, a contract implies that the parties will not attempt to defraud each other by knowingly making false statements or misrepresentations.

Such a contract is thought to exist between shareholders and the officers and directors of companies. The officers and directors contract, for a fee, to manage the company's resources for the shareholders' benefit. It is conceivable that the 'fee' could be stated as 'whatever the officers and directors take for themselves' and include use of inside information for their private benefit. If a shareholder invests in such an enterprise, he should have no complaint. However, such contracts are rarely (if ever) written. There is rather an implied contract that the officers and directors will act in the best interests of the shareholders. To this end, the managers may decide to publish a very limited amount of or even no financial data because they believe that competitors or they themselves will benefit more from this than shareholders. Alternatively, a considerable amount of data would be audited by independent experts and published if shareholders appeared to demand this practice (which was generally the case before government regulations were enacted). Presumably, the quality and extent of the audits would reflect investors' demands and the cost of auditing. Why, then, should government interfere with this contract by requiring more disclosure?

One reason for government interference is its obligation to provide the means whereby contracts can be enforced. While the shareholders could always sue officers and directors who violated their contracts to manage the shareholders' resources as fiduciaries, it might be less expensive for society to prevent or reduce the need for such suits. This would be the case if initial and periodic financial disclosure provided a sufficient incentive for officers and directors to manage shareholders' resources according to the implied contract. Independent auditors would be required to provide assurance that the enterprise was not being operated fraudulently and that the figures presented provided shareholders with an adequate report of how their resources were managed. The rationale for government interference, then, is the belief that the costs to companies (and hence to their shareholders) of disclosure which shareholders otherwise would not have demanded is less than the cost to government (and hence to all taxpayers) of enforcing contracts between the shareholders and the managers.

Fairness. A second reason for government required disclosure is people's desire for the admittedly elusive quality of 'fairness'. Though the concept is not easily defined or measured, it is nevertheless real and politically powerful. One aspect of 'fairness' is the belief by investors that they possess an implied contract which requires that no investor receive useful information before any other. In particular, they may believe that the officers, directors and other 'insiders' are bound to act as fiduciaries, even though such an agreement has not, in fact, been signed. Alternatively, shareholders may knowingly agree to a contract that allows management to profit extraordinarily at the shareholders' expense. But when the shareholders realise how much they have been 'taken in' they often petition government for a redress of the 'damage' done to them. As is discussed above under contract enforcement, it may be less expensive for government to insist on specific disclosure that, for example, makes managers' potential conflicts of interest clear to shareholders. Then shareholders might forebear from entering into contracts which they later regret and dishonest promoters might find it more difficult to deceive investors. Honest promoters, though, would have to substitute more formal compensation arrangements in place of potential gains from trading on inside information.

Protection of non-shareholders Protection of people other than shareholders who deal directly with companies is another reason given for government required disclosure. These people include creditors and employees of companies. The arguments in support of such protection are the same as those previously given – it is presumed less expensive to prevent or reduce damage due to fraud or mis-assessment of risks to creditors and employees than to attempt redress in the courts.

Some people also argue that employees have a vital interest in the success of their employer. Disclosure of financial results, they believe, is useful for motivating managers to operate the company well. At the very least, employees may learn that the company is not doing well or is doing better than the managers claim in wage bargaining sessions. Even if these beliefs are correct, though, it is not at all clear why government should intervene to help employees at the expense of shareholders and consumers. In any event, it must first be determined whether financial data are useful for this purpose.

Improved efficiency of resource allocation This major benefit is based on the presumption that financial disclosure facilitates and may even be necessary for resources to flow to those companies in which the marginal return (net of risk) is greatest, thus tending to maximise the wealth of the nation. 'How else can investors determine where to place their resources,' the argument runs, 'without access to the information disclosed in financial statements?' This belief underlies the disclosure provisions of the US Securities Acts. As the SEC puts it, disclosure of financial information is essential so that 'investors may make a realistic appraisal of the merits of securities and thus exercise an informed judgement in determining whether to purchase them.'[1] This presupposes that financial statements.contain information useful for investment decisions and that the information is made available to investors in time for them to use it and before it is 'known' to and acted upon by others. It also assumes that the decisions alluded to affect and improve the production decisions of firms. An additional important assumption is that adequate disclosure would not be forthcoming unless required by law.

Whether or not assumptions about the value to investors of published financial information are correct, one must still ask why government should require disclosure. Considerations of fraud aside (since these were considered earlier), one would expect managers to provide security holders with information to the extent that the marginal cost of production and distribution of the information is not greater than the marginal value of the information to security holders. While estimates of these amounts are admittedly difficult to make, one would expect corporate managers to be capable of making better estimates than government officials.

One reason supporting government required disclosure is the possible existence of positive externalities in the production and distribution of information. Each company, individually, might not choose to publish much financial data so long as other companies do not publish similar data. This behaviour might be based on the realisation that, while the shareholders of the company pay for the production and publication of the reports, non-shareholders cannot be prevented from using them. Thus the reports produce a benefit that cannot be fully captured by the owners – a positive externality. As a consequence, managers produce and distribute less information than all investors (shareholders and potential shareholders) would want, were there some way to get all who use the information to pay for it. This externality might be captured were *all* companies required to produce and distribute financial data, thereby presumably getting all investors to share the costs. As a collateral benefit, the advantage a competitor might receive were information published by only a few companies would be mitigated. If *all* firms were required to publish similar data, the 'public spirited' firm would not be unfairly penalised.

A second externality claimed from the required publication by all companies of financial reports is a general reduction in the costs of distributing and analysing information. Efficiency increases because investors need not individually make inquiries of companies but could rather receive or easily acquire standardised financial reports. These economies of scale may result in lower costs. Costs of checking the figures for accuracy and honesty should also be reduced if investors could put more trust in figures produced in compliance with a statute than those that would have been voluntarily published.

A third source of benefits assumed is increased public confidence in the stock market. If the public fears investing in securities because it either cannot get sufficient information about companies or does not trust the information available, it may invest in other types of contracts, e.g., real estate, and/or reduce its otherwise desired level of savings. Financial disclosure, mandated and supervised by the government, is presumed to alleviate this problem.

Improved government administration and the public's and employees' 'right to know' Administration of government and the public's and employees' 'right to know' might require specific information of companies, such as the amount of various products exported, the amount of charitable contributions, expenditure on anti-pollution equipment, sales (turnover) of various products, profits from specific products or plants, etc. Of course, this information could be obtained by government directly. However, it may be that publication in financial statements is less expensive than alternative means. Publication may also be the best (perhaps the only) way for the public at large to obtain the information.

Political considerations Passing laws that show that the government is taking action to redress presumed wrongs and correct a 'scandalous' situation is perceived as an important product of legislature. Since the cause of the 'wrong' or 'scandal' (or even whether or not it really exists) and the means of its resolution are not generally known without a considerable amount of difficult research (if then), the laws passed often exacerbate rather than correct the problem or result in new problems or in gains to one group at the expense of another. (As is discussed below, there is reason to believe that this occurred in the US in the early 1930s.) Consequently, it may be less costly to avoid a scandal than to 'correct' one. Disclosure of financial information may reduce the probability that firms will fail spectacularly or that wrongs appear done to innocent people whom the government should protect. If this were the case, required disclosure would be desirable assuming, of course, that the expected costs of the requirement are less than expected benefits from not having 'bad' legislation enacted.

To recapitulate, then, governments may require financial disclosure of privately owned companies to prevent or reduce fraud (and similar violations of contracts between managers and shareholders and between companies and creditors, employees and others who contract with companies); to get 'insiders' to act as fiduciaries towards all shareholders; to reduce the costs to investors of making rational decisions (thus improving the allocation of resources in the economy); to provide information needed by the citizenry of a democracy; and to prevent or reduce the probability of scandals that give rise to precipitous 'calls for action'. The two basic questions to be considered are therefore: (a) is mandated financial disclosure effective in serving these purposes; and (b), if so, do the costs of required disclosure exceed the expected benefits?

The following sections begin this inquiry by considering the reasoning and evidence which support government required disclosure by private corporations. The arguments discussed above are grouped into ten subsections; the final subsection provides a summary of and lists conclusions drawn from the previous ten.

4.2.2   Fraud on investors and others

Fraudently prepared financial statements are not unknown either in the UK or the US, although charges of fraud are much more frequently claimed in the latter country. Only a few such claims have been made in the UK. Tom Hadden (1968), in his comprehensive paper on UK company fraud, does not mention fraudulently prepared financial statements as a problem, except for subscription frauds where the perpetrators rely '. . . on their ability to disappear at the first signs of serious police investigation, leaving their unfortunate "front" men to face the music' (p. 295). Since this, however, two instances of *possible* fraud have surfaced, but whether these are instances of honest differences of opinion, misrepresentation (discussed further below), or fraud has not yet been determined.

The number of instances of claimed and proven fraud in the US exceed those in the UK by a wide margin. Among the well-known cases in which fraud has been alleged are BarChris, Yale Express, Green Department Stores, Continental Vending and most recently, National Student Marketing, Equity Funding and Home Stake Production. Several reasons may be cited for this difference, including the greater number of companies in the US, the more restrictive law governing sales of securities in the UK (the Prevention of Fraud (Securities) Act 1958), and US laws that permit and even encourage law suits.[2] Nevertheless, requirements governing financial disclosure in the US far exceed those in the UK, a fact

104

which leads directly to the question under consideration, namely, is the frequency of fraudulently prepared financial statements *reduced* by government regulation? To answer this question, US data predominantly from before 1933 are examined, since prior to 1933 there was little state and no federal regulation of the content of financial statements.

A review of the available US literature failed to find many reports of fraudently prepared financial statements before government controls were instituted.[3] In a comprehensive study of the legal responsibilities of accountants published in 1935, Wiley D. Rich states: 'An extensive search has revealed not a single American case in which a public accountant has been held liable in a criminal suit for fraud' (1935, p. 100). Nor were many instances of fraudulently prepared financial statements cited during the extensive hearings before the US Senate preparatory to the passage of the Securities Acts.

The lack of evidence on fraud should not be taken as proof that all financial statements were honestly prepared. Before passage of the Securities Acts, law suits against certified public accountants may have been difficult to prosecute, due to the prevailing rule of privity which maintained that only the person for whom the statements were directly prepared (usually the company) could sue, unless the auditor had made a reckless misstatement or insincere profession of an opinion. Under common law, the courts held that 'negligence or blindness, even when not equivalent to fraud, is nonetheless evidence to sustain an inference of fraud, at least . . . if the negligence is gross.'[4] Under present US law any person who acquires securities registered with the SEC may sue the accountant who certified the statements whether or not he is the accountant's client. Under the 1933 Act, the investor need not even demonstrate that he has seen the statements, so long as the statements include a false statement or misleading omission. The accountant must establish that he was free from negligence or fraud by proving that, after reasonable investigation, he believed the statements he certified were true. Thus the Securities Acts made it rather easy to sue public accountants. Had there been a pent-up desire to sue public accountants for negligence or fraud that was suppressed by the difficulty of maintaining a suit, one would have expected this change in the law to have brought forth a rash of lawsuits. But almost no cases were filed against public accountants until the 1950s. Even then, very few were filed until the 1960s. Thus the lack of lawsuits claiming fraudulent or misleading financial statements prior to 1933 does not appear to be due primarily to the difficulty of maintaining a suit.

From what, then, is the often stated belief derived that financial statements were not trustworthy before passage of government statutes? One source (in the US) is published complaints by 'crusading' economists and journalists about financial reporting in the 1910s and early 1920s. An examination of this literature – particularly of William Z. Ripley's influential works (1916 and 1927) and others discussed in Benston (1969a, pp. 51–3) – leads to this conclusion. The evidence presented was anecdotal and concerned primarily with charges of 'watered stock' (inflated asset valuations). But once the public became actively involved in the securities markets in the middle 1920s, securities traded on the major stock exchanges were subjected to the auditing and disclosure requirements of the exchanges. These requirements seem to have been effective in reducing or even in eliminating most financial statement fraud.

A second source of the belief that financial statements (particularly those included in prospectuses) would be fraudulently or misleadingly prepared in the absence of government regulations is complaints and propaganda by prestigious investment bankers and issuing houses who were hurt by competition from independent promoters and 'cut-rate' houses. Public interest in corporate securities increased considerably after World War I, especially in the US. Many people who had not previously owned securities became relatively wealthy after the war. Established investment bankers had to compete with newer firms for their funds. This competition was costly to them in two ways: first, their prestige was damaged by the frauds perpetrated by securities salesmen of unethical firms: hence they found selling securities to new investors more difficult; secondly, competition with the new firms, who often found it desirable to cut prices, was 'distasteful'. Therefore, the established firms sought government regulation to reduce fraud and competition.[5] In the US, federal regulation was also desired to alleviate the necessity of dealing with each state's laws and regulations individually.[6] In the UK, the MacMillan report on losses by investors after the 1928/29 boom, presumably in part because of misleading prospectuses, was influential in the adoption by The (London) Stock Exchange in 1930 of its first rules governing disclosure, and in the passage of the Prevention of Fraud (Investments) Act 1939 (which severely restricted the public sale of securities). However, I am not aware of any analysis of the extent to which fraudulent financial reports were actually influential in causing losses to investors or were even associated with such losses.

This leads to the third source of the belief that financial statements were untrustworthy before the intervention of government – losses by investors after booms collapsed. When the economy is booming, confidence abounds and people seem willing to invest in ventures that they previously

106

had scorned and later might regret. In these situations, it is not clear whether people are fooled by the promises of securities salesmen or fool themselves with imagined prospects of great wealth. In any event, the price/earnings ratios which characterise many securities in these periods indicate that people seem to be basing their investment decisions much more on future expectations than on past performance as reported in financial statements.[7] When these expectations prove false, blame is often put on the prospectuses, which in the light of the bust, may seem fraudulent or misleading. Though it seems likely that some prospectuses were prepared with fraudulent intent, I know of no study that shows whether this practice was rare or widespread or whether it was greater in the 1920s than in the 1930s. In fact, former SEC chairman Ray Garrett Jr recently stated: 'We have had cases of fraud and of mismanagement and disregard of investor interest that rival anything known to the men of 1933 who set about to construct a system that would make the world safe for small investors . . .' (1974, p. 91).

In any event, it seems likely that even had fraudulent or misleading financial statements been a serious problem in the 1920s, these practices would be reduced considerably by now, simply as a result of growing public awareness of their possibility. Consequently, in the absence of government regulations, promoters and managers would probably find the services of an independent certifying group, such as Chartered or Certified Public Accountants, useful. These auditors would provide the requisite independence, honesty and expertise, since otherwise their signatures on financial statements would be of little value. It may be, then, that private actions would be and are more useful than government actions in reducing or preventing fraud.

Nevertheless, some proponents of government regulated financial reporting assert that one cannot assume that independent auditors are independent, since they are engaged, paid and dismissed by company managers and directors.[8] Although evidence of the actual effect of this arrangement on the presentation of fraudulent or misleading financial statements has not been presented, the possibility must be acknowledged. In particular, there appears to be some danger that managers and directors who have operated an enterprise particularly badly over time may not want to report the results to the shareholders and thus management may bring pressure on their auditors to accept misleading accounting practices. Another danger is the possibility that managers and directors or promoters may violate their implied contract with investors by making self-serving (rather than company-serving) arrangements with suppliers, customers, etc., using company resources for their private benefit, or even directly misappropriating company funds. In these situations, it may be necessary to oblige the auditor legally to report such situations to the shareholders in order to prevent subordination of the auditor's duty.[9] The required reporting of violations of managers' fiduciary responsibilities towards shareholders, then, would reduce their incentive to be dishonest. Depending on the form of the required reporting, it may be that the benefits would be greater than the costs.

It is important to note, though, that auditors have a powerful incentive to report poor or dishonest performance by managers. One of the most valuable assets possessed by auditors is their integrity. Their signatures on financial statements are valued in large measure because auditors are assumed to be independent of management. Consequently, should an auditor be discovered colluding with managers to deceive shareholders, creditors or others, the auditor would suffer the severe penalty of losing his 'stock in trade', his reputation for integrity.[10]

Required disclosure of promoters' compensation, relationships with the company, and promises with respect to the proceeds from securities issues might also be effective in reducing potential fraud.[11] Again, little is actually known about the prevalence of fraudulent statements before their contents were regulated by government. However, it seems clear that fraud would be reduced if the relationship of promoters to their promotions were made explicit. In addition, law suits against promoters would be facilitated by the existence of financial prospectuses. (Of course, these benefits must be compared to the costs of preparing and publishing prospectuses, discussed below in section 4.3.)

In summary, then, there is little evidence of fraudulently or misleadingly prepared financial statements, before or after government regulations were imposed. Much of the belief that such statements would abound were it not for government regulation appears to be based on some experience from the 1910s and early 1920s and from a desire to attribute *ex-post facto* bad investment decisions to bad financial statements. The available evidence, then, does not support the belief that required disclosure is needed to prevent fraud. Nevertheless, there is reason to believe that required disclosure of possible violations of the fiduciary responsibilities of managers, directors and promoters may be desirable. Independent auditors are, to some extent, servants of the managers, directors and promoters who hire and fire the auditors who are charged with reporting on their stewardship. Hence without an explicit legal obligation auditors may lack the power or desire to report fully on the actions of the managers, etc.

108

4.2.3 Misrepresentation in financial statements

Reporting the results of income and operations, assets and liabilities so as to hide or obscure bad performance or to give the illusion of good performance, even though figures are not falsified or 'accounting principles' violated, is believed by many to be a much more serious problem than fraud. Critics of financial reporting practices point to the existence of alternative acceptable methods of depreciating fixed assets (by straight line, double declining balance, etc.), recording revenue from sales (upon delivery, receipt of instalments, as a percentage of contract completion, etc.), realising revenue (by choosing which asset to sell when assets are recorded at historical cost), capitalising or charging costs to expenses (such as research and development, oil well drilling, and advertising), reporting mergers and acquisitions as a pooling of interests or purchases, etc.[12] These critics claim that, as a consequence, managers can report almost whatever they want with the approval of their Chartered or Certified Public Accountants. Furthermore, many of those disturbed by this situation believe that government regulation can alleviate what they perceive to be a problem.

Considering that the contents of financial statements can be 'manipulated', several questions must be answered affirmatively before government regulation should be considered a benefit. First, to what extent does manipulation actually occur? Secondly, if manipulation occurs, is the public 'fooled' in the sense that its evaluation of management, the market price of securities, or the credit extended to the enterprises is altered? Thirdly, can government regulation affect the incidence of manipulation?

With respect to the first question, there is very little evidence on the extent of manipulation. Claims that financial statements are designed to mislead investors appear to be based primarily on anecdotes. For example, Abraham Briloff has pointed out how specific US companies report events, such as acquisitions of subsidiaries, in ways that do not make clear that increased sales and earnings per share are due to the acquisitions rather than to the growth of internal operations.[13] In a few instances (such as Penn-Central), he is able to quote memoranda that indicate management's intent to increase reported net income by manipulating accounting figures. One of the few other documented instances of apparent discretionary use of accounting numbers is provided by Michael Schiff (1966). He analysed the practices followed by Chock Full O'Nuts in deferring and charging-off advertising expenses, and concluded: 'It is difficult to avoid the conclusion that a concerted effort on the part of the management was made to examine various accounting methods and select that one which makes for happy, though confused, stockholders.' (1966, p. 66). A few such charges have been made in the UK. In particular, R.C. Morris and G.H. Breakwell (1975) mention some companies who were charged with transferring exceptional losses directly to reserves (Cunard, The Thompson Organisation), capitalising research and development expenses (Rolls-Royce) and increasing profits (Wright-Hamer Textiles).

The existence of manipulation of accounting numbers was also studied by testing the hypothesis that managements attempt to smooth reported net income. Morris and Breakwell (1975) summarise the many studies that have been published. They also test the hypothesis that British firms use discretionary accounting methods to improve their reported performance in 'bad' years. They conclude: 'The results, though decidedly weak, tend to bear out the American experience. In short, it appears that very few companies openly manipulate profits, but where firms suffering ''bad'' years change their accounting practices they are more likely to increase income than decrease it. However, though the impact of some of these changes was sizeable, for the most part the effects on reported profits were immaterial. No evidence was found to support the long-term smoothing hypothesis, which implies that if firms have such a long-term strategy the number which actually manipulate accounting practices to achieve this goal must be very small indeed.' (1975, p. 182)

Despite this evidence, criticism of specific accounting practices will probably continue, in part because a few companies probably do attempt to manipulate their reported earnings. However, I believe that most of the criticisms in both countries stem from the dismay of journalists, politicians and analysts over the way different companies can report seemingly similar events in quite different ways. Since different financial results can be reported, these critics believe that manipulation is possible and, therefore, must exist.

Assuming for the moment that manipulation may exist on more than a minor scale, the second question can be considered – is the public 'fooled' or does it recognise that accounting data need not be valid measures of wealth and income? A few careful studies have been published that address themselves to this question. These studies attempt to measure how the market prices of securities were affected by changes in reported income that resulted from a change in an accounting procedure.

Eugene E. Comiskey (1971), T. Ross Archibald (1972) and Robert S. Kaplan and Richard Roll (1972) analysed the effect of reducing the amount of depreciation expense, thereby increasing net earnings, by changing from the double declining balance or sum of the years' digits method to the straight line method. Comiskey examined the stock market response, measured by changes in price/earnings ratios, to the 1968 change by eleven steel companies from accelerated to straight line depreciation and compared them with a control group. He found that the ratios of the steel companies generally declined while those of the control group increased. Thus the evidence rejected the hypothesis that the market was 'fooled' into thinking the accounting change had increased 'actual' net income. Archibald used the 'market model' (described below in section 4.2.6) to account for general stock market changes that affect individual share prices. He then plotted changes in share prices (net of general stock market changes) in the months before and after a change from accelerated to straight line depreciation by sixty-five firms over the period 1955–66. His conclusion was that the increase in reported net earnings had no immediate substantial effect on share price performance. Kaplan and Roll also used the 'market model' technique for their examination of the effect on share prices (adjusted for changes in general stock market prices) of a change from accelerated to straight line depreciation of seventy-one companies over the period 1962-68. They also studied the effect on share prices, net of the market, of 332 companies who switched to flow-through accounting for the tax savings from the investment credit from a deferred method, thereby increasing reported net earnings. They found that, on average, share prices tended to increase more than expected, but that the increase was temporary.[14] By the time of the first quarterly report, it had been reversed on average. Thus, if investors were 'fooled' by changes in accounting methods, the effect was reversed within a short time.

John L. O'Donnell (1965 and 1968) and Francis A. Mlynarczyk Jr (1969) also studied the effect of alternative methods (flow-through versus deferral) of reporting lower taxes that result from accelerated depreciation or the investment credit. In his 1965 study, O'Donnell examined the price/earnings ratios of thirty-seven electrical utilities or holding companies over the period 1949–61. He concluded that investors can adjust for accounting differences. O'Donnell's 1968 paper reported a replication using data from sixty-nine companies over the period 1961–66 from which the same conclusion is drawn. Mlynarczyk used a regression model with share price as the dependent variable and accounting earnings as one of the independent variables. The equation was used to measure investors' valuation of the net earnings of ninety-five electrical utilities over the period 1958–62. He concluded that investors are able to adjust for differences in the methods of reporting net earnings employed by the utilities.

Shyam Sunder (1975) studied the effect on share prices of changes in the methods by which companies value inventories (stocks). He analysed data over the twenty-one years from 1946 to 1966, during which period 126 companies changed to the LIFO method and 29 companies abandoned this method of accounting. A variant of 'the market model' (described in section 4.2.6) was used to control for differences in the riskiness of shares, after which changes in share prices were measured over the twelve months before and after the change to or from LIFO inventory accounting. Sunder concludes: 'This study does not support the view that the reduction in the reported income of a firm which accompanies a change to the LIFO method of inventory valuation is viewed by the stock market as a sign of adverse performance on the part of the firm. The results also do not support the view that corporate managers can, on the average, manipulate the stock price of their firms by adopting or abandoning the use of the LIFO method of inventory valuation'. (1975, p. 314)

The effect on share prices of alternative methods of accounting for the earnings of life insurance companies was studied by George Foster (1975). These companies must report their earnings to regulatory commissions (and to the public) according to statutory rules. Since 1973 all life insurance companies are required to report earnings adjusted according to generally accepted accounting principles (GAAP). Foster studied the effect on share prices of companies whose changes in annual earnings differed in size according to whether the earnings were measured according to the statutory rules or GAAP. He found that 'The aggregate market appears to behave as if it made adjustments to the life–health statutory measure in the years before the accounting profession required the reporting of GAAP underwriting earnings.' (1975, p. 696)

The effect of a vigorously disputed Accounting Principles Board Draft Opinion ('Cost Center for Exploration, Development and Producing Activities of the Oil and Gas Industry', 22 October 1971) on the share prices of companies whose reported earnings would be affected was studied by Dennis H. Patz and James R. Boatsman (1972). The proposed Opinion would have required oil and gas producers who capitalised the exploration and drilling costs of unsuccessful wells (full-cost companies) to charge these costs to expenses much more rapidly. The Opinion was strongly opposed by bankers, security analysts, accountants and others who believed that the share prices of full-cost companies would be adversely affected if the alternative accounting procedure were used, especially in the case of smaller companies. Patz and Boatsman analysed changes in the share prices (adjusted with the 'market model' for changes attributable to general market conditions) of 30 full-cost and 19 write-off (successful well completion cost) companies in the two weeks before and two weeks after the Opinion was announced (the impact period). They conclude: 'Therefore, on the basis of this research, the common stock prices of full-cost companies were not adversely affected at any time during the impact period. Likewise, small and large full-cost companies were not affected differently.' (1975, p. 402)

The most complete study published to date (Ray Ball, 1972, published in 1974), analysed the effect on share prices of 267 accounting changes made by 197 New York Stock Exchange (NYSE) firms over the period 1947–60. He used a sophisticated version of the 'market model' to separate changes in share prices that result from changes in general market conditions from those that possibly result from changes in reported accounting data. He concludes: 'The market appears to ignore the effect on income of a change in accounting technique . . .' (p. 27). Nor did he find a significant difference in the share price changes whether the effect of the accounting change was disclosed or not, and if it was, whether it was positive, negative or classified as immaterial.

Finally, R.C. Morris (1975) measured the impact on share prices of investments of net earnings that reflect general price level changes. The markets' reaction to the publication by R.S. Cutler and C.A. Westwick (*Accountancy,* 1973) of the inflation adjusted accounts of 136 major companies was estimated in two ways. First, changes in share prices were examined to determine if a downward adjustment in reported earnings was accompanied by a downward shift in share prices, and vice versa. Second, with the 'market model' used to account for changes in general market conditions, the residual 'abnormal' gain or loss that an investor would have made by investing in shares whose earnings were restated downward or upward was calculated. The data were also grouped according to whether changes in earnings were over 20 per cent and over 30 per cent. Morris concluded: 'The inference is clear that the market found little information content in the publication of the inflation adjusted figures – either because it had already made its adjustments; or because it chose in general not to regard such data as being relevant to its deliberations.' (1975, p. 86)

On the whole, the extant studies indicate that securities prices are not substantially affected by a 'manipulation' of earnings based on changed depreciation methods, the deferral or non-deferral of possible future income tax obligations and other changes in accounting techniques. From this evidence, it would appear either that investors are not deceived by the accounting method of measuring net income adopted or do not use the financial statement data reported for investment decisions in the manner studied. In either event, 'manipulation' of the type identified does not appear to be a problem calling for remedial action.

Of course the samples analysed and statistical tools used may be inadequate to reveal the effect of manipulation. A more cogent criticism, though, is that if manipulation exists, it is more subtle than obvious changes in depreciation accounting, etc. Therefore the last question should be considered – can government regulation reduce the incidence of possibly misleading manipulation?

The answer to this question may be derived from an analysis of why the data reported in financial statements are not and cannot be unambiguous measures of wealth and income. Such measurements require knowledge of the present value of cash flows or current market values of assets and liabilities. This information is rarely objectively known. Future cash flows are difficult to estimate with a low degree of uncertainty, nor can anyone be sure of the rate at which these flows should be discounted to determine present values. Easily verifiable, objectively determined current market values do not exist for many assets or liabilities, nor is there much certainty that the values estimated will prevail should an exchange actually be made. Consequently, the economic value of an enterprise and/or of its individual assets and liabilities can be determined only by subjective estimates of cash flows, discount rates and market values. These subjective estimates would be subject to ready manipulation by a management so inclined.

However, one might believe that objective values can be drawn up to obviate subjective estimates and thus reduce manipulation. Indeed, public accountants have attempted to do this by requiring that assets and liabilities be stated at historical costs (possibly adjusted by an index number to account for inflation, where this is permitted). Even so, judgement and estimates cannot be excluded. For example, allocations of an asset's original cost to time periods (depreciation) depends on assumptions about its useful life and the rate at which it will be used or lose its value. The rule that revenue is not realised until a market transaction occurs may eliminate the need for valuing work in progress and finished goods. But judgement must be used where an annual accounting is made of long term contracts. And when payment for sales of, say, property, are made with notes, some estimate must be made of the present value of the notes received. If it turns out that the notes bear a market clearing rate of interest and are paid when due, income should be realised at the time of the exchange. But if the notes are not paid, this procedure might be seen as misleading. Thus, judgement cannot be excluded.

Even if a set of rules were devised that would obviate judgement, the figures reported in financial statements would necessarily be misleading for some firms. A single method of recording a sale must result in an under- or overstatement of 'true' revenue for some companies. Thus elimination of alternative acceptable accounting procedures is not possible except at the cost of some necessarily misleading or uninformative financial statements.

It appears, then, that little can be done to alleviate the fears of those who believe that the contents of financial statements *can* be manipulated. Their fears are based, in large measure, on the unrealistic assumption that accountants can measure wealth and income unambiguously, but often do not. The accounting and legal professions still hold to the myth that there exists a 'true and fair' view of the firm or an 'objective and correct' measure of values and that it is the accounting profession's responsibility to find and report it. The truth is that a large number of different estimates and procedures can be justified, *ex ante,* even though, *ex post,* other methods clearly would have been preferable. Therefore the only protection that readers of financial statements can have is not to expect too much from them. However, readers may expect that the statements were not prepared to mislead them. But this is a matter of intent on the part of the company and its certifying accountant. While the laws of fraud deal with this situation, it would seem that the desire of public accountants and issuing houses to protect their reputations for integrity may provide more meaningful protection, particularly when one considers the cost of law suits and the present value of the expected damages awarded compared with the costs of audits.

4.2.4   Security price manipulation and disclosure

As is discussed above, government may believe it should prevent or reduce the manipulation of securities prices. Financial disclosure is thought to be useful for this purpose. With disclosure, it is claimed, manipulators would find floating rumours (which would persuade people to purchase securities at inflated prices or sell securities below their 'true' values) more difficult. In particular, the SEC apparently believes that the 'pools' formed to manipulate US security prices in the late 1920s and pre-SEC 1930s were able to operate because of lack of financial disclosure. They believe that security price manipulations

  . . . resulted in a situation in which no one could be sure that market

115

prices for securities bore any reasonable relation to intrinsic values or reflected the impersonal forces of supply and demand. In fact, the investigation record demonstrated that during 1929 the prices of over 100 stocks on the New York Stock Exchange were subject to manipulation by massive pool operations. One of the principal contributing factors to the success of the manipulator was the inability of investors and their advisers to obtain reliable financial and other information upon which to evaluate securities . . .[15]

One might argue that prevention of manipulation by government is justified because traders believe they have a *de facto,* if not *de jure,* contract with insiders and other traders that forbids share price rigging. Or it may be that investment would be discouraged, to the detriment of the efficient allocation of capital in the economy, if people believed that share prices were manipulated. But what logic or evidence is there to support the SEC's assertion that periodic financial disclosure would affect share price manipulations?

Logic tells us that rumours about important happenings, such as a great invention, oil discovery, contract award, collapse of union negotiations, etc., can rarely if ever refer to events reported currently in financial statements. Few if any of these events affect revenue, expenses, assets or liabilities, as recorded by accountants, until some time after their economic significance is known. An effective manipulation must rather rely on people bidding up or down the price of a security over a relatively short time, after which the manipulators sell or buy the security. Annual or even quarterly financial statements should have little effect on this process.

As for evidence, an analysis was made of the reporting practices of the 100 plus companies whose stocks were subject to manipulation by pools in 1929 (Benston, 1973a). All had financial statements published in *Moody's Investors Service* for at least the two years before their securities were allegedly manipulated, for the year of pool and for the next year. All provided investors with balance sheets and income statements audited by CPAs. The major lack of disclosure was non-reporting of sales (turnover) and cost of goods sold. Of the 103 corporations whose securities were included in the 1929 pools, some 39 per cent did not report sales and 50 per cent did not report cost of goods sold.[16] In comparison, the percentage of *all* companies listed on the NYSE in 1929 and not disclosing sales was 39 per cent and the percentage not disclosing cost of goods sold was 61 per cent.[17]

Thus, it does not appear that the fact or degree of financial disclosure

116

affected the existence of securities pools. This conclusion is corroborated by the fact that the number of pools decreased from 103 in 1929 to 30 in 1930, 6 in 1931, 2 in 1932 and 12 in 1933, while the extent of disclosure by NYSE traded corporations changed hardly at all. Further evidence on this question is derived from UK experience. Until the passage of the Companies Act 1967, many companies listed on The (London) Stock Exchange did not disclose sales (turnover) and most do not at present disclose their cost of goods sold or gross profit. Yet extensive (or any) stock price manipulation is not charged.

4.2.5 Fairness to non-insiders

If 'fairness' is to be defined operationally, it would seem to mean that a purchaser or seller of shares paid or received only the amount that his claim on a company was worth. Since a share is a claim on the future, which by definition is unknown, the price paid or received is almost always too high or too low, viewed in the light of subsequent events. Nevertheless, share prices would be 'fair' and the stock market would be 'a fair game' if the market price of shares at all times measured, without bias, the intrinsic value of the claims they represent. In this event, the market price would reflect (discount) completely the best estimate that can be made of the economic effect of all known and anticipated events (in what has been termed the 'strong form') or all publicly known events (in what has been termed the semi-strong form).[18] Then, should a corporation's plant burn down or its president be in a serious accident, should it receive a potentially lucrative contract or discover a great invention or mineral deposit, the price of its shares would fully reflect the present value of these happenings. While the economic effect of future events cannot be known with certainty, the unbiased nature of share prices means that the present market price of a share is as likely to be an over- as an underestimate of the 'true' value of the firm in the light of the subsequent events. Thus any person buying or selling a share will pay or get whatever the share is worth – the stock market is a fair game.

Of course, the stock market cannot be a fair game in the extreme. It is not physically possible for all shareholders and potential investors to receive all information about all possible investments simultaneously. Nor can all people evaluate information equally well. The question, then, is whether the required publication of financial reports tends to make the stock market more of a fair game than it otherwise would have been. (Another aspect of fairness is the 'cheating' of one group, e.g., naive investors, by another, e.g., insiders, by the publication of misleading data or withholding of valuable data. This aspect is considered below.)

Before the available evidence is reviewed, it is important to point out that the publication of financial information cannot be *sufficient* for markets to be 'fair'. Consider the situation where information about companies is obtained by investors solely or even largely from financial statements. Even if the statements are published monthly, and even if the statements report meaningfully the economic effect on the company of events, and even if all investors received the statements simultaneously and can interpret the information equally quickly and well, stock prices may not be 'fair'. Investors who trade on other that statement publication dates will pay or receive prices that do not reflect the events that occurred between the statement dates. Thus someone will be treated unfairly. Of course, statements are almost never published as often as once a month, accounting data often provide poor and inadequate measures of economic events, and all investors cannot obtain the reports at the same time or display equal ability in using the reports. Hence, if information about companies is obtained solely or largely from financial statements, investors cannot expect stock prices to be fair.

Not surprisingly, financial statements do not appear to be the sole or even the principal source of information about companies. Rather investors appear to base their decisions on specific knowledge about company management, products, production facilities, labour relations, markets, competitors, government relations, etc. gathered from field research by analysts, knowledge about the industry and markets, intimate familiarity with the company, etc. The evidence reviewed in section 4.2.6 below is consistent with the belief that when financial statements are published, they appear either to confirm what investors have already learned from other sources or are ignored. If the statements provide information not otherwise available or if they simply confirm what investors learned from other sources, publication of the statements contributes to making the stock market a fairer game. The statements may also help investors to form rational expectations about companies. Whether this contribution is greater as a consequence of government required reporting is the question now considered.

Some indirect evidence on the question can be derived from studies of the statistical behaviour of share price changes. Paul Samuelson (1973) has shown that if information is impounded into share prices completely and without bias within a time period, successive share price changes would be independent, appearing to follow a random walk (with or without a trend). Thus knowledge of the past behaviour of share prices (whether they increased or decreased, what the pattern of changes or levels was, etc.) would not enable one to predict what the next change would be. In statistical terminology, changes in share prices are independent. A finding that these changes were not independent, so that future prices changes could be predicted from past prices, would be evidence that information contained in financial statements was not fully and rapidly impounded into share prices. The dependence in the time series of share price changes would result from the incomplete absorption by the market of the information. However, it should be stated that evidence that share price changes were independent would not prove that the market is a fair game. It is only consistent with the hypothesis, it does not prove it.

A fairly large number of studies have been made of the statistical properties of share price changes. Most studies of US shares listed on stock exchanges are reviewed by Fama (1970) and, to some extent, by William Beaver (1972). Monthly price changes of over the counter shares were studied by Robert L. Hagerman and Richard Richmond (1973). I analysed the behaviour of New York Stock Exchange monthly share prices in the period before compared with the period after the passage of the Securities Exchange Act 1934 (Benston, 1973a). In the UK, the statistical behaviour of share prices was analysed by Myles Dryden (1970).[19] This extensive volume of research shows that, whether share price changes are measured daily, weekly, or monthly, they appear to be successively and systematically independent. Furthermore, the researchers have shown that a number of plausible trading rules that give buy or sell decisions based on patterns of past share price changes do not give rise to trading profits that exceed transactions costs. Thus the evidence is consistent with the hypothesis that stock markets are a fair game.

The studies of share price behaviour also consider directly the question of the usefulness of required disclosure. Although much greater disclosure of periodic financial data is required in the US than in the UK, the studies of share prices in both countries show an equivalent lack of dependence. My study of the share price behaviour of corporations who were considerably affected by the provisions of the 1934 Act by having to disclose their sales revealed that both groups' share prices conformed to a random walk before 1934. Thus required disclosure does not appear to increase the extent to which the stock market is a 'fair game' as measured by the independence of share price changes.[20]

Another measure of a stock market as a fair game for investors is the extent to which large share price changes occur. Of course, large price changes may be due to large 'real' changes in the economic affairs of

119

companies rather than to discontinuous realisations that change has occurred. In this event, the market would not be fair unless share price changed. Nevertheless, many people (particularly legislators) believe that large price changes are undesirable. While gains and losses from large price changes may be symmetric, complaints to legislators are frequently not.

Some evidence of the effect of required disclosure on the incidence of large share price changes and on the variance of prices is found in two studies. My analysis of the prices of NYSE companies that did and did not disclose their sales prior to the 1934 Act reveals that the percentage of large price changes was almost the same for both groups before and after the passage of the Act (Benston, 1973a). This study also reveals that the monthly variance of prices was almost exactly the same for both groups before and after 1934. R.R. Officer (1973) studied the causes of variability of monthly returns of an index of NYSE shares over the period 1892 to 1969. He concluded that the decrease in variability that followed the end of the 1930s depression was not due to the creation of the SEC, since 'The variability of the market factor in the 1920s and before is similar to the postwar variability, and the SEC was not formed until 1933' (p. 436). Large relative price changes are rather related to fluctuations in business conditions. Thus the published evidence is inconsistent with the belief that required disclosure reduces the variability of share prices and the incidence of large price changes.

Fairness might also be measured as a function of the probability that investors incur losses as a result of the unexpected bankruptcy or near collapse of companies in which they invest. Of course, investors must take risks in the hope of greater expected returns. But some people argue that these risks should be minimised. Others believe that minimising risks would remove a principal function of a securities market and thus reduce the wealth of the nation. In any event, the available evidence should be examined.

In the only empirical study of the effects of required disclosure on newly issued share prices, George J. Stigler (1964) calculated the average return from investments in small companies for each of the five years between 1922 and 1927 (before enactment of the Securities Act of 1933) compared with the period 1949–55. His data (as corrected by Irwin Friend and Edward S. Herman (1964) who discovered numerous errors) show that these investments, relative to general stock market prices, yielded almost equal returns in both periods. However, the variance of the returns was considerably greater in the pre- than in the post-1933 Act period. Thus it appears that if the companies and their environments other than the securities laws are comparable (a key assumption on which no evidence was presented in the papers), the 1933 Act did not decrease net losses to investors but did decrease their chances of making large gains or taking large losses. Some observers, such as Friend and Hermann, view this reduction in the variance of a cross-section of returns as 'a good thing', since they interpret this finding as a reduction in risk with no compensating reduction in yield. However, this interpretation is applicable to the variance of an individual security rather than to a cross-section of securities. To determine whether lower cross-section variance is 'good' (gross of costs), one must know whether the decrease in variance was a consequence of the SEC's preventing fraudulent securities from being sold to the public (in which event the mean return should have been higher), or whether the SEC simply prevented the public from investing in companies with greater potential gains and losses. If the latter is the case, the lower measured variance may be a consequence of a constraint upon the set of alternative opportunities available to investors and, therefore, a reduction of their well-being (utility).

Some additional data are provided in my study (1973a) of NYSE listed corporations that did not disclose their gross income in 1929 (before this was required by the Securities Exchange Act of 1934).[21] During the period 1929–34, 12 per cent of the 'disclosure' corporations were struck off the lists of the New York Stock Exchange compared to 7 per cent of those that did not disclose their gross income. During the period 1934–37, the percentage struck off was 4 per cent for the disclosure compared to 2 per cent for the non-disclosure group. By 1941, 21 per cent of the disclosure group had been struck off compared to 11 per cent for the non-disclosure group. Hence, it appears that disclosure was, if anything, more an indication of weakness than of strength.

Finally, the question of whether required publication of financial statements reduces or eliminates 'unfair' practices by certain market participants (e.g., insiders) on others (e.g., small investors) should also be considered. Insiders might cheat other investors by withholding favourable information until after they had purchased shares at bargain prices from shareholders, by withholding unfavourable information until after the insiders had sold their investment (or sold shares short), or even by publicising misleading or incorrect information about the company's financial status or prospects.

Though the question cannot be answered conclusively, the evidence presented in previous sections provides a partial answer.[22] As is discussed in section 4.2.2, there is no evidence that fraudulent financial statements were prevalent before the US Securities Acts were enacted. Nor is there evidence that financial statements were more or less misleading as a consequence of the financial disclosure provisions of the Acts (section 4.2.3). The study reported in section 4.2.4 shows that manipulation of share prices by pools of brokers or insiders was not affected by the disclosure or non-disclosure of specific information. Thus, while it is possible that insiders (or others) may have 'unfairly' profited at the expense of outsiders (or others) before financial disclosure was mandated, there is no evidence that this type of unfairness was affected by mandated disclosure or even has been reduced by legislation.

In summary, the available evidence is not consistent with the hypothesis that government mandated disclosure is needed to make the markets fair for investors. Studies of the statistical behaviour of share price changes indicate that the prices follow a random walk in the UK (where less disclosure is required than in the US) and in the US before and after passage of the Securities Exchange Act of 1934. These data are consistent with the belief that share prices are unbiased estimates of intrinsic values in the sense that they fully reflect all publicly available information. Studies of the extent to which large changes in and greater variability of share prices characterised the NYSE before and after the passage of the 1934 Act were also reviewed. These studies indicate that required disclosure had no effect on reducing the extent of share price changes. Finally, the effect of required disclosure on losses by investors was considered. One study found no greater average gains or losses on investments in relatively small companies before the passage of the Securities Act of 1933, but greater variance in the returns (though the data are really not adequate to support a conclusion). The other study reviewed revealed that a smaller percentage of the New York Exchange listed companies that did not reveal their gross income before 1934 were struck off the list (before and after 1934) than were companies that did disclose their gross income.

The other definition of fairness considered is the production, suppression or misuse of information by insiders to 'cheat' outsiders. Again, the available evidence does not support this hypothesis. Considering the near impossibility of measuring and reporting in financial statements the economic effects of many events that affect the value of companies, it seems unlikely that insider trading can be eliminated or even reduced by required financial disclosure. It appears, then, that neither evidence nor logic supports the contention that requiring publication of financial statements in the form specified by the government affects the extent or degree of fairness to non-insiders.

122

4.2.6 The usefulness of published financial statements for investment decisions

A cornerstone of the rationale for the disclosure provisions of the US Securities Acts and, to a somewhat lesser extent, the UK Companies Acts is their usefulness, their indispensability even, for investment decisions. As was discussed above, this belief is based on several assumptions: (a) in the absence of legal requirements, corporations would not publish sufficient or adequate financial information; (b) the prospectuses and annual statements which government requires them to publish contain information that is potentially useful to investors; and (c) the information published as a consequence of government mandated disclosure laws is sufficiently timely to be of value to investors.[23] Each of these assumptions is now considered.

Basic concepts of economic rationality would lead one to conclude that a company would provide investors with the information they desired to the point where the marginal cost of providing the information did not exceed its marginal value to security holders. After all, investors need not purchase or hold the securities of a specific company. If they believe the information published is insufficient for their investment decisions, they can direct their funds to companies which provide 'adequate' information. A company must also realise that refusal to publish financial statements, to have statements audited by independent accountants, or to continue publishing data previously made public would also be 'information' to investors. Thus, as public interest in securities increased, one would expect increased publication of financial statements, as a way to assure investors that the company had nothing to hide.[24]

Yet many present day proponents of government required disclosure appear to believe that either scanty or no financial statements would be published were it not for government requirements. However, the evidence from the US and the UK, reviewed below, indicates otherwise.

Prospectuses before and after securities legislation In the UK, prospectuses of companies newly selling securities to the public generally exceed legal requirements. For example, the practice of having a respected firm of chartered accountants (reporting accountants) attest the data in addition to the firm's regular auditors is customary, but not required. Forecasts of sales (turnover) and earnings are often published, but are not required. In part, these and other disclosures are 'suggested' by the Quotations Department of The (London) Stock Exchange, which serves as a quasi-legal body. Consequently, it is difficult to determine whether the disclosure is truly voluntary or not.

The contents of prospectuses are much more detailed in the US than in the UK, primarily because of the requirements of the Securities Act 1933 (see section 3.7). Although the extent of financial disclosure before 1933 has not been carefully studied, there seems little doubt that pre-1933 prospectuses contained much less data than are required to be disclosed by the 1933 Act. In pre- and immediately post-1933 editions of his comprehensive work on *The Financial Policy of Corporations,* Arthur S. Dewing (1934) devotes almost no space to the financial statements included in circulars and prospectuses, which leads one to conclude that they were not considered very important before the passage of the 1933 Act. Other works of the period, even those devoted to problems of financing enterprises, show a similar lack of interest in financial statements.

This neglect is subject to conflicting interpretations. One is that investors did not want detailed financial statements. As Dewing says:

> Probably 99 out of 100 prospective investors in the securities of a new company have neither the training, inclination, nor the will to carry on any independent investigation of their own, no matter how much information is put at their disposal. In the last analysis, it is the authority of the investment banker that inspires confidence in the new enterprise and not the investor's reliance on his own powers of analysis. And the investor knows, moreover, that the banker has spent far more time in investigating all the ramifications of the undertaking than he is likely to spend; and he knows that the banker's reputation is bound up in the success or failure of the undertaking. (Dewing, 1934, pp.1018–19.)

The alternative interpretation is that investors were not provided with sufficient information to make informed judgements and, as a consequence, were misled and defrauded. Another contemporary observer of the time (Head Economist for Kuhn Loeb and Co. before he became Director of the Research Division of the SEC) agrees with Dewing, but goes on to say: 'Unfortunately, there were cases where the investigation [by investment bankers] was so perfunctory as to be of no significance, and when this occurred the mechanism was weakened at its very base, and investment banking became susceptible to serious abuse.' (Paul P. Gourrich, 1937, p. 47.)

These statements apply to securities issues by 'reputable' corporations. All writings of the period which I was able to locate contend that promoters of 'speculative' securities rarely burdened their prospects with detailed financial statements. For example, Dewing (1934, pp. 408–11) describes and illustrates the marketing of low grade securities as follows:

> With the sucker list before him, the promoter is prepared to distribute his high pressure 'sales literature'. This consists of a circular describing the fabulous fortune to be made in the promoter's stock. It is usually very well written. The circular is graphic, couched in generalities, and usually graced with illustrations.
>
> No specific information is ever given in these circulars, no specific facts, earnings, or capitalization of the new enterprise. The purpose of the circular is to excite the interest of the prospects. And this is done chiefly through emotional appeals, either to the prospect's avarice or to his vanity. Less frequently, the appeal is made to such common motives as saving for illness or old age, or the protection of family; but in the vast majority of cases avarice or vanity alone, without any garnishments, is the sole basis of appeal.

From the statements made at the US Senate hearings on the Securities Act of 1933 and from other writings, it appears that sales of these 'low grade' issues were the target of the legislation. Legislators and reformers alike seemed appalled at the quality of securities offered to and purchased by investors who, they believed, needed protection from their own folly. Whether or not financial statements, which necessarily refer to the past, would be meaningful where people are buying a chance on a very uncertain, though potentially lucrative, future does not appear to have been considered.

In any event, complaints about the inadequacy and/or uselessness of the financial data presently included in US prospectuses are voiced today. Some 'friendly' critics, such as Carl W. Schneider (1972), want the SEC to remove its prohibition against issuers including 'soft' information, such as sales and earnings forecasts and appraisals, in prospectuses. As he puts it, '. . . SEC filings generally have an artificial or unreal quality. They purport to be full disclosure documents but, as a matter of convention, they exclude important types of information investors consider relevant, and stress much information investors consider irrelevant or relatively unimportant.' (1972, p. 264.) Homer Kripke, another eminent authority generally identified as a supporter of the disclosure laws, writes: 'I have reluctantly come to the conclusion that the Securities Act of 1933 is not operating as it should and that the prospectus has become a routine, meaningless document which does not serve its purpose. Trying to keep from going entirely academic on the ivory shelf by maintaining my contacts with the practising bar, I have reached the conclusion that most lawyers agree with me, and think of the registration process as simply a useless, but lucrative bit of paper', (1973, p. 631; see also Kripke, 1970.) In addition, the disparaging comments made by government officials about people's willingness, during a 'hot issues market', to invest in speculative companies without regard to prospectuses that present a dismal report of past performance and pessimistic expectations about the future are similar to complaints that were made about people's gullibility in buying shares in mining and oil exploration companies in the 1920s.

Although specific instances could be cited to show that the registration required by the Securities Act of 1933 prevented apparently fraudulent or, at the very least, ill-conceived companies from selling shares to the public,[25] it is not clear whether or not the law succeeded equally in preventing them from benefiting from 'bonanzas'. The only published study that concerns itself directly, though imperfectly, with this question (Stigler, 1964, corrected by Friend and Herman, 1964) is discussed above in section 4.2.5. Although the findings reported are consistent with the view that the Act has reduced opportunities for gains and losses that otherwise might have been available to investors, the quality of the data and the model do not allow one to draw conclusions with much confidence.

Periodic reports before and after securities legislation Some evidence on the extent of voluntary reporting by UK publicly trading companies may be obtained by considering the extent to which sales (turnover) were disclosed by publicly trading companies before this disclosure was required by the Companies Act 1967. For this exercise, the financial statements (as reported in *Moody's Manual*) were examined for companies whose shares were listed on The (London) Stock Exchange during the years 1965–70. A sample of 223 companies was drawn from all companies included in the Financial Times Actuaries' Index with available weekly share prices over this period. Only sixty-six (30 per cent) of this sample did not report sales (turnover) by 1967, when the law required this disclosure.[26] Thus, it appears that a considerable majority of publicly trading companies provided investors with sales (turnover) information before the law required it of them.

As is the situation with prospectuses, the extent of the items disclosed in financial statements is much less in the UK than in the US. In large part this difference is due to the more extensive legal requirements obtaining in the US (detailed in chapter 3). However, differences in the extent of public interest in and ownership of securities probably also play an important role, as is shown below.

The proportion of the population that directly owned securities in the US in the 1920s probably equalled or exceeded that proportion today in the UK. Perhaps for that reason, periodic disclosure by US publicly trading corporations before it was required in 1934 was about as extensive as it is today in the UK. Data on the extent of corporate periodic disclosure before 1934 was gathered from *Moody's Manuals* for all NYSE listed companies, starting with 1926 (Benston, 1969b). In the year, *all* companies published balance sheets, including separation of current assets and liabilities, and income statements. CPAs audited 82 per cent of these companies. By 1934, that percentage increased to 94 per cent. In 1926, sales (turnover) was reported by 55 per cent. The percentage reporting sales rose to 61 per cent by 1929, and 62 per cent by 1934. Cost of goods sold was reported by 45 per cent of the NYSE companies in 1926, and 54 per cent in 1934. The percentage reporting depreciation was 71 per cent in 1926, and 93 per cent in 1934. Thus disclosure was more the rule than the exception before it was mandated by the 1934 Act. Indeed, the extensiveness of disclosure in the US before 1934 in many respects exceeded that common in the UK today. This fact at least is consistent with the hypothesis that voluntary disclosure is a function of the demand for, amongst other things, information, which, in turn, is a function of the extent of public interest in securities. Also consistent with this belief is the observation that many companies, particularly those whose shares are held by a large number of persons, generally disclose more information than is required by law or stock market listing agreements.

While the evidence reported above indicates that financial disclosure was forthcoming before it was required by government, some would argue that this disclosure was and would be inadequate to allow investors to make rational decisions. This allegation may be examined by considering evidence on the inherent meaningfulness of the data presented in financial statements and the timeliness of periodic financial statements.

Published financial statements and security prices   The meaningfulness of data reported in financial statements has been questioned by many observers. Some of these criticisms are reviewed in section 4.2.3 above (misrepresentation in financial statements). It should not be necessary to add to the well known 'list of horribles' here. Suffice it to recall that the accounting procedures generally required by government regulatory agencies (particularly historical rather than present or market value numbers) because they reduce the extent of subjective, not easily auditable

127

judgements, may also reduce the meaningfulness of financial statements for investment decisions.

However, periodic statements may provide investors with some information that they could not obtain from other sources. In this event, the publication of the statements should affect investors' expectations about companies.[27] This change in expectations should be reflected in changes in share prices at or after the time when the statements became available to investors. If share prices changed *before* the statements were made public or were not affected by them, their usefulness to investors is questionable.[28] Evidence on this hypothesis is reviewed next.

As was outlined in chapter 3, detailed regulations governing periodic disclosure are for the most part directed towards annual reporting by corporations. These statements provide investors with much more extensive data than the rather brief semi-annual or quarterly reports. Hence studies on the relationship between annual reports and share prices are particularly relevant for this analysis.

At the outset, one fact seems clear. Investors, corporate management and others are interested in financial reports. Casual supportive evidence abounds, such as the reporting of periodic results by the press, subscriptions to services (such as *Moody's* and *Standard and Poor's*) that report and compile financial data, preparation and publication of financial statements even when not required by governments, arguments and even law suits by comptrollers and public accountants over changes in accounting procedures, etc.

Relatively large scale statistical studies also indicate the public's interest in published financial statements. William Beaver (1968) studied the variance of the number of shares traded and the price per share on NYSE traded shares in the weeks before, around, and after the announcement of annual earnings per share. He found greater variability in those weeks than in weeks when financial results were not announced. Robert Hagerman (1973) performed a similar exercise on commercial bank stocks traded over the counter. He found statistically significant, greater than usual variability in the weeks in which annual earnings were announced.

But how should these results be interpreted? Does the publication of financial results simply provide stockbrokers with an excuse to call their customers to suggest portfolio changes in order to generate commissions (churning)? Does the receipt of the reports remind some investors about the companies, thus 'triggering' trades in the companies' shares? Or do the investors use the information contained in the statements to revise their expectations about the return from or risk of owning shares in the companies whose statements are analysed? If they do, is the value of the

128

information contained in the statements greater than the cost of trading on it and producing it?

Although 'churning' may be the explanation for the greater than usual activity in shares around the dates when financial reports are announced, there are no available data to test this hypothesis. However, a number of studies have been made that relate the publication of financial statements to changes in share prices and risk (rather than simply to changes in the variance of share prices and numbers of shares traded). These are reviewed next.

The most useful studies are relatively large scale statistical analyses that attempt to account for changes in share prices due to the publication of financial reports, whilst accounting for the effect of other factors.[29] In general, regression analysis is used to account for changes in the price of a share due to changes on the stock market as a whole, based on the capital asset pricing theory which postulates a stable relationship in the absence of information that affects investors' expectations.[30] Share prices are also adjusted for stock splits and stock dividends. The following relationship, then, is estimated statistically with data from periods other than the ones in which financial statements were made public:[31]

$$R_{jt} = b_0 + b_1 R_{Mt} + u_{jt}$$

where R_{jt} = relative price changes of share j in period t.

= logarithm $(P_{jt} - 1 + D_{jt})/P_{jt})$, where $P_{jt} - 1$ and P_{jt} are the market prices per share of share j at the beginning and end of the period, adjusted for stock splits and stock dividends, and D_{jt} is cash dividends declared on share j during the period.

R_{Mt} = a similarly constructed relative price for the market as a whole (a market index such as the *Standard and Poor's* 500 is often used).

u_{jt} = residual relative price change of share j in period t, the expected value of which is presumed equal to zero in periods when financial information is not released to the public.

The estimated coefficients b_0 and b_1 then are used to predict the residual price change ($u_{jt} = R_{jt} - b_0 - b_1 R_{Mt}$) for periods in which the financial statements were published. If the statements contained information that affected investors' expectations about the value of the company, the actual u_{jt} is expected to be other than the expected zero value.

One more aspect of this research design should be mentioned. Investors' expectations about the accounting data reported must be specified in some way. Otherwise, one cannot interpret whether an increase in net earnings, for example, is 'good' (greater than expected) or 'bad' (less than expected). Consequently, researchers have used various 'models' to estimate expected net earnings, including averages of previous net earnings (levels and changes), amounts based on previous relationships with the earnings of other firms, and 'naive' models (which turned out best) that say that the most recent change in net earnings is expected to prevail.

The model presented above was used to estimate the relationship between changes in monthly share prices and the announcement and publication of financial results (Benston, 1967). The sample included 483 companies whose shares were traded on the New York Stock Exchange in 1964. Several definitions of net earnings per share (including and excluding extraordinary. items and including and excluding depreciation) and investors' expectations were used. Only a minimal (though statistically significant) economic relationship between reported net earnings and share prices was measured in the months before and including the announcement of annual reports. Specifically, a doubling of the percentage change of an unexpected increase (or decrease) in reported net earnings per share was associated, on average, with a 2 per cent increase (or decrease) in the rate of return on shares. Sales, though, seemed more important. A doubling of the percentage change of sales was associated with a similar 18 per cent change in the return on shares.

Several other studies examined the relationship between annual financial data and share prices over the year of the data, including the time (after the year end) when the financial results were announced and published. Raymond Ball and Phillip Brown (1968) used a procedure similar to the one just described, except that they cumulated the residual share price change ($\geq \hat{u}_{jt}$) over the year to which the financial statements pertain through several months after their release. Their sample consisted of 261 NYSE firms whose data were included in the *Standard and Poor's Compustat* tapes over the period 1946-66. They found a positive association between abnormal (i.e., greater than expected after considering general changes in the stock market) increases or decreases in share prices and unexpected increases or decreases in net earnings per share. Thus if one knows which company's earnings would increase (unexpectedly), one could make better than random choices of shares to buy or sell. But they also found that by the time the financial results were announced, at least 85 to 90 per cent of the information content of the statements had already been anticipated.[32]

A study by William Beaver and Roland Dukes (1972) used procedures similar to those used by the studies outlined above and corroborated those findings. Beaver and Dukes studied a sample of 123 NYSE listed corporations over a five-year period, 1963–67. They restated net earnings in three ways: (a) income taxes less amounts deferred as liabilities; (b) income taxes paid (flow through); and (c) net cash flow. They found that knowledge of a year's earnings (preferably stated as flow through or net cash flow) at the beginning of the year enabled one to purchase or sell shares profitably. But, they reported, '. . . there were no abnormal returns to be earned from investing . . . after the release of the announcement.' (p. 331.)

Phillip Brown (1970) studied the relationship between financial statements and share prices for 118 companies listed on the Australian stock exchanges over the period 1959–68, using the same procedure followed by Ball and Brown. Since the Australian disclosure requirements were similar to those prevailing in the UK, his findings are particularly interesting. With respect to annual reports, Brown found results similar to those reported by Ball and Brown: '. . . once the annual report has become generally available there are no further opportunities for abnormal profits.' (p. 282.) However, he did find (as did Ball and Brown) a significant adjustment in share prices, equal to about 20–25 per cent of the total, also taking place in the announcement month. Thus the financial statements do seem to convey some information, but most of this information appears to be 'known' to the market by the time the statements are publicly released.

Foster's (1975) study of the reaction of insurance company shares to published financial reports provides a further test because these shares are traded over the counter. He also used the 'market model' method to analyse annual data from 73 firms over the period 1964 to 1972. His study included separate analyses of insurance companies' earnings from underwriting, investment and capital gains. He concludes:

> Prior studies into the relationship between accounting earnings and security price changes have found that once annual earnings are publicly announced, there is little difference between the security price behaviour of firms with positive earnings changes and firms with negative earnings changes. This result is consistent with a semi-strong efficient market in which new information is rapidly and unbiasedly impounded into security prices. Similar conclusions appear to hold for the market for insurance stocks over the 1965–71 period. (1975, p. 694.)

A criticism that can be made of the studies reviewed is that they focused on a single number – earnings per share. Hence studies by Nicholas J.

Gonedes (1971b and 1974), which relate accounting measures other than net earnings to stock prices, are of greater interest. Gonedes' earlier study (1971b) considered separately the effect on share prices of 'unexpected' changes in the percentage change of four accounting statement ratios: net income/common equity; current assets/total assets; total debt/total assets; and net income/sales. The dependent variable used was a measure of a percentage change in investors' share price expectations over the three months before and four months after the fiscal year end. The tests were computed for eighteen years' data (ending with 1966) from 80 NYSE firms chosen at random. These tests '. . . fail to disprove the null hypothesis that the measured impact of the selected accounting data from annual reports on investors' expectations is not significantly different from zero . . .' (p. 550.)

Gonedes' later (1974) paper also analysed the relationship of 'unexpected' changes in a number of accounting ratios with stock prices. He tested seven ratios: (current assets/current liabilities)/total assets; common equity/total assets; operating income/total assets; earnings per share; total assets/sales; net income/total assets; and net income plus depreciation plus amortisation/preferred stock plus long term debt plus current liabilities. The ratios were combined into an index with a procedure (multiple discriminant analysis) that maximised the explanatory power of the ratios. Sophisticated variants of the 'market model' (discussed above) were then used to separate the effects of changes in general market conditions and the interrelationships among companies' earnings reports from the effect of a specific company's reports on its share prices. The 'market model' was also used to adjust share prices for changes in general market conditions. The data for this study included 244 firms of the 261 used by Ball and Brown (1968) in their study. Gonedes found that using detailed data from financial reports, separately and in combination, resulted in only a slight improvement over using net earnings. Most importantly, he found, as do the studies reviewed above, an economically unimportant and weakly statistically significant ($t < 1 \cdot 46$ in a validation sample) contemporaneous relationship between the data in the reports and share prices in the periods when and after the reports were announced.

The statistical evidence on annual reports, then, is generally consistent with the conclusion that the information content of financial statements is essentially 'known' by the time the statements are available to the public. This conclusion is also derived from the research that analysed the effect of changes in accounting methods on share prices (see section 4.2.3). And the evidence is consistent with the findings that the stock markets in the

132

US and UK are 'efficient' in that the independence of successive share price changes implies that information is quickly and completely impounded into share prices.

Published financial statements and estimates of risk   Although published financial data do not appear to be useful to investors in the sense that their publication affects share prices, they may aid investors in determining the riskiness of shares. Improved information about the riskiness of shares may enable investors to purchase those shares that meet their desired combinations of risk and return and to combine shares in portfolios that reduce aggregate risk. Of course, it may be that the cost of using the information contained in financial statements may not exceed the benefits derived therefrom. But first the usefulness of the statements for assessing risk should be determined.

Several studies have considered this question. The measure of risk that it is assumed investors want to estimate is referred to in financial literature as 'systematic risk'. This is the risk that investors cannot diversify out of by purchasing portfolios of shares in which an expected, say, positive variation in the prices of one share is offset by a coincident negative variation in the price of another. 'Systematic risk' is the variation in share prices associated with variations in the market in general. It is measured by the b_1 term in the equation given above (known as the beta of the 'market model'). (It may also be measured similarly for portfolios of shares, a procedure which reduces the 'noise' of random fluctuations.)

One of the first studies to examine this question was that of William Beaver, Paul Kettler and Myron Scholes (1970). They used reported accounting data to calculate several measures of risk. Data from 307 companies for two ten-year periods, 1947–56 and 1957–65, were used for the tests. Of the various accounting-based risk measures calculated, they found the payout ratio, average asset growth, average leverage, earnings/price variability, and an 'accounting beta' (co-variability of a firm's earnings/price ratio with that of all firms in the sample) significantly correlated with the market-based measure of risk (market beta). R. Richardson Pettit and Randolph Westerfield (1972) also report a similar finding for contemporaneously determined data. However, Gonedes (1973) conducted a further analysis for ninety-nine firms over the period 1946 to mid-1968. He transformed his data differently and failed to find the relationship reported by Beaver et al. (1970). He concluded: '. . . .I *suspect* that our results differ primarily because of differences in the scaling methods used for the income numbers. In scaled income numbers by another accounting number, viz., total assets. Beaver,

Kettler, and Scholes scaled income numbers with *market prices.* But market prices also appear in the variables of the market model; consequently, the estimated B_i [beta] *coefficients of the market model are functions of market prices . . .* Hence, their results may simply reflect 'spurious correlation . . .' (p. 436, italics in original).[33] Though Gonedes' work does not support that of Beaver et al., he does find a statistically significant (though weaker) relationship between the overall accounting-based and market-based measures of risk over contemporaneous periods. (That is, the variances of the adjusted accounting and market numbers are positively and significantly correlated.)

The papers reviewed studied the contemporaneous relationship between financial statement data and share price data and, hence, cannot answer the question of whether or not financial statements are useful for investment decisions. However, one aspect of the Beaver et al. (1970) study does consider this question. They attempted to predict the share price risk (market beta) in the second ten-year period with the accounting-based variables calculated with data from the first ten-year period. The prediction errors from this exercise were compared to those generated by predicting the second decade's betas with the first decade's betas, and it was found that the accounting-based variables predicted with slightly lesser errors, particularly when predictions were made for portfolios rather than for individual shares. As yet, their findings have not been replicated.

Thus only the Beaver et al., study indicates that financial statement data might be used for investment decisions. But they did not suggest any procedure that investors might use to predict riskiness or estimate the riskiness of shares or portfolios. Furthermore, it is not clear whether the costs of such an exercise would outweigh any benefits derived therefrom.

Additional evidence from studies of 'sophisticated' users Nevertheless, all the statistical studies can be criticised because they may not have used the 'best' representation of investors' expectations about financial data to be published or may not have used methods as effective as an experienced analyst's evaluation of the data. It may be that when the wealth of detail published in financial statements, particularly the detail required by the SEC, is reviewed by an astute investor or analyst, better decisions would be made than if financial statements had not been reviewed.

This hypothesis may be examined empirically by considering the returns realised by a group that spends considerable resources analysing published financial statements (among other data) – mutual funds (unit trusts). One would expect that, were such information useful for investment decisions, the funds (trusts) would garner higher returns from their portfolios, net of risk, than would be earned from a random selection of securities. This test is biased in favour of establishing the usefulness of published financial reports for investment decisions, since fund managers obtain information about companies from sources other than the reports. But if it appears that the funds do not perform better than the market (i.e., yield abnormal returns, given risk), these findings at least would be consistent with the findings from the statistical studies reviewed above.

Many studies have been made of the performance of mutual funds. One of the earliest was by F.E. Brown and Douglas Vickers (1962). They analysed the performance of 152 funds over the period 1953–58. Each fund's performance was compared with the performance of a market index constructed to approximate the funds' holding of bonds, shares, etc. This study was extended to cover the period up to June 1968 by Irwin Friend, Marshall Blume and Jean Crockett (1970). William F. Sharpe (1966) used a more sophisticated technique to account for differences in the riskiness of each fund's portfolio. He studied the performance of thirty-four funds over the twenty-year period 1943–63. The most theoretically valid study was, however, made by Michael C. Jensen (1968). He used the capital asset pricing model (discussed above) to account for risk in his study of the performance of 115 funds over the ten-year period 1954–64. All of these researchers reached similar conclusions. In Jensen's words: 'The evidence on mutual fund performance . . . indicates not only that these 115 mutual funds were *on average* not able to predict security prices well enough to outperform a buy-the-market-and-hold policy, but also that there is very little evidence that any *individual* fund was able to do significantly better than that which was expected from more random change.' (p. 24.)

The only study of UK mutual funds of which I am aware was made by James R.F. Guy (1974, chapter 5). He analysed the performance of fifty investment trusts (the twenty-five largest plus twenty-five selected at random) over forty-three quarters from 31 March 1960 to 31 December 1970. As with the US studies, a number of procedures were used to account for differences in the riskiness of the funds and a number of performance measures were constructed. Guy concluded, as do the investigators of US mutual fund performance, that '. . . in the long run no fund outperformed the London market.' (1974, p. 130.)

Of course this evidence is not conclusive. It may be that mutual fund managers obtain useful information from the statements but use it for themselves rather than for their funds. Or the analysts employed by the funds may not be as astute as individual analysts or investors. Some additional evidence on the ability of investment firms and individual analysts to use financial data for investment decisions is therefore considered next.

Lyn P. Pankoff and Robert Virgil (1970) conducted a controlled laboratory study in which they allowed security analysts to 'buy' the actual financial statements and other data of companies (whose identities were disguised) for the purpose of making decisions about share purchases. They found that the ability of an analyst to purchase shares that outperformed a random selection of shares was not at all associated with whether or not the analyst saw the financial reports. Nor is the record of the research departments of brokerage houses any better. R.E. Diefenback (1972) studied the market performance of shares whose purchase or sale was recommended by twenty-five US institutional research services. He found that, were their recommendations followed, these shares would have yielded returns equivalent to those earned by investments in the *Standard and Poor's* 500 Index.

Other explanations of interest in financial statements   Considering the evidence that annual financial statements, *when published,* do not appear useful for immediate investment decisions, why are people so obviously interested in them, as casual observation attests? One reason may be that earnings reports at least provide investors with a better than random history of the economic progress of companies. Some evidence that supports this hypothesis is presented next.

All the statistical studies reviewed above that analysed the relationship between annual earnings and stock prices over the year to which the earnings pertain found a positive economic as well as statistically significant correlation. Ball and Brown (1968), Beaver and Dukes (1972), Brown (1970), Gonedes (1973b) and Foster (1975) found abnormally high or low earnings (compared to previous or 'expected' earnings) associated with abnormally greater increases or decreases in share prices, such that an investor having knowledge of the earnings at the beginning of the year could have profitably bought or sold shares. These findings are corroborated by several other studies. R. McEnally (1970) analysed the procedure of using low or high price/earnings ratios to choose portfolios of shares. He found no significant difference (statistical or economic) in the returns realised by portfolios chosen according to this rule, a result consistent with the studies cited above. He then created portfolios using price/earnings ratios constructed with perfect forecasts of a year's earnings, by assuming that the actual earnings reported after the year end were known at the beginning of the year. The portfolios formed with low price/earnings shares outperformed these formed with high price/earnings shares. Henry Latane and Donald Tuttle (1967) and John Hammel and Daniel Hodes (1967) reported similar results. Finally, Niederhoffer and Regan (1972) examined the fifty NYSE shares that experienced the greatest price decrease, the fifty that experienced the greatest price increase, and a control sample of fifty shares chosen at random in 1970-71. They found that the earnings changes of those companies mirrored to an extraordinary degree their share price changes.

Thus the evidence is consistent with the belief that reported earnings provide a meaningful, though perhaps crude, history of changes in the economic value of companies as measured by the market prices of their shares. The evidence also indicates that knowledge of earnings after the close of the year (at or around the time they are announced, which almost always precedes the time when disclosure is required by government) appears not to be useful for the purposes of investing. But knowledge of a year's earnings at the beginning of that year would be very useful information. This observation gives rise to a final hypothesis that should be considered before conclusions about the usefulness of published financial statements for investment decisions are drawn.

If the data reported in a financial statement provide a reasonably good history of the economic status and progress of a company over the period on which it reports, the reports may serve to *confirm* information otherwise obtained during the year and also provide data for assessing expectations. Thus, when investors receive information about a company's sales (turnover), expenses, inventories (stocks), etc. from analysts and brokers, they can trust the information because, at the year end, an accounting will be available in the form of audited financial statements. In this event, the statements are desired as useful checks on the accuracy of data received otherwise.

This hypothesis is difficult to test directly. An indirect indication of its correctness is the fact that all companies listed on the major stock exchanges in the US published fairly complete statements before publication was required by the Securities Act of 1934. And, in the UK, a large number of companies publish more detailed data than are required by the Companies Acts. Presumably, these data are and were published to meet public demand.

One important aspect of the hypothesis was tested directly: are data which the government requires to be published used by (and hence considered useful by) investors? This question was examined empirically by measuring the changes in share prices that occurred in the US when the Securities Act of 1934 required disclosure of data that some companies had not previously published (Benston, 1973a). The particular circumstances surrounding the passage of the 1934 Act allows this examination. The Senate hearings, which preceded the passage of the Act in June 1934, began in February 1934. Prior to that date, few observers thought such legislation would be enacted: hence there was probably little pre-release of the data required to be disclosed. The 1934 Act applied to companies whose shares were traded on all major stock exchanges, of which some 70 per cent of transactions were on the NYSE. As was discussed above in section 4.2.2, the major financial statement item not disclosed by a large number (38 per cent) of NYSE listed companies prior to the Act was sales (turnover). Hence, it is possible to test the hypothesis that the required disclosure of sales provided investors with information that they previously did not have and would have wanted. The test is predicated on the model which says that if sales are 'information' and were not known before the government required their disclosure, investors' expectations and perceptions about a company newly disclosing sales would change, as measured by a change in the market value of the company's shares or in their riskiness.

Changes in the share prices over the period February 1934 to December 1935 of the 62 per cent of NYSE companies who had previously disclosed their sales were compared to the 38 per cent who were required to disclose sales by the Act. Share prices of both groups were adjusted for general changes in the stock market, as described above. The analysis shows clearly that changes in the share prices of both groups over that period were almost identical. Changes in riskiness measured were, if anything, less for the companies newly disclosing sales. This evidence is inconsistent with the hypothesis that government required disclosure provided investors with useful information.

Some confirming evidence is provided by Robert Hagerman's study (1973) of over the counter commercial bank shares. As was discussed above, he found greater variation in share prices in the weeks around the publication of banks' financial statements. However, in an earlier related study (1972) he also found no difference regarding this activity between national banks, who were simply required to publish financial statements, and state chartered insured banks, who were required to publish much more detailed statements according to regulations promulgated by the Federal Deposit Insurance Corporation. While publication of financial statements, as such, may be meaningful to investors, there appears to be no evidence that specifying the contents of the statements increases their value.

The conclusions of these studies are somewhat tempered by the

138

findings of two studies of the usefulness of reporting product-line revenue and earnings. Richard F. Kochanek (1974) assumed that the stock market discounts future reported earnings, from which he hypothesised '. . . that if the additional data did in fact enable investors to predict future earnings and, correspondingly, to currently value securities in line with these expectations, then one would expect higher correlations between current period stock price changes and future period earnings changes for "good" reporters than for "poor".' (1975, p. 822.) He analysed the financial reports of thirty-seven companies for the period 1967 to 1970. (The SEC first required product-line data to be reported in 1970.) Twenty-four of these companies were considered 'good' reporters and thirteen were labelled 'poor' reporters. As hypothesised, changes in the 'good' reporters' current share prices were statistically more highly correlated with their future earnings changes than were similar correlations computed for the 'poor' reporters. However, the significance of these findings was challenged by Russell M. Barefield and Eugene E. Comiskey (1975), who questioned the assumption underlying Kochanek's hypothesis and, consequently, substituted the percentage error of financial analysts' earnings forecasts (compared to the actual amounts) as the criterion against which 'good' and 'poor' reporters should be tested. They also pointed out that Kochanek did not account for differences among the companies with respect to the number of product-lines on which they might report, which could account for the significant differences in the correlation between current share prices and future earnings changes. Barefield and Comiskey's new analysis was consistent with Kochanek's findings in that they also found lower forecast errors for firms classified as 'good' reporters than for those classified as 'poor' reporters. But, when the firms were separated according to the number of product-lines upon which they might have reported, the significance of the difference was reduced considerably. In a reply to this 'Comment', Kochanek presented some additional data that further weakened his earlier conclusion. He tested a hypothesis, mentioned in his first paper (Kochanek, 1974), that the market could have obtained information about the companies from sources other than their published financial statements. He reports that a survey of the Wall Street Journal Index '. . . revealed that the number of articles appearing for "good" reporters was significantly greater than for "poor" reporters'. The statistically significant relationship he found, then, may have been due to greater newspaper reporting rather than to more detailed financial reporting.

Even more important than the limitations discussed, Kochanek's study does not consider the economic significance of reporting data on product-lines. Daniel W. Collins (1975) attacked this question directly. He developed and tested share trading strategies that depended on knowledge of product-line data compared to strategies using consolidated data only. The 1970 SEC requirement that companies disclose revenue by lines of business required them to reveal these data for 1967 to 1969. Collins used these figures together with industry specific data that were publicly available to estimate the annual earnings of 92 companies for the years 1968 to 1970. He then compared the gains an investor might make by trading the shares of companies according to the following rule: buy (or sell short) shares of a company whose earnings, forecasted with product-line data are greater (or less) than its earnings forecasted with consolidated data. (The 'market-model' was used to eliminate market related movements of share prices.) Fifty-seven of the ninety-two companies he analysed had reported product-line data during the period, giving Collins a control group against which he could measure the usefulness of publicly available information compared to non-publicly available information. He found that for two of the three years (1968 and 1969) the trading rule would have given investors significant gains (averaging about 18 per cent per annum) when applied to shares of the thirty-five companies who did not disclose their revenue by product-lines until required to do so by the SEC. Small and statistically insignificant gains, however, were found for the fifty-seven companies who published similar data. For one year though (1970), small and statistically insignificant gains were found for both groups (though the gains were greater for the thirty-five non-disclosing companies). When the three years' data were combined, the total gains were not significant. Thus, it is not clear whether or not investors would have benefited had product-line revenue been reported.

Thus, on the whole, the evidence does not support the hypothesis that published annual financial statements are useful (net of investment costs) for investment decisions, when published, or that government required disclosure provides investors with useful information. However, there is some evidence that people use or, at least, seem affected by the publication of financial statements, since share price changes are greater in the periods when net income is announced. In addition, there is some evidence that quarterly financial statements provide investors with information.[34] And there is some reason to believe that published financial data are useful to investors to confirm what they have learned from other sources. Additionally, one can argue that the primary function of financial statements is to show shareholders that an independent auditor has examined the accounts of their company and has either not discovered any gross frauds or serious mismanagement or has reported

140

them.[35] In any event, the studies analysed do not indicate that detailed financial information or specific information disclosed as a consequence of government mandate improves the usefulness of financial statements. Consequently, the conclusion of this section is that while annual financial statements may be of some value for investment decisions, this value is undemonstrated. Furthermore, it appears that basic information desired by the investing public is published voluntarily by a substantial number of publicly owned companies and that government required disclosure of additional data is of little, if any, additional value.

4.2.7 Externalities in the production and distribution of financial information

The publication of financial information in a form, quantity and quality mandated by government may give rise to two related, though essentially different, positive externalities (benefits that cannot be captured by those who incur the costs of producing the information). The first is lower costs to security analysts and investors of gathering, checking and processing information about corporations. The second is improved resource allocation to corporations where the marginal return on investments is the greatest (net of risk).

The externalities with respect to both of these possible benefits occur because corporations cannot garner all of the benefits derived from the information, although they must pay the costs of producing and distributing the information. Consequently, it can be demonstrated that corporate management does not necessarily produce and distribute as much information as investors in total (security and non-shareholders) would be willing to pay for. Security holders pay for the information indirectly because they own the corporation that incurs the expense. But there is no way to require non-security holders to pay. Yet they can acquire published financial statements as quickly as can security holders. Hence, if corporate management produces and distributes financial information to the point where the marginal costs of the information to the corporation equals the marginal revenue gained from it by security holders only, less information than would be desired by all investors would be forthcoming.

However, it is important to note that corporate information is not entirely a 'public good', the distribution of which to non-security holders benefits them at no cost to security holders. A distinction must be made between information that is used for share trading decisions and information that is used for decisions which result in resource use by producers. Considering trading decisions first, information on a corporation's past achievements, economic position, and prospects is not a public good, such as television broadcasts, where consumption by one person does not reduce its value to others. Indeed, the contrary is the basic quality of information that is useful for trading decisions. Knowledge about a change in a corporation's affairs is valuable because it is *not* known by all, because the information allows its possessor to purchase or sell a security *before* the price changes to reflect the economic impact of the previously unknown event. Hence information considered as a 'public good' is not a valid argument for required disclosure.

However, where the information is used for decisions that allocate resources among producers (corporations and others), its prior use by one person does not entirely destroy its value to another. Knowledge about the prospective returns that may be earned from resources invested in a specific enterprise may increase the amount of resources made available to that enterprise and also affect the amounts made available to other enterprises. As a consequence, the economy as a whole benefits, since resources tend to be used in those enterprises where their marginal returns (net of risk and other considerations) are the greatest.

Considering that an overwhelming proportion of transactions in shares are for trading rather than for resource allocation decisions, one should ask why corporate management wishing to maximise the wealth of security holders would make financial statements publicly available. One reason is that shareholders may be willing to pay for publication to enhance the marketability of their shares and the ability of the corporation to raise additional funds. Another is to gain non-shareholders' scrutiny of management's performance, which benefits shareholders. In any event, as described in section 4.2.6, financial information was published voluntarily before it was required by statute.

Nevertheless, proponents of required disclosure argue that positive externalities would accrue if *all* corporations were required to publish essentially standard financial statements. Investors could assimilate and analyse the information more quickly and less expensively were they able to obtain standard statements as a matter of course. As a consequence, it is argued, investment opportunities would be evaluated more efficiently and effectively. Investment resources would then flow to where their use would produce the greatest marginal value and the 'discipline of the market' would be applied more effectively to corporate management.[36]

Against this positive externality, a negative external effect should be mentioned. A corporation might be required to publish information about products, markets, processes, etc., that would be of value to

142

competitors. Aside from the loss that disclosure would impose on shareholders (which is not an externality), required publication of such information would reduce the amount corporations would be willing to invest in developing products, markets, processes etc. In effect, a corporation is required to share some benefits from its investments with others yet cannot require them to share the costs. The optimal investment amount, therefore, is reduced to the detriment of the economy, in general. Of course, it is possible that a corporation can disguise or 'bury' meaningful information and so evade the disclosure statutes. But then why require disclosure of meaningless data?

This argument for secrecy is opposed by the claim that, were *all* corporations required to disclose financial and statistical data, none would get an unfair advantage on balance. But the validity of this conclusion is doubtful. It would seem that large, diversified corporations are able to hide or bury information more effectively than their small, single product competitors, although required product line disclosure does limit this opportunity somewhat. Even then, proponents of required disclosure point to predictions before disclosure legislation was enacted of the dire effects such legislation would have on business. The proponents say that these predicted events did not occur. Unfortunately, one cannot know whether or not a small corporation did not succeed or a product was not developed because of the law, whether the law was successfully evaded or whether the externalities for individual corporations cancelled out. Let us turn, then, to the claimed positive externality of cheaper, more effective analysis of information.

There is no direct way to determine whether fund flows to the 'most promising' investments were enhanced by required disclosure. Some indirect evidence on the effect of required disclosure in the US on securities flotations is presented in the next section. This evidence indicates that the Securities Act of 1933 may have hindered rather than aided such flotations. The evidence on the efficiency of the UK and US securities markets presented in section 4.2.5 also considers this question. The studies of the character of share price changes in the UK and in the US before and after the passage of the Securities Acts are consistent with the hypothesis that the shares market was and is 'efficient'. These studies do not show any increase in the 'efficiency' with which information appears to have been impounded in security prices before extensive financial disclosure was required in the US as compared with afterwards (Benston, 1973a). Nor do they show that the US is more efficient than the UK shares market (Dryden, 1970).

Direct evidence on the effect of required disclosure in reducing the costs

143

to security analysts and investors of making trading decisions (and resources allocation decisions) is also not available. Indirect evidence must therefore be considered. The contents of the major private information gathering services, *Moody's Manuals* and *Standard and Poor's,* which were published prior to and after passage of the US securities laws and new versions of the UK Companies Acts, were examined. The data published by these services show very little change before and after the disclosure statutes were enacted. To be sure, the amount of sales (turnover) is published where previously these data were not available for some corporations. But the wealth of required detail which is disclosed (particularly in the US) is not published. This leads one to question whether investors find these additional data useful.

The net effect of these conflicting benefits and costs is difficult to assess. Unlike the material discussed above, well-specified statistical studies have not been made. It would be well, then, to consider the evidence on public confidence in the securities market before a conclusion is drawn.

4.2.8 Public confidence in securities markets

One of the major arguments for government required financial disclosure is that it is necessary to 'restore public confidence in the securities markets'. As this phrase implies, the passage of legislation often follows what appears to be a loss of confidence by the public. Before some evidence on the effects of required disclosure on the public's willingness to invest in securities is presented, some obvious, yet very important, facts should be mentioned. In the US and the UK the public has increased and decreased its participation in the securities market in seeming disregard of the extent of disclosure. Interest in securities boomed and declined before and after various versions of the UK Companies Acts. In the US, the 1920s was a boom period which collapsed before 1933 and did not recover until after World War II, some fifteen to twenty years after the passage of the Securities Acts. While passage of securities legislation appears motivated by rapid declines in public participation in the securities markets and by the desire of some to destroy or hobble their competitors, it appears to have had little if any influence on the public's desire to invest. Instead, public participation and variations in share prices are primarily reflections of general business conditions.

Quantitative, though somewhat indirect, evidence on the effect of required disclosure on investors' confidence (in the US) may be obtained by considering the possible effect of the Acts on the suppliers of funds as an indication of how they perceived buyer (investor) demands for securities floated in the public market. The extent of corporate flotations of securities before and after the passage of the Securities Acts provides some evidence on this question. One would expect that relatively more corporate capital formation would be financed with shares had the Securities Acts made investors more willing to invest in shares. This question was studied by measuring the amount of new security issues (net of redemptions to account for issues floated merely for refinancing) sold by US manufacturing and mining corporations, stated as a percentage of expenditure on plant and equipment over the period 1900 to 1953 inclusive, the last date for which the required data were available (Benston, 1969a, pp. 66-9). Expenditure was measured as gross and net (gross less capital replacement measured by depreciation adjusted for changes in replacement costs). To account for changes in general economic conditions not reflected by the amount of expenditure on capital assets, the percentages of net new issues to gross and net capital expenditure were averaged over thirteen minor and four major business cycles. Other institutional changes, in particular changes in personal and corporate taxation in 1938 which make the financing of capital investments internally (retained earnings) preferable to externally raised funds, must also be considered, although exploit adjustments could not be made for them.

The data show that from 1900 to 1924, net new issues averaged 30·9 per cent of gross capital expenditure and 58·3 per cent of net capital expenditure. From 1919 to 1929 these percentages averaged 36·8 per cent and 354·3 per cent.[37] (1924–27 was the period of the greatest percentage of net new issues to net capital expansion.) In contrast, there was a net capital redemption from 1932 to 1938 and net new issues of 6·5 and 51·2 per cent of gross and net capital formation from 1932 to 1940. The World War II period was understandably one of few new share issues. However, the percentages for 1946–53 were 21·9 per cent and 59·9 per cent, not quite as great as from 1900 to 1924 and far less than the previous economic boom period of 1919–29. Thus this evidence does not support the hypothesis that required disclosure increases the public's desire to purchase shares. However, because many other factors may also have affected corporate flotation of new securities, it cannot be claimed that the SEC's regulations necessarily decreased the relative amount of new issues.

Some additional evidence may be obtained by considering the effect of the US disclosure statutes on public and private placement of securities. US laws and regulations exempt from registration securities purchased by a small group of knowledgeable investors. Except under very restrictive conditions, these exempt securities cannot be publicly traded. Before the passage of the Securities Act of 1933 these private placements were rare. As a leading authority on this market notes, 'In the thirty-four years from 1900 to 1934, about three per cent of all corporate debt cash offerings, or approximately $1 billion were [privately] placed. However, in the ensuing thirty-one years, from 1935 to 1965, 46 per cent, or $85 billion, were directly [privately] placed.' (Avery D. Cohan, 1967, p.1.) Of course, the considerable relative and absolute growth of private placements is probably due to many factors, including the growth of life insurance companies over this period who tended to place their funds directly with corporations. However, these and similar investors were important suppliers of funds before 1933. Therefore it is fair to conclude that, at the very least, these data are consistent with the hypothesis that the SEC's regulations decreased rather than increased corporate willingness to use the public markets, apparently because increased flotation costs were not offset by the positive effect of increased public confidence, if there were any.

A supplementary test of the hypothesis was made by considering the differential effect of the SEC's accounting disclosure regulations on specific industries (Benston, 1969a, pp. 67–73). Data on the percentage of debt issued publicly and privately are published by the SEC for eight industries since 1953. The SEC's conservative accounting rules (which, among other things, forbid publication of appraised values of minerals, oil and other extractive resources, the economic effect of contracts and airline route awards, etc.) impart a differential bias to the financial statements published by corporations in these industries. If these rules impose a significant cost on corporations of communicating their economic prospects to the general public, we would expect them to place some of their debt privately. To test this hypothesis, the eight industries were ranked by several professional accountants according to the negative bias imposed by the SEC's accounting rules. These rankings were compared to annual rankings (1953 to 1966) of the percentage of debt privately placed. Even discounting the fact that other institutional factors support private debt placement by some industries (such as railroads) or require placement of securities by competitive bidding (as is the case with public utilities), the rankings are almost perfectly correlated – the greater the bias imposed by the SEC, the higher the percentage of debt privately placed.

Thus the evidence on public flotation of securities by corporations is inconsistent with the belief that government required disclosure enhances public confidence in the securities markets. Indeed, the evidence indicates that the US regulations, at least, impose costs on issuers that appear to decrease public investment in new issues.

4.2.9 Government administration and the public's and employees' 'right to know'

A gross benefit might result from required publication of financial reports if their publication reduces the cost of government administration. (Of course, the costs to corporations may exceed the benefit to government.) Government might need information on sales (turnover), cost of sales, salaries, depreciation, net income, specific assets and liabilities, etc., to administer laws and consider actions needed to control inflation, reduce unemployment, break up monopolies, etc. Aside from the question of whether these items or other information reported in financial statements are useful for the enumerated or other accepted governmental purposes, it is clear that government can and does obtain specific information from other sources, such as tax returns, census surveys, and special reports and surveys. Before the cost of providing the information presumably needed is imposed on all corporations subject to an act (such as the Securities Exchange Act or the Companies Act), it should be determined that gathering the required data from samples of enterprises is not more efficient than continuous reporting by all enterprises. The flexibility of specifically designed surveys as opposed to continuous reporting should also be considered, since the needs of government for specific information often change over time.

This argument does not apply to the public's 'right to know'. This reason for requiring publication of financial data is based, in large part, on the belief that government officials may not act 'in the public interest'. Therefore it is necessary that the press and the public generally be informed directly of the actions of corporations. It is argued that since non-government corporations (publicly or privately owned) control most of an industrialised nation's wealth, employ most persons and produce most of the goods and services consumed, their efficiency and operations are a matter of public concern. In the absence of required disclosure, it is argued, shareholders might not demand as much information as the public would wish, because shareholders cannot capture the externality (a 'better run economy') the information provides.

It is difficult to determine whether such an externality actually exists and, if it does, whether it exceeds the cost to shareholders (corporations) of providing the information. Nevertheless, if this type of information is useful to the general public, it would appear limited to rather broad data such as net income, sales (turnover), changes in capital investments and inventories (stocks), etc. It is difficult to imagine how detailed information on allowances for depreciation, accrued expenses, sub-categories of revenue, etc., can be assimilated, much less used, for general analysis of the economy. While at specific times, specific information (such as expenditure on pollution control equipment or charitable contributions, or the sales of a specific product) may be desired by some people, it would seem that the cost of requiring all corporations to report data that are, at best, meaningful to a few, would result in costs that exceed any benefit. However, it should be noted that the additional direct cost to corporations of providing specific data, once disclosure in general is required, may be small. Nevertheless, it appears that the 'public's right to know' alone is a weak reed on which to support government required detailed disclosure.

The contention that employees have a right to know their employer's financial data is based on the belief that corporations have as much responsibility to their employees as to their shareholders. The validity of this belief is debatable. As a minimum, the implications of dual responsibility toward employees and shareholders for people's willingness to invest in corporations and for the quality and quantity of products and services provided to consumers should be examined. But these important questions are beyond the scope of this analysis. Instead, a more limited question is considered – would government required disclosure of financial data provide information that is relevant to employees?

In most instances, it would appear that having detailed financial statements would not be useful to employees and might indeed be dysfunctional. As is discussed above, accounting statements provide rather crude measures of the economic condition and progress of an enterprise. The managerial efficiency of specific corporate officers is difficult if not impossible to measure with the type of data reported in financial statements. One really needs estimates of the opportunity costs of decisions, numbers which are not recorded in accounting records. The probability that a company or any one of its plants will offer continued employment at any given level also cannot be determined from financial statements. Instead, special studies are required. Neither can the ability of a company to pay a wage increase be determined from its earnings report (except, perhaps, where the company has clearly absorbed large losses). Consequently, there are few benefits from required reporting to employees that may offset the costs imposed on shareholders and the economy.

148

4.2.10 The political role of government

Legislators and political leaders are expected to solve problems. However, because of the relatively short range of their political horizons, the appearance of solving a problem is generally an acceptable and often preferable substitute for its actual solution if the desired benefits are achieved at a lower cost. Study of the cause of problems and the effectiveness of proposed solutions is usually too time-consuming to be pursued. In addition, studies often result in the uncovering of additional, even more intractable problems and ambiguous conclusions. Therefore, when faced with a crisis or scandal, government tends to take immediate action, any action.

The specific action taken depends on the ability of the lawmakers and their staff to understand the situation and draft legislation and on the skill of special interest groups in getting their views represented in the bills. These special interest groups are in an advantageous position for having laws drafted in their favour since they generally have well-defined views whose implementation via legislation is well thought out. Therefore it is not surprising that laws passed to alleviate a crisis or correct abuses discovered as a result of a scandal often turn out to serve quite different purposes.

Specifically, versions of the US securities laws had been proposed for years before their passage in 1933 and 1934.[38] Investment bankers wanted a law that would bring their smaller competitors 'up to their standards'; some reformers, appalled by some reporting practices, wanted legislation to enforce acceptance of their ideas; other reformers wanted a government agency to pass on the merits of securities; corporations that disclosed more wanted similar practices required of their competitors; some accountants wanted a means to require clients to follow practices the accountants thought correct, etc. Virtually no group had prepared studies to support their beliefs. The legislation passed was a function of the special interest groups' demands, newspaper reporting of a few scandalous happenings in the late 1920s, and the demand that the government 'do something'.

The history of UK Companies Acts and their passage demonstrates the advantages of the alternative approach. The 1948 and 1967 Acts were preceded by studies, a report of a select committee and legislative debate. Groups of individuals had ample opportunity to voice objections, although it must be conceded that those who had no special private interest were unlikely to take the time and effort to make their views known. As the analysis presented in chapter 5 shows, the result is, in many important respects, preferable to the US securities laws.

In any event, if some disclosure of financial information and the required auditing of financial statements by independent accountants prevents or reduces the incidence of scandal, the benefit from avoiding circumstances in which punitive or special interest legislation can be passed may exceed the cost to private corporations. In this regard, it would seem that more emphasis should be placed on auditing to prevent or reduce misappropriation of resources and similar frauds, events which are considered 'scandals' when they occur. Prevention of general precipitous declines in share prices would also be advisable politically (although if they are a consequence of precipitous declines in the economy or the fortunes of specific firms, equity would not be served unless share prices similarly declined). Unfortunately, there is no reasoning or evidence that supports the contention that required financial disclosure would play this role.

4.2.11 Summary and conclusions

In a free society, government ought not to require private companies or persons to do anything unless, at the very least, the requirement resulted in a net benefit to society. Why, then, should financial disclosure be required of privately owned companies? Several reasons for believing that this requirement provides gross benefits (before consideration of costs) were delineated and discussed in section 4.2.1. The arguments and evidence that support or reject these reasons were presented in the following nine sections. The possible benefits considered in these sections may be grouped into three categories: first, prevention or reduction of fraud, misrepresentation and unfairness to non-insiders; second, improved efficiency in the allocation of resources and in the operation of security markets; and third, improved government administration and availability of information for the general public and employees.

Evidence on the existence of fraud and misrepresentation in financial statements was considered in sections 4.2.2 and 4.2.3. A review of the available information reveals very little evidence of fraudulently or misleadingly prepared financial statements in the US before the federal Securities Acts were enacted, or in the UK, where disclosure requirements are not as detailed. Nevertheless, there is little doubt that some fraud existed before the securities laws. Nor is there much doubt that it still exists today: Equity Funding, National Student Marketing and Home Stake Production certainly rival the revelations of the unregulated 1920s. But the evidence does not support the belief that fraudulently or misleadingly prepared financial statements were a serious problem requiring corrective legislation or that the enacted legislation prevented or even ameliorated fraud. Nor does it appear that the market is 'fooled' by changes in accounting techniques that affect reported net income. Rather it seems that the presumption of misleadingly prepared statements is based on scandals from the pre-1920s and on unrealistic expectations about the ability of accountants to measure wealth and income unambiguously.

However, there is reason to believe (though there is no supportive evidence) that auditors may not be willing or able to report possible conflicts of interest or misrepresentation which obscures unfavourable operations by the management which employs them. Therefore government required disclosure that is directed towards preventing or reducing the incidence of management violating its fiduciary responsibilities to shareholders appears justified and beneficial.

The considerable evidence reviewed in sections 4.2.4 and 4.2.5 does not support the belief that financial disclosure has any effect on share price manipulation. The evidence on the behaviour of share price changes in the US before and after enactment of the federal securities laws and in the UK is also consistent with the hypothesis that the stock market is a 'fair game'. Information about companies appears to be absorbed rapidly by the market, making the quoted price of shares an unbiased (though not necessarily correct) estimate of their 'true' value. This property of stock market prices is observable in the US before and after disclosure was mandated by the Securities Exchange Act 1934, for companies that were not essentially affected by the Act and in the UK where less disclosure is required than in the US. Hence my conclusion is that government required disclosure is not beneficial for reducing security price manipulation and fairness to non-insiders, except, perhaps, where it reduces fraud by insiders.

The value of required disclosure for improving the allocation of resources was considered in sections 4.2.6 to 4.2.8. First, evidence on the publication of prospectuses and financial statements before they were mandated by law was considered. The (scanty) available evidence indicates that prospectuses in the US before enactment of the Securities Act of 1933 were not very detailed. Speculative issues appear to have been sold without reference to detailed (in many cases, any) financial reports. However, there is considerable doubt that such statements were wanted by investors, who based their investment decisions on the reputation of the issuing house or their hopes for great fortune. Considerable doubt exists today as to whether investors read or are in any way influenced by the very

151

detailed prospectuses required by the 1933 Act. Nor does the little available evidence support the view that the current prospectus requirements benefit investors. In the UK, prospectuses generally exceed the requirements of the Companies Act 1948. Therefore, unless the evidence supports the view that specific detailed information is required for rational investment decisions, mandated disclosure does not appear to be beneficial.

Evidence on the extent of voluntary periodic reporting before 1934 by US corporations whose securities were traded on the New York Stock Exchange was examined. All these companies published financial statements: most were audited by CPAs and about two-thirds gave shareholders such detailed data as sales (turnover), depreciation and cost of goods sold. In the UK, most companies report more data than are required by law. Publication of much financial data by a large proportion of publicly owned corporations, then, does not appear to be due primarily to government requirements.

To determine whether periodic disclosure is useful to or at least appears to be used by investors, a large number of studies were reviewed that seek to establish the relationship between share prices and published statements. These studies report almost no relationship existing at or around the time the statements are published other than that the number of transactions and the variance of price changes are greater in the weeks around the publication dates than in other periods. Other studies show that security analysts and mutual fund (unit trust) managers do not appear to obtain above average benefits from analysing financial statements and from other 'research'. The question of whether the required publication of sales (turnover) in 1934 affected share prices was also tested empirically. No economically significant effect was discovered.

The hypothesis that externalities in the production and distribution of financial information would necessarily reduce the amount of useful information voluntarily published was considered in section 4.2.7. The examination does not support the hypothesis. The belief that greater public confidence in the securities market is a consequence of required disclosure was examined in section 4.2.8. The evidence reveals that public confidence is basically unrelated to the extent of required financial disclosure by corporations. Indeed, data from the US shows that the SEC's administration may have reduced public ownership of securities as a consequence of having imposed onerous regulations on issuers. Thus, most of the evidence and analyses do not support the belief that required disclosure benefits investors.

The benefits of required disclosure as regards improved government

152

administration and increased information for the general public and employees were examined in sections 4.2.9 and 4.2.10. First, it is likely that government can obtain information needed for policy development and implementation more efficiently from samples of companies and specific surveys than from continuous detailed reporting by all publicly owned corporations. Second, 'the public's right to know' may be served by corporate financial reporting, but it is doubtful if more than general data, such as sales (turnover) and net income, could be useful and whether the benefits from detailed disclosure warrant the costs imposed on corporations. Employees would also find detailed published financial statements a poor source of useful information. But assuming they have a 'right to know', detailed analyses germane to a specific question would have to be required. Third, the government's desire to 'take action' by enacting legislation is considered as a reason for required disclosure. This argument is found to have some validity if required disclosure reduces the probability of scandals whose dramatic exposure leads to passage of special interest or ill-conceived, punitive legislation.

In sum, the above analysis leads to the conclusion that government required disclosure benefits the public primarily by helping the government enforce management's and insiders' implied contracts to act as fiduciaries towards shareholders. Disclosure may reduce the incidence of fraud, self-dealing, and poor performance by managers. Government required disclosure may give auditors the responsibility and power to protect shareholders' property rights. The requirements should be directed towards these goals. However, since there is little evidence supporting the view that required disclosure aids investment decisions, this role for financial statements should not be emphasised by the government, as it is now.

These recommendations are made on the assumption that the benefits from required disclosure exceed the costs thereof. Whether or not this assumption is valid is considered next.

4.3   Costs of government required disclosure

4.3.1   Types of costs

Because companies would prepare and publish financial statements in the absence of government imposed requirements (as is discussed above), the *total* costs of the statements should not be charged to the requirements. Only the *additional* costs of fulfilling the requirements should be considered.

The costs to companies, government, investors and the general public of government required disclosure may be categorised as direct, indirect and opportunity costs. Direct costs are incurred by companies in producing and distributing the required data and by government and investors in assimilating them. Indirect costs are also incurred by these groups, but they are not recorded as 'expenses' in accounting records and so are more difficult to measure. Opportunity costs are the most difficult to measure, since they refer to alternatives foregone as a consequence of the disclosure regulations. Although these categories are not mutually exclusive (e.g., economists measure all costs as opportunity costs), they provide a useful heuristic framework for analysis. Each is discussed briefly, following which the costs of periodic disclosure and of prospectuses are considered.

The direct costs of required disclosure include the *additional* expense of keeping records, auditing, organising accounting numbers, typing, printing and distributing statements that would not have been incurred in the absence of the disclosure statutes. While all companies would keep some accounting records and most would prepare and distribute audited financial statements, some of the required data probably would not be recorded. In particular, few companies in the US would be likely to record all of the specific data required by the SEC. Were it not for the law, some companies also might not employ the services of certified or chartered accountants (particularly the very small, private, owner managed companies that are subject to the audit requirements of the UK Companies Acts). And, were it not for the legal liabilities imposed by the US securities laws, the audit fees of CPAs would be lower. Neither would US companies use legal services to the extent they do now, were it not for the Securities Acts. In addition, in the US issuers of securities must pay filing fees to the SEC and incur higher underwriting costs for legal services and printing.

The direct costs of required disclosure incurred by government include the cost of reviewing and processing the statements filed. In the UK this cost is rather small, since the statements are generally not reviewed. The review process in the US uses a considerable amount of resources. The cost of this review is not available, since the SEC does not disclose the amount of expenditure on each of its major activities in its annual Report. ('Line of business' data are apparently not considered useful to the public.) However, the SEC's Annual Reports do state that fees paid by corporations for all purposes (registrations, annual fees, etc.) reimburse the SEC for some 70 per cent of its annual expenditure. Thus most of the government's costs are borne by a segment of the public.

154

Investors incur almost no direct costs as a consequence of required disclosure. On the contrary, non-shareholders obtain a 'free good' at the expense of shareholders, to the extent that the data they receive in financial statements is information (i.e., newly affects their expectations.)

Indirect expenses include the time that corporate officers, government officials and investors otherwise would not apply to fulfilling the requirements of the disclosure statements. These costs are greatest for corporate officers, particularly in the US. The potential legal liability imposed on officers and directors should a prospectus or periodic statement be materially misleading is great. Directors of US corporations are finding that they can no longer simply sign the statements prepared for them by their expert auditors and lawyers. Reliance on these and other experts is often not an adequate defence in lawsuits. As a consequence, it is reported that many US corporations are finding it difficult to obtain the services of outside directors who cannot take the time to 'audit' the corporation's officers. It is not clear whether the cost of not obtaining such services exceeds the benefit from having directors actively oversee corporate officers and experts. Nevertheless, the cost should be recognised.

Government and investors incur few discernible indirect costs as a consequence of the disclosure requirements. Indeed, government may be thought to benefit, since the laws enable an expansion of its bureaucracy. Investors may also benefit to the extent that the data filed reduce the cost of financial analysis.

The opportunity costs of required disclosure are greatest for companies who want to raise capital from the general public. These costs include the cost of delay (particularly in the US, where the SEC can and often does take several months to accept a registration statement) and the cost of not being able to offer the public the issue where the regulating authorities raise objections that cannot be overcome. The SEC also restricts the type of information that can be included in a prospectus. The opportunity cost to the public and investors is the foregone opportunity of having products and services and profits provided by ventures that could not be funded because of costs imposed by the authorities. Of course, off-setting these opportunity costs are the opportunity benefits to investors of not losing their resources by investing in ventures that would have failed had they been funded. Periodic reporting requirements may cause incurrence of the opportunity cost to shareholders and the public from firms not investing in product development, research, etc., where they fear that required disclosure will give the benefits of the investments to competitors.

Another possible opportunity cost that applies to new issues and periodic reports is the failure of investors to develop what might be termed 'immunity' against fraud. Those who would defraud investors may use the fact that a government regulatory agency reviews financial statements to imply either that the government approves the statements (despite the explicit disclaimer that it does not) and/or that the government would not allow the really important 'facts' about the investment to be included in the statements. Hence the customer would have to rely on the security salesman's 'inside information'. Were there no disclosure laws, investors would be aware that their only recourse would be a lawsuit for fraud should the numbers be wrong or misleading. Consequently, they would have to review the data carefully and/or check the reputation of the issuing house and certifying accountant. *Caveat emptor* may therefore be a better defence against fraud than government regulation.

4.3.2   Costs of periodically required disclosure

For relatively large companies, the additional costs of meeting the periodic reporting requirements might not be too much above the amount they would otherwise expend.[39] UK requirements, in particular, are not so detailed as to require many companies to maintain records that they otherwise would not have kept (see chapter 3). In addition, The Stock Exchange's disclosure requirements generally require publication of more data (though relatively little more in comparison with US requirements) than are required by the Companies Acts. The Acts, therefore, impose relatively few additional direct costs on listed companies. US disclosure requirements are much more detailed than those of the UK, as the comparison given in chapter 3 shows. Although most US companies whose shares were traded on the major stock exchanges published fairly complete financial statements before the enactment of the Securities Exchange Act of 1934, that Act has probably caused them to incur additional direct costs. While the larger companies would probably keep the detailed records necessary to provide the data required by the SEC, few would publish the numbers required by form 10-K. The additional costs of completing the requirements of form 10-K include somewhat higher accounting and legal fees, because of the legal liabilities imposed on accountants and directors, and somewhat greater book-keeping and typing costs.[40] If the SEC insists that all security holders receive the 10-K report (as they seem to be doing), companies will have to incur significantly greater printing and distribution costs, particularly those companies who do not now send glossy public relations documents to

156

their shareholders.

For smaller companies, the direct and indirect costs can be onerous. In the UK, many small unlisted (private) companies would probably not use the services of a chartered accountant, were it not for the Companies Act requirements. Small US corporations subject to the Securities Acts must incur an even greater burden, since US disclosure requirements are much more detailed. Relative to their resources, their auditing costs are often much greater than those of large corporations; this is particularly true of those small companies that do not have extensive internal audit or control systems. The cost of preparing and distributing the detailed 10-K report is also relatively more onerous for small than for large companies. And the indirect cost to management and directors may also be great where out of the ordinary events occur. Therefore, whether this relatively higher cost is worth the benefit to the shareholders is much more questionable for small than for large corporations.

The opportunity costs to small companies are also greater than those incurred by larger companies. The principal opportunity cost is disclosure of information about sales, costs and profits to competitors. Large diversified companies can hide meaningful figures by grouping data that might be of value to competitors, government regulators or trade unions with other data. Small, single product companies do not have this option. In the US, increasing emphasis on line of business reporting has decreased this advantage for conglomerates somewhat, although it should not be difficult for most to 'bury' their more useful data. The required disclosure of proprietary information also results in an opportunity cost to the public if companies do not invest in product and market development because they will not be able to gain the full advantage from projects, should they succeed, but must pay fully for any failures that occur.

The direct costs to government of processing the periodic reports are not readily measured. Although the SEC requires corporations, brokers and security dealers to report a large amount of detailed financial and activity data, it does not publish similar data on its own operations. The SEC's financial report occupies one page of its 177 page 1973 annual report, in which no breakdown is given of the cost of administering the various laws under its jurisdiction. In total, $29,761,000 was budgeted for the fiscal year 1973, of which approximately $21,726,000 (73 per cent) was collected from fees, for which no breakdown is provided; some 1,656 persons were employed (Securities and Exchange Commission, 1974, p. 176-7). The DT's budget and personnel is smaller. Although the DT is concerned with some 600,000 'live' companies who are registered at Company House, it does not make a detailed examination of annual

157

reports and prospectuses, but rather acts as a repository. Some 900 personnel are employed at Company House (almost all are office staff). Of these, only about six people regularly deal with inquiries regarding breaches of the Companies Acts, for which additional staff and qualified accountants are called in as necessary.

Investors both gain and lose as a consequence of required disclosure. Non-shareholders gain by having available (at no cost) data provided by corporations [41] and, hence, by shareholders. Both sets of investors gain if the standard reporting imposed by government regulations reduces the cost of analysis. However, in the US, investors incur the opportunity cost of not having information that the SEC prohibits companies from providing. In particular, companies cannot reveal appraisal values of assets, forecasts of sales and earnings and other 'soft' data in prospectuses.[42]

In summary, it appears as if government required periodic disclosure imposes but relatively slightly higher additional costs on large diversified companies. In the US, few companies would otherwise produce the detailed statements required by the SEC. The SEC's new rules for computing such information as interest costs affected by compensating bank balance will probably increase accounting costs. Should the SEC continue to encourage, if not require, the sending of the full 10-K report and more detailed proxy material to all shareholders, then printing and postage costs will also increase substantially. Thus costs to larger companies might increase considerably. However, the greatest cost impact of the law, present and potential, is on small companies. In the UK, many would not otherwise use the services of chartered accountants. In the US, many are forced to record data that they would not otherwise keep. The statements they must prepare are costly, compared to their resources. They must hire experts who are familiar with SEC rules. They may be forced to reveal valuable data to competitors. Should these costs reduce the availability of goods and services, then the public bears the consequent opportunity cost.

4.3.3 Cost of new security issues

In the UK, the additional costs to issuers of securities are very similar to those imposed on companies who report periodically. For most issuers, these additional costs are not great. The practical prohibition of public sales of all except securities admitted to listing on The (London) Stock Exchange makes the Exchange's more extensive prospectus requirements of overriding importance, as detailed in sections 2.3.1 and 3.7. Moreover, the prospectus requirements of the Companies Act 1948 are not very onerous (see section 3.7); it is doubtful if the costs of preparing a prospectus for companies whose shares are privately issued are much greater than they would have been had it not been for the Act. However, it should be noted that the Prevention of Fraud (Investments) Act 1958, which effectively prevents development of an over the counter market, and The (London) Stock Exchange's listing requirements, which do not admit 'unseasoned' companies to trading, prevent the public from investing in new or speculative enterprises. As a consequence, losses and potential gains to investors may be reduced (a portion of the set of preferred investments – efficient frontier – is excluded). Perhaps of greatest importance is the fact that the availability of capital to new and unusual ventures is also reduced and the public does not get the products and services that are not developed.

US prospectus requirements are much more detailed than those required by the Companies Act 1948 or The (London) Stock Exchange (see section 3.7). Consequently, the cost of preparing a prospectus is relatively greater in the US than in the UK. Although some effort was made to measure the costs of issuing a security in the US compared to the UK, comparable data could not be obtained. US data on the primary costs of an issue are compiled by the SEC (Securities and Exchange Commission, 1970) but similar data are not available in the UK. Even were such data recorded, it would be very difficult to separate the costs of market risk and institutional arrangements from the costs of fulfilling the disclosure requirements of each country. Consequently, the comparison that follows is not as explicit as one would like.

Direct costs of a US prospectus are greater than would be incurred in the UK because US requirements call for much more data (see section 3.7). The greater detail increases auditing and statement preparation costs. Perhaps the greatest increase is in printing costs. US prospectuses are much longer than those prepared in the UK, where required prospectuses are printed on one to two pages of two London daily newspapers (though prospectuses distributed to the public are often longer). In contrast, US prospectuses usually run to fifty or more 7½″ × 9″ pages. US law also makes legal fees a much more important cost of a security issue. It is difficult to determine the effect of the disclosure laws on issuing houses' and underwriters' fees. It seems clear that the greater legal liabilities imposed by US law increases underwriters' risk and hence their fees. However, for larger, well-established companies at least, there may be little increase over what otherwise would have been charged.

Indirect costs are probably greater in the US than in the UK, primarily because of the legal liability imposed on officers and directors and because of the complexity of US regulations. Directors in particular must expend time and resources to check the statements made by officers and experts. The officers of the company must also familiarise themselves with the SEC's regulations rather than simply rely on experts. Perhaps the most important indirect cost, though, is the time required to get a prospectus accepted by the SEC. The SEC operates much more formally than does its UK counterpart, the Quotations Department of The (London) Stock Exchange. In the UK, an auditor can call the manager of the Department, discuss the question of whether a requirement is met by a particular procedure or can be modified to meet a special circumstance, and can often get an answer the same day or within no more than about three days if a decision is required of a panel of members. Usually, no more than a few days will elapse between the day a prospectus proof goes to the Quotations Department and the time of its acceptance for further proofing. Completion of the work necessary to comply with the comments of the Department is usually achieved within one week.

In the US, procedures are much more formal and often more time-consuming. Though the SEC staff will answer many telephoned queries, important rulings are rarely given quickly. Often conferences are needed involving the top officers, senior auditors and legal counsel of the company and SEC officials. The SEC's Annual Report states that in 1973 '. . . the median number of calendar days between the date of the original filing and the effective data was 41.' (Securities and Exchange Commission, 1974, p. 31.) This delay also gives rise to higher direct costs, since underwriters, accountants and lawyers are under great pressure to work overtime to meet objections from the SEC's administrative staff and prepare final proofs of the prospectus quickly in order to reduce the time between the initial determination that a security should be sold and its offer to the market.[43]

Another major difference in the costs of security flotations in the US and the UK is the issues to which the laws apply. The coverage of US law is much broader than that of the UK. The most important differences are the requirements for rights and secondary offerings, and employee stock option and stock purchase plans. In the UK, these offerings do not require a prospectus, though one may be used in connection with a rights or secondary offering should the issuing house and company feel this to be desirable. In the US, *all* issues of securities by a company require registration and a prospectus. Unlike the prevailing rule in the UK, it does not matter whether the security issued is in all respects similar to securities currently being traded and quoted on a stock exchange. In addition, UK law applies only to security issues by a company and by underwriters who are acting in a professional capacity. In the US, however, secondary offerings by persons to whom securities were privately issued are subject to the SEC's regulations (which are very restrictive). As a consequence of these differences, it is estimated that from one-half to two-thirds of all registration statements filed in the US would not be required in the UK (Robert L. Krauss, 1971, p. 64).

To summarise, the more detailed and extensive prospectus disclosure requirements in the US no doubt impose greater direct and indirect costs of issuing securities than those of the UK. Except for the expense of printing the fifty or more prospectus pages required, large companies may not expend much more than they otherwise would have incurred had only a fraud statute been in effect without specific required disclosure. However, the US requirement that all security issues, including rights offerings, be registered with the SEC, has probably resulted in essentially unnecessary expenses for companies who were already reporting their operations periodically. Small companies, though, appear more negatively affected than large companies. As was discussed above, the disclosure they must make may benefit their competitors more than their investors. Their accounting, printing, and legal expenses are also relatively (if not absolutely) greater than those incurred by large companies.[44] Interestingly, though, the disclosure costs of a security flotation for a totally 'untried' company are less in the US than in the UK. Since such a company has no financial past, it has no statements to audit and report. In the UK, however, the costs of a public issue are infinitely high, since companies without at least three (often five) years of successful operations are rarely allowed to list their shares on The Stock Exchange.

Although the evidence reviewed does not, on the whole, support government required financial reporting, it is doubtful that laws requiring disclosure will be repealed. The continued existence of such laws is therefore assumed and the question raised is whether administration of the laws by an active regulatory agency, such as the SEC, is desirable. The next chapter considers this question by comparing the US system with the UK system of passive government regulation (by the DT) and active private regulation (by The Stock Exchange).

Notes

[1] Securities and Exchange Commission (1967), p. 1.

[2] A major reason also often mentioned is the existence in the US of an agency that presumably actively investigates and uncovers fraud, the SEC. The validity of this possibility is examined in chapter 5, pp. 166–92.

[3] See George J. Benston (1969a), pp. 51–5.

[4] *Ultramares Corp. v. Touche* (225 N.Y. 170; New York 1931).

[5] See Henry G. Manne (1974) for a fuller exposition of this hypothesis.

[6] See Michael A. Parrish (1970) for an extensive account of the activities of the Investment Bankers Association and the events that preceded the passage of the Securities Act of 1933. However, the legislation passed added federal requirements without eliminating state requirements.

[7] As brokers put it, 'investors are discounting not only the future, but also the hereafter.'

[8] The most recent and prominent of these critics are Abraham Briloff (1972) and Edward Stamp (Stamp and Marley, 1970).

[9] The Companies Acts and the SEC's proxy rules in effect impose this requirement.

[10] See George J. Benston (1975b) for a more complete exposition.

[11] These disclosures are required by the Companies Acts and the Securities Acts.

[12] A very large number of articles could be cited here. In particular see articles and books by Edward Stamp in the UK and Abraham Briloff in the US, and the weekly column 'The Numbers Game' in *Forbes Magazine.*

[13] Abraham Briloff (1972) and various articles in *Barrons.* However, see my review of Briloff's book (Benston 1973b).

[14] Ray Ball (1974, pp. 30–31) questions the statistical accuracy of this increase.

[15] Securities and Exchange Commission (1959), pp. xi–xvi.

[16] The financial statements of companies whose stocks were included in pools in 1930 to 1933 inclusive were also examined. The percentage not reporting sales and cost of goods sold decreased to 30 per cent and 40 per cent for the thirty companies whose securities were included in the 1930 pools. The percentage was similar for the six 1931 pools, two 1932 pools and twelve 1933 pools. See Benston (1973a), Table 1, p. 136 for the complete data.

[17] The percentages are very similar for the years 1926 to 1934. See Benston (1969b), Table 1, p. 519 for details.

[18] See Eugene Fama (1970) for an extensive and rigorous exposition of the concept of the stock market as 'a fair game'.

[19] Alexander G. Kemp and Gavin C. Reid (1971) also published a study

of share price behaviour. However, in an unpublished note, Dryden points out a number of problems that make their results suspect.

[20] It is possible that the costs of maintaining a 'fair game' market are different as a consequence of required disclosure. Some evidence and reasoning on costs is presented in section 4.3. However, I know of no evidence or reason to believe that the total costs of disclosure (including costs to companies) are lower in the UK or the pre-SEC US, while there is some reason to believe they are higher (see section 4.3).

[21] Non-reporting of gross income was considered a major lack of disclosure in the late 1920s. See L.H. Sloan (1931), from which the initial list of corporations who did and did not disclose gross income was taken.

[22] Disclosure of insiders' (or anyone else's) share holdings and transactions is not the subject of this study. Such disclosure may or may not be useful in reducing insider trading before or after the costs of such disclosures are considered. See Henry G. Manne (1966) for a view that insider trading is beneficial to investors, Roy A. Schotland (1967) and other articles referred to in note 2, p. 547 of Manne (1970) for a critique thereof, Manne (1970) for a reply, and Jeffrey F. Jaffe (1974) and other works cited therein for evidence that greater than normal profits are realised on trades by insiders who report their transactions to the SEC.

[23] The cost of required disclosure must also be considered, since it may exceed the benefits. This is discussed in section 4.3.

[24] Fraud and misrepresentation are considered above in section 4.2.2.

[25] Edward G. Cale (1937) reviews individual statements filed under the Securities Act of 1933 that were considered 'ineffective' by the SEC. He concludes '. . . available information indicates that the ineffective investment trust and precious metal mining issues would have constituted poor risks for investors.' (p. 43.)

[26] The non-reporting companies were generally smaller than the reporting companies: total market value of the sales (turnover) reporting companies was 1·65 greater than that of the non-reporting companies.

[27] Obviously, data presented in one company's statements may affect investors' expectations about other companies. The impact of this possibility is very difficult to assess.

[28] The 'model' on which this fairly obvious statement is based is expressed formally in Benston (1967) and at greater length and formality in Gonedes (1971a).

[29] See Benston (1967) and other studies cited below for a detailed description.

[30] See Michael C. Jensen (1972) for a rigorous exposition of the theory and review of evidence.

[31] Several studies subtract the risk free rate of return from R_{jt} and R_{Mt} in accordance with the Sharp–Lintner capital asset pricing model.

[32] The contents of the annual statements may have been anticipated by the disclosure given in quarterly reports published by NYSE companies. The SEC's monthly 8-K reports did not require disclosure of extraordinary items as early as 1966; therefore, they were not a means whereby the annual data were anticipated.

[33] The validity of the Beaver et al. findings is the subject of some controversy as revealed by Beaver and Manegold (1975) and Gonedes (1970). Though further discussion is not appropriate here, the reader is advised to consult the professional literature further.

[34] Robert May (1971) reports results for quarterly statements similar to those reported by Beaver (1968) and Hagerman (1972). C.P. Jones and R.H. Litzenberger (1970) and Henry Latane (1970) show how past quarterly earnings per share can be used to select portfolios of shares that apparently outperform randomly selected portfolios with the same risk characteristics.

[35] See Benston (1975b) for an extended discussion of this.

[36] This argument is also based on the assumption that information provided as a consequence of securities laws is useful for resource allocation decisions. See studies discussed in section 4.2.6 which report findings contrary to this belief.

[37] The large (354·3 per cent) figure is a consequence of a large amount of issues floated in 1919–21 and a relatively small net capital expansion in 1924–27.

[38] See Ralph F. de Bedts (1964) and Michael E. Parrish (1970) for narrative, non-analytical histories.

[39] However, it took British Petroleum over two years to prepare its statements in a manner acceptable to the SEC. The cost of this effort is not available.

[40] It is common for auditors to charge 25 per cent above standard fees for SEC work.

[41] The undemonstrated assumption, again, is that published financial statements contain information that is both useful and unknown before it is received.

[42] The SEC has indicated that forecasts may be permitted in the future. In its *amicus curiae* brief to *Gerstle v. Gamble-Skogmo* [1973], the Commission stated that good faith offers to purchase assets must be disclosed if their omission would be materially misleading.

[43] The consequences of the SEC's twenty-day 'cooling-off period' are not considered since this is not directly related to the extent of required

disclosure.

[44] Although the SEC allows somewhat simpler procedures to be followed for issues of under $500,000 (Regulation A), the difference in the requirements is not great.

5 Administration of corporate financial disclosure laws

5.1 Introduction

The SEC is given the authority to prepare and administer regulations governing financial disclosure mandated by the Securities Act of 1933 and the Securities Exchange Act of 1934. In contrast, the Companies Acts stand on their own in the sense that the specific disclosure required is given in the Acts rather than in regulations promulgated by the DT. Although the DT has the power to investigate failures of directors to conform to the requirements of the Acts, particularly when such an investigation is requested by security holders, it serves primarily as a repository for the statements filed pursuant to the Acts. In the US, however, the SEC actively investigates situations that its staff believes may mislead investors and obtains stop orders preventing trading in or issuance of securities. It also reviews the financial statements filed in accordance with the Securities Acts and reject those which, in its opinion, do not conform to regulations. This 'screening' is particularly extensive with respect to prospectuses. In the UK, a somewhat similar function is performed by private regulatory agencies, e.g., the Quotations Department of The Stock Exchange and the issuing houses.[1]

The costs and benefits of the US compared to the UK system of required disclosure are considered in this chapter. As an introduction and background to this analysis, the forces governing behaviour by a regulatory agency such as the SEC are first briefly discussed (section 5.2). In the light of the concepts outlined, the SEC's administration of the Securities Acts is then analysed (section 5.3). Analysis of the administration of the Companies Act by UK private regulatory agencies follows (section 5.4), and the presumed benefits from administration by an active public regulatory agency are described and evaluated in the light of the prior discussion (section 5.5). In the penultimate section (5.6) the effect of public and private regulatory agencies on the practice and profession of accounting is briefly considered. Conclusions and recommendations are presented in the final section (5.7).

5.2   Forces governing the behaviour of a public regulatory agency

In analysing the performance of an active administrative agency, such as the SEC, it is essential to remember that agencies are administered by people who are subject to the same sort of needs as are other people. They respond to rewards and punishments as much as do the accountants, directors, brokers, lawyers and bankers whose work they oversee. The factors that motivate the behaviour of privately employed individuals are fairly obvious – long term personal gain in the form of monetary rewards (present and future), social status, personal pride, desire to see justice done, public reputation, personal security, etc. There is no reason to believe that employees and directors of public regulatory agencies are in general motivated differently, although they might value non-monetary rewards more than their counterparts in private industry. Naturally, public regulatory agency personnel may profess that they always put the public's interests before all else, and they may believe that they do so, but they are still self-interested human beings.

Yet the public regulatory agency's mission may allow its employees to emphasise some non-pecuniary personal rewards. In particular, public regulatory agency officers may be attracted to that line of work because they are especially concerned to see justice done and 'truth' prevail. Such would be the situation where the particular mission of the agency is believed to be the uncovering of falsehood and establishment of truth. Having discovered wrongdoing, many (perhaps most) people wish to see its perpetrators punished. Having searched for truth, many (again, perhaps most) people eventually claim to have found it and wish to see it proclaimed and adhered to. In most circumstances, wrongdoing must be proved in an adversary proceeding and truth cannot be imposed, but must be voluntarily accepted.[2] But, within the constraints of law, public opinion and private influence, the public regulatory agency is granted the power to punish wrongdoing and impose the truth. This power might be very appealing to persons who wish to serve the public and who believe that, without their help, the public (particularly its less informed and weaker members) would be ill-served.

Aside from these individual considerations, people's behaviour is affected primarily by the reward structure of their organisation. The employees of any organisation are rewarded for enhancing the utility of their supervisors who, in turn, are rewarded for enhancing institutional values. In private enterprise, the institutional values include maximisation of the wealth of the owners (some would say this is the only institutional value), which requires efficient production and distribution of goods and services to consumers.

A public agency, on the other hand, is not controlled by a market which dictates the aggregate level of services demanded by the public, but rather receives its funds through an imperfect political allocation system which at best attempts to tap societal demands for the public good. Public revenues are raised differentially from the various segments of society, usually on the basis of ability to pay and not on a basis consistent with the value of the benefits received from public expenditure. Hence the public agency usually seeks to maximise the quantity of the services it can provide, given its budget. Over time, the public administrator can only increase the level of his agency's services through larger budgets.

Consequently, the optimising behaviour of the public agency does not result in maximisation of net public benefit (or social welfare) in the way the profit maximising behaviour of a privately owned enterprise operating in a competitive market results in a Pareto optimum allocation of resources. The agency seeks rather to maximise the resources with which it can work – its budget. For some (perhaps most) agency directors, budget maximisation is a goal because only by this means can they maximise their own monetary rewards and prestige. For others, budget maximisation is desired so that they can better serve the public. Since the public generally does not pay for the services provided, the usual market constraint on production is not present. For the public agency, the constraint is the limited resources available to the legislature which must be allocated among competing agencies and other governmental functions. In seeking to maximise its budget, the public agency must be concerned with the government (legislature and executive) and with the part of the public that can influence the government. Thus its officers may not be able to prosecute the public good, as they see it, as zealously as they might like. On the other hand, the public agency is not as dependent upon brokers, companies and others whom it regulates as is a private regulatory agency, such as The (London) Stock Exchange.

Several hypotheses about the behaviour of public regulatory agencies can be drawn from this analysis. First, a public regulatory agency will tend to serve organised and relatively enduring groups (who can serve as lobbyists in the political process of securing larger agency budgets) rather than the diverse, unorganised general public. However, the agency may also act zealously to serve the public, should its officers feel this need strongly and should other factors allow this action. Secondly, the agency will act to expand and rarely to contract the scope of its operations. Thirdly, the agency will seek to avoid scandals and situations which might cause the general public and other government officials to conclude that

168

it is not 'doing its job', and consequently to question future budgets. Hence the agency avoids risks and institutes formal rules that prevent someone from blaming a specific person for an error of judgement.

5.3 Administration of the Securities Acts by the SEC

I suggest that the SEC's administration of the Securities Acts reflects essentially, though not completely, the above behavioural description of a public regulatory agency. First, although the SEC is concerned with protecting and otherwise aiding individual investors, its actions indicate that it is primarily interested in serving organised enduring groups whose demands it believes to be proxies for the public's needs. Several easily identified groups are concerned with financial disclosure. Most prominent among these are security analysts, stock brokers, investment bankers, certified public accountants, financial executives and business groups. All except the last two would prefer that corporations provide more information, since they do not pay for the information directly but may benefit from its production.[3] Corporations (and therefore shareholders) pay for the production of information which the SEC requires to be disclosed. Corporations who sell shares to the public must pay registration fees to the SEC. These groups, therefore, are expected to oppose additional disclosure, unless they believe that present shareholders would benefit thereby. Since relatively few companies issue shares very often and since annual reporting tends to be routine after the first reports are filed, corporate officers are not in regular contact with the SEC. However, security analysts, brokers, investment bankers and certified public accountants tend to be in regular contact with the agency. In addition, as Henry G. Manne (1974) points out, larger, established companies and groups generally find regulations less onerous than their smaller, newer competitors. Having filed the required reports before, the established firms are able to prepare updates at much less cost and with much less uncertainty than can newcomers. Thus more extensive and detailed regulations serve to give established firms a competitive edge over their newer rivals that may be well worth the cost (to older firms) of meeting the regulatory agency's requirements. This predominantly once only expense is a barrier to entry for some potential firms and a deterrent to others. Although the magnitude of the barrier or restriction is not known (in part because the additional total cost of meeting the SEC's requirements has not been estimated, and in part because the effect on entry of this cost would be very difficult to separate from the effect of other factors), its direction is clear. Consequently, it is not surprising that the agency tends to understand and sympathise with the 'Establishment's' problems and needs.

However, the SEC is also concerned with protecting the general public from what it considers to be rapacious or, at best, irresponsible professionals and companies. Perhaps because regulatory agencies were ostensibly established to protect the public which, by assumption, could not protect itself, regulators find it necessary to establish and maintain 'honest, correct' procedures and relationships among people. With respect to financial disclosure, this concern is reflected in the establishment of 'better' accounting and reporting rules and the disallowance of what are believed to be misleading practices. The extent to which an agency, such as the SEC, attempts to establish 'truth' appears to depend on the personal views (or needs) of its officers as much as (if not more than) on the current circumstances of the institutions and markets the agency regulates. In particular, after its early years, during which rules and regulations were promulgated, the SEC became a rather inactive force with respect to the establishment of accounting principles or procedures. Rather it emphasised procedures that allowed for relatively easy administration, such as disallowance of estimates, appraisals, and other 'soft' information that is inherently difficult to verify. Whether or not this approach was justified, it appears to have been as much a consequence of the philosophy (or needs) of the SEC's chief accountants and commissioners as of stock market or other 'real' conditions. In the last several years, though, perhaps coincidental with the replacement as chief accountant of Andrew Barr (who retired after twenty-five years in office) by John (Sandy) Burton in 1972, the Commission has become very active, particularly with respect to accounting (disclosure) matters. Although the stock market has been troubled by general economic events over part of this period, there is no evidence or reason to believe that misleading or poor accounting practices have been either widespread or in any way responsible for more than, at most, a few business failures. Nevertheless, the SEC has put forth more changes in required accounting procedures in the last few years than in most of its history after the codification of its basic rules and regulations.

Several factors may explain this increase in activity. One is that it simply reflects its times. As an article critical of the SEC by Walter Guzzardi Jr concludes: '. . . anyone focusing on the SEC's recent aggressiveness might note that the three chairmen who presided in this period were all appointed by Richard Nixon, and served at his pleasure. The atmosphere in which they operated was one of growing executive power, and declining respect for the rights of individuals. No continuous national policy gave these chairmen a proper environment in which to work.' (1974, p. 202.) Or the activity may reflect the beliefs of the particular individuals who happen to occupy positions of power in the SEC. Or the agency may simply be reacting to public and press distress at declining share prices with action that might be interpreted as showing that the SEC is 'doing something'. While the Commission cannot affect the losses investors are experiencing, it can indicate its concern and give the impression of acting correctively by criticising accountants (and others) publicly, imposing what appear to be strict rules and prosecuting civil and (through the Justice Department) criminal cases against alleged wrongdoers.

The second type of behaviour desired by a public regulatory agency – expansion of its activities – is supported by the congruence of interests between the SEC and established firms, security analysts, public accountants, lawyers and other professionals and by the SEC's appearance of protecting the public by establishing better accounting rules and by prosecuting miscreants. The established groups demand additional data or, at the very least, do not oppose expansion of the amount of data reported and the number of reports filed. It is in their interests to reduce the bad publicity that results from the alleged misdeeds of non-establishment firms and professionals. The established firms and professionals therefore tend to support the agency's similar desire to reduce risks and expand operations. The public is also likely to support expanded surveillance by the SEC, since people can generally empathise with the plight of an investor who appears to have been cheated of his savings. It appears much more difficult for people to appreciate that a process that screens out the risk of great loss also tends to screen out the possibility of great pain.

The scope of the Securities Acts also changes in response to specific situations that give rise to public indignation. Since a public agency generally seeks to expand its activities and hence its budget, it tends to stretch its mandate whenever possible. The SEC has done this by expanding the definition of a security to cover such situations as sales of merchandising franchises and condominium apartments. When the questionable, perhaps fraudulent, practices of some promoters of these ventures came to public attention, lawsuits were brought against them contending that they were offering 'securities' to the public without prior registration with the SEC in violation of the Securities Act of 1933.[4] While the public might applaud action taken against apparent miscreants, a precedent is established as to what is subject to the Securities Acts.

Originally the Acts were designed to provide information to the investor who entrusted his resources to a management he did not directly supervise. The wording of the statute is very broad to avoid the simple renaming of a security to avoid the law. But in 1946 the Supreme Court established a test. They held in *SEC v. W.J. Howey Co.* that the law referred to an investment contract characterised by: '(1) An investment of money in (2) a common enterprise and (3) profits to come solely through the efforts of others' (Mofsky, 1973, p. 399). Recent attempts (some successful) by the SEC to expand this relatively clear definition have injected uncertainty into financing arrangements. This uncertainty necessarily introduces additional costs into the establishment of business relationships. While some individuals might benefit from having an experienced agency such as the SEC intercede in arrangements that are thought to be fraudulent, it is not at all clear that the potential benefits exceed the legal and other costs imposed.

In any event, it appears that the SEC is increasingly becoming (willingly or not) a regulator of much more than security market transactions. The securities laws were clearly intended by the US Congress to provide the public with information rather than bar them from purchasing securities that failed to meet the standards of a government agency. Yet in 1938 the SEC promulgated Accounting Series Release 4, which declares that:

> . . . where financial statements filed . . . are prepared in accordance with accounting principles for which there is no substantial authoritative support, such financial statements will be presumed to be misleading or inaccurate *despite disclosures* contained in the certificate of the accountant or in footnotes to the statements provided the matters involved are material. (Italics added.)

By refusing to accept registration statements or by objecting to specific items in order to delay repeatedly the date at which registrations become effective, the SEC has used its power to deny the public the right to purchase securities in ventures which the staff felt were inadequately described or which could not be adequately described within the conservative accounting rules and disclosure regulations enforced by the Commission. Most recently, Accounting Series Release 115 made formal the SEC's refusal to accept for registration the statements of corporations who appear to have inadequate working capital to operate successfully.[5] While these actions may be undertaken to protect investors from their own folly and from presumably unscrupulous promoters, such was not the intent of the Securities Acts.

The SEC also insisted from its earliest years that appraisals of assets should not be reported, that goodwill be eliminated from balance sheets and that only 'hard figures' (rather than estimates) be included in financial statements. These and similar prohibitions seem contrary to the disclosure philosophy of the securities laws. After all, the SEC is not supposed to approve or disapprove financial statements.

The move towards 'blue sky' merit regulation in place of 'disclosure only' is understandable when one considers the third type of behaviour described, the natural aversion of a public agency towards risk. Unlike a privately owned company or individual who bears risks and reaps rewards, a public agency is rarely rewarded for risks it undertakes.[6] Thus if a company undertakes a risky research project, it may lose its investment, but if the project proves successful, it gains the benefits. However, if a public agency allows a company to publish subjective estimates of the value of the research, it risks public criticism if the estimates prove over-optimistic, but gains nothing should the estimates prove correct. Similarly, if a new company turns out to be a failure, in retrospect its prospectus may appear misleading, even fraudulent. Even though the prospectus states (in block letters), that 'these securities have not been approved or disapproved by the Securities and Exchange Commission nor has the Commission passed on the accuracy or adequacy of this prospectus', purchasers of the company's securities may blame the SEC for 'passing' the registration. Therefore it is not surprising that the SEC prohibits appraisals of assets (since these later may prove vastly incorrect), forbids estimates (since these cannot be 'objectively' determined), and requires reporting of very detailed data and analyses by all companies despite the relevance of these numbers to relatively few companies and situations. If even one fraud or scandal is prevented thereby, or if it occurs and the SEC is not blamed, to the agency the benefits exceed the costs since it does not assume the costs imposed on the general public, including the cost of not getting possibly useful information (such as valid appraisals and estimates).

For this reason, and because it prefers larger to smaller budgets, an agency such as the SEC will rarely contract its activities. Specific items are added to the list of requirements by the SEC in response to specific situations. In a particular case, analysis of the depreciation accounts of individual groups of assets might be helpful to an analyst. In another case, knowledge of the amount of specific intangible assets not yet written off may be valuable. An analyst might want to know the amount of the provision for doubtful accounts, or royalties, or advertising expenses, or maintenance and repairs, etc. Addition of each requirement seems to place only a small burden on corporations and may yield some benefits. But, even after it is clear that the amount of the benefit is non-existent or very small, the requirement for disclosure remains and is imposed on all registrants. Aside from the natural aversion of public regulatory agencies towards contracting their activities, the SEC must be on the alert in case it drops a reporting requirement that someone later claims would have been useful in a specific case.

The SEC's most recent expansion is required reporting to shareholders. Amendments to the proxy rules have been adopted that require annual reports to shareholders to include a five-year summary of earnings, information about the nature and scope of the company's business (including data by line of business and classes of products and services), disclosure of the principal occupation and employer of each director and executive officer, and information about the trading market and price of the company's shares and the dividends paid and the company's dividend policy. In addition, the complete 10-K report must be provided to shareholders free of charge upon request.[7] It would seem that this latter requirement is imposed because the SEC does not believe that shareholders have cared enough about receiving the information reported in the 10-Ks to have reviewed them in the SEC's offices, requested copies (and paid a cost per page charge) from the service which supplies them, or received summaries prepared by security analysts who review the filings. Nor does the SEC seem to believe that the information contained in the 10-Ks would get to the market were the reports not sent to shareholders. Although the cost of printing and mailing the 10-K report may seem relatively trivial, there is little reason to believe that the benefits exceed the costs to shareholders. And while large, consumer oriented, public relations conscious companies might not find these additional requirements onerous, the costs are not trivial for smaller companies compared to their net profits.

The net result of this expansion of requirements may be seen in chapter 3. The reader might review the specific reporting requirements outlined there and ask how specific required items might be used and, if an item appear to have some value, if it is likely to have been worth the cost of producing and reproducing? It seems as if the SEC chooses not to ask such questions and subject the answers to some type of validity test, statistical or otherwise. Rather it expands and rarely, if ever, reduces its list of requirements.

As the discussion in section 5.2 indicates, the tendency of the SEC to serve enduring, established groups, to expand its activities and budget, and to avoid risks is neither peculiar to it nor particularly malevolent.

Most, if not all, public regulatory agencies act similarly. The Interstate Commerce Commission tends to serve shippers more than consumers, the Civilian Aeronautical Board tends to be concerned more with airlines than with travellers, etc. While even a superficial analysis that supports this observation is considerably beyond the scope of this study, it is useful to note that the SEC's budget has grown at much the same rate as have the budgets of other US regulatory agencies.[8]

5.4 Administration of the Companies Acts by The (London) Stock Exchange and issuing houses

The Quotations Department of The Stock Exchange serves as a private regulatory agency with respect to prospectuses. Since almost all publicly traded securities must be listed on the Exchange, the Quotations Department's authority is virtually absolute. Because the UK stock market is smaller than that of the US, and because in the UK security issues that are the same as issues already listed need not be floated with a prospectus, the volume of registrations handled by the Quotations Department is much smaller than the volume handled by the SEC. Nevertheless, some useful comparisons can be made.

First, essential differences between a private and public regulatory agency should be considered. As was discussed above (section 5.2), both types of regulatory agencies are run by human beings who are similarly motivated. The private regulatory agency, however, receives its support from private individuals and persons who benefit from its services. These private groups include broker members of the Exchange, issuing houses, accountants and the companies whose shares are listed. Several consequences, positive and negative, result from the Exchange's having to serve this constituency compared to a constituency served by a public agency, such as the SEC.

On the positive side, The Stock Exchange's Quotations Department is encouraged to be efficient and cost-conscious. The expenses of the Department are paid by the Exchange and, consequently, by persons who use its services rather than by taxpayers in general. As a consequence, there is a closer link between the resources received by the private regulator and the benefits derived by its constituents from this level of resources. The Department operates with 40 principal people, including 15 professionals. Although the SEC admittedly processes more prospectuses than does the Quotations Departments, the SEC's hundreds of employees appear greater in proportion to its activities than those employed by The Stock

Exchange.[9] Of even greater importance with respect to costs, the Department expedites filings, answers questions and resolves disputes more quickly than does the SEC. A week to ten days is generally required for a draft prospectus to be accepted by the Exchange prior to final printing. If necessary, this can be speeded up. In contrast, Alan B. Levenson, Director of the Division of Corporation Finance of the SEC, said in August 1972: 'At present, the average time between the receipt of repeat filings and issuance of initial staff comments is 14 days. The average time between receipt of a first time filing and issuance of initial staff comments is 45 days.' (Annual Report, 1973, p. 533.)

Another positive aspect of the private UK system is that The Stock Exchange must balance the desire of brokers and analysts for more information (for which they do not pay) against the resistance of companies and issuing houses to greater disclosure. The net result of this 'push and pull' is a prospectus that can be printed on two or fewer pages of a national newspaper but is supported by a detailed accounting report filed by a prestigious firm of (reporting) chartered accountants. The prospectus contains, at the minimum, the items required by The Stock Exchange (see section 3.7) plus additional disclosures of items particular to the specific company, including sales (turnover) and earnings forecasts when these are deemed useful. Additional materials are filed with the Exchange and are available to the public.

The issuing houses also serve as private regulatory agencies. In an important sense, so do the reporting accountants. In conjunction with The Stock Exchange's Quotations Department, they determine the content of prospectuses and the investigations of company data that underlie them. The issuing houses and reporting accountants have a very great incentive for ascertaining that the prospectuses they issue and sign are not fraudulent or misleading – protection of their reputations. The issuing house's reputation is a direct function of the post-issue performance of the companies it sponsors. Should subsequent events show that the prospectuses issued misstated the companies' economic position and prospects, then the issuing house will 'pay' by losing public confidence. Similarly, the signatures of reporting accountants are valued in prospectuses because they are known to be independent, careful auditors. Should the public's faith turn out to have been misplaced, the auditors' perhaps most valuable asset, their reputation, may be lost or seriously damaged.

The nature of the constituency served by a private regulator such as The Stock Exchange gives rise to charges of negative behaviour. Some critics (most notably Edward Stamp, 1970) allege that an 'old boy network' develops in which insiders may get information that the ordinary investor does not receive and poor performance and other embarrassments are not revealed. While few (if any) such instances are actually cited by the critics, they claim that the limited disclosure required by The Exchange does not allow revelations that would otherwise occur. An additional related charge is that the informal system, wherein the Quotations Bureau answers accountants' questions and determines what information need and need not be given, benefits established accountants and issuing houses over their smaller competitors.

Private regulators tend to act analogously to public regulators with respect to reduction of risk and costs to themselves and their constituency. As is the situation in the US, The Stock Exchange and established firms and professionals are damaged if the public loses investments in ventures that, in retrospect, appear to be fraudulent or to have been more risky than was realised. While the public and the economy might benefit from investments in risky enterprises, established firms generally only lose. If the new ventures are successful, the newcomers provide unwanted competition to established firms and few gains to The Stock Exchange. If they are unsuccessful, investors may blame their losses on poor administration by Exchange officials. Perhaps as a result of these considerations, The Stock Exchange rarely permits a company to have its shares listed until it can demonstrate five years or more of successful operations. The Stock Exchange is also now the only market on which shares can be publicly traded. In contrast, a new company in the US is not restricted by the SEC from offering its shares to the public, regardless of its 'track record'. Indeed, the shorter its financial history, the less onerous are the SEC's prospectus requirements. This difference between the US and the UK may be a consequence of the fact that the SEC's constituency is more diverse than is The Stock Exchange's, since several stock exchanges and over the counter stock brokers and dealers vie for the public's business in the US compared to the monopoly situation obtaining in the UK.

To summarise, the UK system of private regulatory agencies is characterised by considerable incentives against misleading reporting of the financial positions and prospects of companies. Issuing houses, reporting accountants and Stock Exchange members bear the cost should the public lose confidence in the fairness of financial reports. However, the system also produces entry barriers, thus restricting competition. The Stock Exchange rarely accepts a new listing for a company with an operating record of less than five years. Issuing houses generally do not accept financial reports signed by smaller, relatively unknown, chartered accountants without a confirming report by a well-known firm. These practices reduce competition by newcomers.

5.5 Evaluation of the presumed benefits of administration by an active public regulatory agency

Several benefits may be achieved by having an administrative agency, such as the SEC, actively regulate financial disclosure. The six benefits outlined are not mutually exclusive nor are they exhaustive. They do, however, give something of the 'flavour' of the arguments for an agency such as the SEC. While they are not authoritative, I believe they are more complete than is the rationale generally found in the SEC's publications and in most textbooks and articles.

The following advantages are thought to flow from a continuing professional administrative agency such as the SEC: (a) adaptability; (b) professional implementation of the securities statutes and regulations; (c) an expert and public interest source of information for legislative changes; (d) uniformity with respect to the type and format of data disclosed; (e) improvement of the quality of information disclosed; and (f) protection of the small investor and prevention of fraud. Each 'benefit' is described and analysed in turn. In the analysis that follows, all of the evidence that I am aware of is applied to the evaluation of the SEC's administration of the Securities Acts.[10] Unfortunately, few 'hard' empirical studies have been published. Consequently, I have had to rely more on reasoning and hearsay evidence than I would have wished. Nevertheless, I believe this evidence is, in general, sufficient for most of the questions considered.

First, an agency like the SEC can be *adaptive* in determining the specific disclosure presumably needed to meet the public's 'legitimate' demand for information. The agency can propose new rules, receive the opinions of interested parties, interpret these opinions in the light of its experience, and draft new disclosure rules and revise old rules to meet the present needs of investors. In contrast, disclosure required of UK companies is specified by Parliament by means of the Companies Act. If a given requirement appears unneeded, ineffective, or inadequate, it is generally not changed except by the passage of a new or amended act.[11] Since passage of new legislation rarely occurs more often than once in each decade (in the past in the UK at about twenty-year intervals), it appears that the Companies Acts lack the currency that can be achieved by the SEC.

However, the SEC's power to promulgate disclosure requirements also serves to reduce the adaptability of the Securities Acts. Because the SEC is given broad power to implement the disclosure provisions of the Securities Acts, they have been forced to specify detailed rules and regulations that necessarily apply to a wide variety of circumstances. At first, the addition of a rule or regulation or publication of an opinion may serve to adapt the law to specific circumstances. But later, circumstances change and the regulations remain. Even though the regulations may no longer be meaningful to a changed environment or to the circumstances of specific corporations, the Commission appears reluctant to eliminate or even to change them: at least, that is an inference that can be drawn from the fact that the SEC's regulations are almost never withdrawn or even changed except to increase their specificity or coverage. Once a regulation is adopted or a rule formally interpreted, the Commission's staff are understandably reluctant to waive a requirement to meet particular circumstances. If they do, they risk being accused later of favouritism or even bribery, should it transpire that the petitioner misled them or proved (or appeared) guilty of fraudulent acts. Thus as time passes, the SEC's administration of the Securities Acts' disclosure requirements tends to become less adaptive to changed environments and individual situations.

A private regulatory agency such as The (London) Stock Exchange can, in practice, be more adaptive than the SEC, since it need not, and in general does not, promulgate a detailed set of rules and regulations. It has the power to adapt reporting standards to the circumstances of individual corporations, since it is not greatly prevented by law or established precedent from waiving or adding requirements. The Quotations Department can also answer questions and resolve problems more quickly than can the SEC's staff because it need not be as concerned with uninformed *ex-post facto* criticism.

It should be noted, though, that the considerably greater number of prospectuses processed by the SEC compared to the Quotations Department necessitates more formal, and hence less flexible, procedures. It may be that were the UK financial market as great as that of the US, then the UK would tend to adopt similar formal written rules and regulations.

Second, an active administrative agency can provide *professional implementation of the securities statutes and regulations.* The SEC is staffed by accountants, lawyers and financial experts who specialise in administering the Securities Acts. Consequently, they are presumed to be much more competent to determine investors' needs and the costs of compliance by companies than are legislators. Few legislators are expert or even very knowledgeable about the securities markets, accounting

179

principles and procedures, financial institutions and the like. Nor do they come into regular contact with market participants and the day to day problems of investors, brokers, accountants, comptrollers, and others who are concerned with financial statements. In contrast, the staff and administrators of an agency such as the SEC are in daily contact with the parties who are affected by the securities legislation. Further, since the agency is charged with enforcing the law, they are assumed to be the best judges of how the regulations should most effectively be written. In particular, an SEC type of agency can plug a loophole in the regulations which allows an unscrupulous issuer of financial statements to mislead the public.

It seems correct to conclude that the SEC provides professional implementation of the law. The agency is well-staffed with lawyers and accountants. However, while many (if not most) of these professionals administer the law they also serve an apprenticeship for private practice in which they will earn fees from clients for steering them through and around the law. For lawyers in particular, a profession that deals entirely with the regulation of the securities industry has developed in the US. The securities bar, as it is called, is perhaps unaware of the inherent self-interest of its position as drafters, interpreters, and defenders of those who try to deal with the securities laws. This conflict and confusion of interest is intensified by the apprenticeship served in and constant dealings with a regulatory agency. As Henry G. Manne describes it:

> To be a leader of the securities bar, one must be on extremely friendly terms with important SEC staff members and even commissioners. Such a 'social' position is not reached automatically by studying lawbooks. Rather, typically, it requires an apprenticeship at the Commission and then practice in one of the important corporate law firms. Then begins the gradual ascendancy through the committee structure of the American Bar Association or related organizations to the exalted position of 'leading securities lawyer'.

> If at any point along the way an individual begins to wonder out loud whether the whole system of regulation is actually in the public's interest, he will not appear to other leaders to have the stuff from which leadership is made. He may also find that he is less able to serve his clients well, since a continuing friendly relationship with the SEC staff is essential to that function. The circle will then be complete, for certainly one cannot be a leading securities lawyer without numerous or important clients. (1974, pp. 94–5.)

The evidence reviewed in chapter 4 indicates that the multitude of rules

180

and regulations, court cases, releases, journal articles and conferences generated by the SEC and the securities bar has benefited investors only slightly, if at all. The bar, though, appears to have benefited itself.

Third, the *expertise and public interest orientation of an SEC can be an invaluable source of information to legislators* in evaluating proposals to change the law. The agency can carry out studies requested by the legislature. Examples in the US are the 1963 Special Study of the Securities Market and the 1972 Study of Institutional Investors requested by Congress, and the 1969 SEC-initiated study of Disclosure to Stockholders (Wheat Report) prepared by the Commission. Since the agency is not directly supported by accountants (as are the AICPA and the ICAEW), lawyers (as are the bar associations), brokers (as are the stock exchanges), or others, it presumably acts in the public interest. In effect, the agency may be thought of as a continuous Royal Commission.

This benefit, though, is of limited value because of the inherent self-interest of the securities bar and of the SEC as a regulatory agency. The more complex a law, the more work for lawyers and regulators. Although simplification and/or elimination of many disclosure requirements may result in a net benefit to investors, the SEC rarely conducts rigorous cost-benefit analyses. The Commission employs few professional economists and sponsors almost no economic research despite the fact that the Securities Acts are based on presumed economic problems. Consequently, the economic effect of its regulations are rarely measured and economic analyses are not undertaken to determine whether the present .regulations are beneficial in any sense, or even effective.

Nor is the SEC necessarily concerned with the interests of the general public when the interests of the latter conflict with those of the analysts, public accountants, investment bankers, brokers, stock exchange officials and others who constitute perhaps the most influential constituency of the former. The general public might not want (in the sense of being willing to pay for) additional detailed disclosure (as evidenced by the relatively few requests by shareholders of 10-K reports)[12] but this silent lack of demand is difficult to balance against the vocal demand by security analysts for 'more'. As a consequence, perhaps, the Commission tends to add disclosure requirements and rarely to remove them, although it has this power.

In addition, the Commission tends to suggest legislative changes that only increase regulation, on the assumption that additional regulation is almost always in the public interest. Thus, despite good intentions, the SEC cannot serve the legislature as an unbiased expert source of information as to what changes in the Securities Acts will best serve the public interest.

Fourth, the SEC can impose a *uniformity with respect to the type and format of data disclosed* by companies. Ambiguities in the interpretation of law and regulations can be reduced by means of published decisions and opinions on accounting practices. This uniformity may reduce the cost of gathering and analysing financial data.

It is questionable, though, that the benefits from detailed regulations exceed the costs thereof (see chapter 4). Non-administered legislation, such as the Companies Acts, can provide analysts and other company data users with specified data which can be processed just as readily by a non-regulatory agency, such as the DT, as by an SEC.

Fifth, proponents of the US system (such as Homer Kripke, 1970) believe that the SEC can also *improve the quality of the financial data available to investors* by enforcing the maintenance of minimum standards with the threat of sanctions should the data be misleading. In addition to the extreme threat of criminal charges, these sanctions include court orders stopping the sale or trading of a security, injunctions against corporate officers and directors, and temporary suspension or barring from practice of public accountants who prepare misleading statements, are not independent, or conduct grossly inadequate audits.

Assuming that the 'quality of information' is an operationally meaningful term, there is little evidence to support the belief that the SEC has improved the quality of information disclosed. As was discussed in section 4.3.2, regulatory agencies tend to avoid ambiguity and judgement to reduce their risk. As a consequence, the data reported are of necessity less useful to investors. As one SEC official, later to become a Commissioner, put it after citing specific examples: 'You could often predict with precision what a prospectus would say about various problems. There was always a consensus that conservatism was the safest course.' (Sommer, 1973, p. 505.) Carl Schneider agreed, saying, 'Historically, certain types of highly relevant information – which I will call "soft" information – have been largely excluded from filings by the SEC.' (Schneider, 1973, p. 506.) He went on to add: 'Generally, filings are treated as insurance policies against liability, and all of the juicy soft information is disseminated through oral selling'. (p. 507.) As Schneider says, the potential legal liability of accountants and others results in rigid conservatism and following the letter (though not the spirit) of the regulations and law. Accountants and managers appear to be concerned primarily with following the rules and regulations in a manner that will avoid lawsuits and problems with the SEC. Unfortunately, this approach also limits presentation of judgements that could be valuable to investors.

Lastly, because a public regulatory agency receives its support primarily from the government, many believe it will be particularly concerned with *protecting the small investor and preventing fraud.* In addition, an agency that specialises in securities laws, such as the SEC, should be able to prosecute criminals and other wrongdoers more efficiently than ordinary police and legal officers. Security law specialists should also be better equipped to promulgate and enforce regulations and propose disclosure and other laws to counter new methods devised by swindlers to cheat the public.

This 'service' offered by the SEC is considered by many to be the most important benefit derived from a public regulatory agency. Many, if not most, small investors see the SEC as their 'ombudsman'. Should they have a dispute with their brokers, not be able to get information from a company, think they were misinformed by a security salesman, etc., then the SEC is there to help. The SEC should assure them that their brokers are executing their order at the best price, that insiders do not profit at their expense, etc., but while many of these expectations are no doubt met, recent and past history indicates a considerable failure by the SEC to meet this obligation to the public.[13] However, these considerations are beyond the scope of this study, since it is limited to financial disclosure of corporations.

Considering fraud related to financial statements, it is difficult to determine whether the SEC has been a more effective 'policeman' than a police fraud squad would have been. It is not useful to compare the record of the US Justice Department (which works with the SEC, since the SEC can only recommend criminal prosecution) with that of the UK police fraud squad, since only arrests for and not commission of frauds is known. Nor can one even know the extent to which fraud was prevented because wrongdoers fear the SEC or the fraud squad.

Nevertheless, it is clear that securities fraud is still a problem in the US and does not appear to be nearly as big a problem in the UK. (The reader is referred to former SEC chairman Garrett's statement cited in section 4.2.2.) The SEC's Annual Report gives a very brief summary of actions taken. Each year, several hundred companies and persons are investigated, stop orders are issued preventing securities from being sold or traded when the financial statements of the companies involved appear materially misleading, and some thirty to fifty cases are referred to the Justice Department for criminal prosecution. While very few of these cases involve certified public accountants and financial statements, the impact of an SEC action of any kind upon an accountant, even a temporary suspension from practice, is great. Even the threat of such an action is powerful. Therefore one cannot measure the SEC's effectiveness in preventing fraudulently prepared financial statements simply by counting the number of cases filed.

However, as was discussed in section 4.2.2, there were very few cases of fraudulently prepared financial statements before the Securities Acts were enacted, and most security specialists believe that SEC prosecution has little effect on anyone who is basically dishonest. In particular, one lawyer who worked for the SEC and the Justice Department said (in personal conversation, after recounting the cases he had worked on and the need for an agency like the SEC): 'I must admit, the principal difference between now and the 1920's is that you need the help of a lawyer to commit a successful fraud. But it's still a good business. These people are almost never caught. If caught, they're almost never indicted. If indicted, they rarely are found guilty. If found guilty, they almost never are fined much or sent to jail. If sent to jail, they get out on parole in a few months or years at most and then are welcomed back to their country club in Westchester.'

While the SEC may reduce the amount of fraud, it may be that an individual investor's best defence is still *caveat emptor*. It is possible that the SEC has made the small investor too complacent about purchasing securities by giving him the impression that the 'bad old days' are no longer with us.[14]

One other dysfunctional aspect of the SEC's role in preventing fraud should be mentioned. Law enforcement officers, in general, often tend to see prevention of crime and punishment of wrongdoers as more important than the presumption of innocence and protection of civil liberties. The courts and even the prosecuting attorneys act as a balance against the understandable bias of the police who, coming into direct contact with the consequences of crime, may become over-zealous concerning the need to punish criminals. Unfortunately, a public regulatory agency such as the SEC has the power of. policeman, prosecutor and judge over an accountant, lawyer or other professional who represents clients before it. When the client (company) wishes to offer a security to the public, the SEC also has almost total power over it by delaying registration.

One prominant accountant, Harvey Kapnick, Chairman and Chief Executive of Arthur Andersen and Co., commented after members of his firm were found innocent of criminal fraud charges brought by the SEC:

Too often today, it appears that the SEC staff is wielding power to attempt to discipline and control accountants with utter disregard for the effect on the public interest at large. The SEC, more so perhaps than other government agencies, should understand that allegations made by it, even though unsubstantiated, are accepted as fact by a large portion of the public. The mere allegation carries more impact than the ultimate resolution of the allegation. In fact, even though certain accountants recently were found innocent of charges alleged by the SEC [Four Seasons Trial], a senior officer of the SEC recently stated publicly that such accountants were not vindicated by the jury but that the jury found that there was reasonable doubt as to their 'criminal conduct.' If this attitude is right, how does a professional ever eliminate the unproven charges? No longer, it seems, is one deemed innocent until proven guilty! (Kapnik, 1974.)

Lawyers have apparently been even more subject to possible abuses of power by the SEC. In a well-documented paper, Monroe H. Freedman (Dean of Hofstra University Law School) concludes: 'In sum . . . securities regulation is characterized by denial of the right to counsel, corruption of the independence of the Bar and of the traditional professional standards of lawyers' obligations to their clients, a police state system of investigations, and denial of a variety of other basic due process rights.' (Freedman, 1974, p. 288.)[15]

5.6 The effect of public and private regulatory agencies on the practice and profession of accountancy

A comprehensive comparative analysis of the effect on the practice and profession of accountancy of public versus private agencies regulating the securities statutes is beyond the scope of this study. Nevertheless, some consequences should at least be mentioned. In particular, auditing and reporting practices and standards and professional prestige will be discussed.[16]

In general, auditing practices are similar in the US and the UK. However, procedures in the US are codified in 'Statements on Auditing Standards', while auditors in the UK rely primarily on the Companies Acts' requirements and on an unwritten understanding of expected professional expertise. For example, a US auditor must observe physical stocktaking and confirm receivables while a UK auditor is expected to follow these practices only to the extent that he deems it necessary to obtain sufficient evidence to support his opinion.[17]

185

The auditor's independence is similarly defined differently in the two countries. In the US, 'independence' is rigidly defined with respect to form as well as substance (i.e., an auditor may have *no* financial interest in a company). The Companies Act 1948 prohibits some relationships (i.e., an auditor cannot be an officer or employee of the company), but independence is more a matter of professional integrity than adherence to a set of rules. (An auditor is not prohibited from having a financial interest in his client.) The auditor is protected from a malevolent management by provisions of the Companies Act 1948 and rules of professional ethics. The Act provides that an auditor will normally be reappointed, requires that special notice must be given of his dismissal before a general meeting, gives the auditor the right to put his case to the stockholders, and allocates responsibility for the auditor's remuneration to the shareholders. In the US, the SEC has recently moved to strengthen the position of auditors by requiring a change of auditors to be reported in the monthly 8-K report, together with a statement of any disputes over material accounting or auditing principles or practices during the two previous annual audits and a letter from the CPAs confirming their clients' statement. (It should be noted, though, that while these practices support the independence of auditors, they also support the position of established accountants with respect to potential competitors.)

Specific reporting practices in the US and UK were outlined in chapter 3. In general, practice in the US is much more codified than it is in the UK. Aside from the Companies Act, Stock Exchange requirements and the few ICAEW pronouncements, the general UK rule is that financial statements must present a 'true and fair' view. Generally accepted accounting conventions and the accountant's professional judgement determine what is 'true and fair' for a specific circumstance and company. In the US, the specific practice that must be followed is 'spelled out' for a large number of circumstances.[18]

In large measure, the existence of the SEC is responsible for these differences.[19] While the SEC has not used its power directly to enforce specific auditing procedures, it has nevertheless been a powerful force.[20] Its investigation of the McKesson–Robbins fraud in the late 1930s was an important determinant of the requirement that inventory counts be observed and accounts receivable be confirmed. The agency was also instrumental in making reviews of the client's internal controls a routine auditing practice. Most important, the SEC's review of financial statements and prospectuses filed with it and occasional public criticism of auditing practices followed in specific instances, makes its opinions and standards of more than passing interest to auditors.

186

One area in which the SEC has been particularly influential is the definition of the auditor's independence. The SEC promulgated the rule that an auditor cannot have any financial interest in his client, no matter how insignificant, in part because this rule is relatively easy to administer. A few years ago, the AICPA adopted the definition as part of its canon of ethics. The SEC also forbids an auditor to maintain the books and records of a client, although it does permit a CPA firm to provide management services.

The SEC has also affected the internal day to day practices of auditors with several important opinions. The *Interstate Hosiery Mills Inc.* case [1939] laid down the requirement that subordinates' working papers be reviewed as follows: 'If not a partner of the firm, such review should, in our opinion, be made by persons who are independent of those actually performing or supervising the audit work as well as those who prepared the draft of the financial statements.' More recently, the SEC has required several large CPA firms to submit their procedures, working papers, quality control, etc., to a review by peer accountants selected by the SEC.

The SEC has also influenced reporting practices and principles, although it has not used its power under Section 19(a) of the Securities Act 1933 and Section 13(b) of the Securities Exchange Act of 1934 to determine

> . . . the items or details to be shown in the balance sheet and the earning statement, and the methods to be followed in the preparation of reports, in the appraisal or valuation of assets and liabilities, in the determination of depreciation and depletion, in the differentiation of recurring and non-recurring income, in the differentiation of investment and operating income, and in the preparation, where the Commission deems it necessary or desirable, of separate and/or consolidated balance sheets or income accounts . . .

Although it has deferred the prescription of accounting principles to the AICPA and its committees or associated groups (the most recent being the Financial Accounting Standards Board), the SEC has been a powerful force in the adoption of specific rules. In particular, it has been influential in having the accounting profession adopt rules related to consolidated statements, mergers and acquisitions, real estate transactions (particularly sales and lease-backs), valuations of securities, contingent liabilities, write-off of intangibles, etc.[21] The SEC has also been effective in preventing revaluations of assets and price level adjusted statements.

In contrast, the ICAEW and its sister organisations have been reluctant, until recently, to dictate auditing and reporting practices to their members. As Bruce G. Picking observed, 'While the Companies Acts lay down requirements with which the auditor must comply, the English Institute has preferred to rely on persuasion rather than compulsion in most instances.' (Picking, 1973, p. 66.) The same attitude governed with respect to reporting practices until formation of the Accounting Standards Steering Committee in 1970. Since then, the relatively few statements issued require conformity on the part of members.

A further important, though indirect, influence on auditing practices by the Companies Acts should be mentioned. Because the Acts apply to all companies, whether their stock is publicly traded or not, minimum acceptable auditing standards tend to be those applicable to the smallest, essentially private, companies. It would seem preferable to distinguish between owner-managed, proprietorship companies and publicly traded stewardship companies managed by non-owners. The auditing procedures applicable to the latter companies might emphasise disclosure of self-dealing, conflicts of interest, etc. However, these procedures are not nearly as important where the owners manage the enterprise or are in direct contact with the managers.

Several related effects of this difference in administration of the securities laws can be delineated. First, US accountants are subject to much greater restrictions than are their UK counterparts. US accountants are penalised for not following the letter of the law and regulations which are presumed to protect the public. In the UK, much more reliance is placed on accountants' professional judgement and integrity and their desire to protect their reputations. Perhaps for this reason, UK accountants appear to enjoy more prestige than do their US counter-parts.[22] Secondly, financial statements tend to be more reflective of the specific circumstances of individual companies in the UK than in the US. Unfortunately, no studies are available concerning this issue. Nor are there any studies that test directly whether the greater control over auditing and reporting exercised by the SEC results in publication of less misleading or fewer fraudulent financial statements. However, casual observation and the evidence reported in section 4.2 does not support the hypothesis that auditing and accounting practices are better in the US than in the UK.

5.7 Conclusions and recommendations

The analysis presented in section 4.2 leads to the conclusion that few discernible benefits result from government required disclosure. To summarise, reasoning and evidence generally do *not* support the presumptions that required disclosure visibly prevents or reduces misrepresentation in financial statements or security price manipulation, ensures fairness to non-insiders, improves efficiency in the allocation of resources, enhances public confidence in securities markets, or improves government administration and fulfilment of the public's and employees' 'right to know'. However, reasoning does support, partially, the belief that positive externalities, such as benefits from improved efficiency, in the production and distribution of financial information may result from required disclosure. Benefits may also be obtained from reduced fraud as a consequence of required auditing of companies, particularly if the auditing is directed towards uncovering and reporting self-dealing, conflicts of interest and the like by officers, directors and promoters. In addition, disclosure designed to prevent frauds which result in scandal may dampen the government's propensity to take action when such scandals erupt. The passage of ill-conceived and special interest laws may thus be avoided. Hence, the primary benefits derived from required disclosure are related to auditing which uncovers or prevents misuse of shareholders' resources by those who owe them a steward's responsibility.

One fact should be mentioned before discussing conclusions with respect to costs. Companies voluntarily disclosed financial data before government requirements were imposed. Financial statements were and are published because shareholders, present and potential, demand them. Furthermore, there is very little evidence that voluntarily published financial statements contained fraudulent or misleading data.

The costs of government required disclosure are incurred primarily by companies and partially by taxpayers in general. Although direct measurements could not be made, the costs imposed on companies seem considerable, particularly for smaller enterprises and particularly for US compared with UK companies. Large companies may not find the periodic reporting requirements (even in the US) very onerous. However, the cost may be considerable for small companies. The greatest burden of required disclosure is on US companies who wish to raise funds from the public, since the SEC's prospectus requirements (including the cost of delay) are quite burdensome.

On the whole, the costs of government required disclosure seem to outweigh the benefits. Aside from required auditing of stewardship companies (whose shares are publicly traded) and perhaps a general requirement that some form of balance sheet, income statement and funds statement signed by a certified or chartered accountant should be published, the case for government required financial reporting is very weak. In particular, little evidence or reasoning supports the belief that required reporting of detailed financial statements generates benefits that outweigh costs.

Nevertheless, it seems very doubtful that the securities statutes which require financial disclosure will be repealed. Consequently, the advantages and disadvantages of the US system of an active public regulatory agency (the SEC) were compared to those of the UK system of an inactive public agency (the DT) and active private agencies (The Stock Exchange and issuing houses). The expected behaviour of a public regulatory agency was outlined first in order to provide some insight into the behaviour of the SEC. Such an agency tends to serve organised and relatively enduring groups, acts to expand and rarely contracts its operations, and seeks to avoid scandals and similar situations that may bring it into public disfavour. In general, the SEC's behaviour fits this description. It tends to require disclosure that benefits larger firms, security analysts and established investment houses more than smaller companies and newcomers. It adds disclosure requirements and rarely, if ever, removes any which might be unnecessary or of insufficient value relative to their cost. It avoids potentially risky situations by promulgating explicit rules and enforcing regulations on all corporations even when they would appear to be applicable to a few potential miscreants, at most.

The private regulatory system of the UK also has some dysfunctional aspects. The Stock Exchange tends to serve its constituents who, perhaps even more than is the case with the SEC, tend to be the established firms rather than newcomers. While The Exchange does not impose as extensive or expensive reporting requirements for prospectuses as does the SEC and has few additional periodic reporting requirements above and beyond those required by the Companies Acts, it does tend to reduce the risk to established firms and to itself by requiring that newly listed companies have at least five years of successful operations behind them before their securities can be listed. Consequently, the risk to investors in purchasing the securities of a new firm is reduced. But then the possible benefits to investors and to the general public from funding new ventures are also thereby reduced.

The less formal procedures of The Stock Exchange's Quotations Department also tend to favour established issuing houses and public accountants. But the procedures also allow for considerable flexibility in applying the general requirement that financial statements present 'a true and fair view' of the company's affairs, and thus tend to reduce the costs to companies of preparing prospectuses and possibly increase the usefulness of data presented to investors.

The UK system relies primarily on accountants' and issuing houses' judgement and integrity and their need to protect their reputations. The US system relies more on specific rules and regulations and on law suits and sanctions imposed by the SEC. Perhaps as a consequence of this, public accountants appear to be held in higher esteem in the UK than in the US. Certainly, UK accountants are permitted to use their professional judgement to a greater extent than are their US counterparts.

Six benefits that may affect the higher costs imposed by an active public regulatory agency such as the SEC were delineated and examined. The first was the ability of such an agency to adapt the securities laws to changing environments and individual circumstances. However, once a rule-making agency such as the SEC promulgates its regulations and publishes its opinions, these tend to become as fixed as are the lists of items which must be disclosed that are given in the Companies Acts. Furthermore, although the SEC is empowered to remove regulations, it rarely, if ever, does so. The second and third possible benefits considered were professional implementation of and a resource for changes in the securities statutes. Some benefits do appear to follow from the establishment of a relatively permanent staff of accountants, lawyers and financial specialists who are knowledgeable of the securities laws, institutions and behaviour of market participants. But the factors that motivate public regulatory agencies in general also act to limit the benefits derived from the SEC. Although the public might benefit from less regulation, it is very difficult, if not impossible, for a regulatory agency to comprehend this. Rather it tends to support extensions in the scope of regulation and resist undertaking or encouraging research that might disprove the value of regulation. Hence its concept of 'the public interest' tends to be as one-sided (though to some, not as obvious) as is the concept of special interest groups such as brokers, corporate executives, stock exchange officials, etc. The fourth and fifth possible benefits considered were the greater uniformity and quality of the information disclosed. Uniformity of reporting can probably be effected more readily by a rule-making agency than by statute (although a private rule-making agency such as The Stock Exchange could also require uniform reporting). Improved quality of the data reported, however, is more difficult to achieve. First, one has to define 'quality' operationally, a task not yet achieved, at least to my knowledge. Nevertheless, there is considerable doubt that the SEC has indeed improved the quality of reported financial data. For one thing, there is little evidence that these data were misleading before the SEC was established. For another, the SEC's adherence to historical accounting rules cannot be said to have improved the 'quality' of the data reported. Nor does there appear to be any reason to believe that the data reported by UK companies is of worse quality than the data reported by US companies (although its quantity is smaller). The final possible benefit considered was greater protection of the small investor and prevention of fraud. The evidence does not, however, support this hope. Although the SEC may be effective in protecting the small investor from some types of frauds, there is little evidence that fraudulent financial statements were either a significant problem before the creation of the SEC or that their incidence has been significantly reduced. To the contrary, there is reason to believe that the existence of the SEC may have cause some investors to forget that *caveat emptor* may still be their best defence.

In conclusion, the evidence reviewed provides little reason to believe that the US system affords the public greater benefits, on the whole, than does the UK system. The cost of the US system, though, appears considerably greater. On balance, then, there is little (if any) evidence that the disclosure regulations promulgated by the SEC provide a benefit, net of costs, to the public. Perhaps, though, the more formal, more explicitly codified, more regulated US system is politically necessary for a large diverse country where there are relatively few restrictions (though considerable costs) on a company that wishes to sell its shares to the public. Such does not appear to be the case in the UK. There is little evidence (hard or casual) to believe that an active regulatory agency such as the SEC is needed there or would be anything other than dysfunctional. Consequently, I believe the British would be ill-advised to establish an SEC-type agency by giving the DTI regulatory powers. The US experience shows that once these powers are granted, they almost never contract and almost always expand, regardless of their demonstrated lack of efficacy for solving problems or propensity to create new problems. Finally, for the US, I would recommend a move towards the UK system by reducing the authority and power of the SEC. The concept of 'disclosure' should be restated to make it clear that the SEC is primarily an agency to which corporations report what they have disclosed to shareholders and how they determine the numbers rather than an agency that determines what and how corporations must report to the public.

Notes

[1]   See section 2.2.2 for a more detailed description.

[2]   An exception is the temporary ability of teachers to impose their views on students. The students, though, soon pass out of the school. The regulated must leave the industry to achieve a similar freedom.

[3]   As was discussed in section 4.2.6, most of the available evidence does not support the belief that corporate financial statements provide 'information' when published in the sense that their publication affects share prices.

[4]   See James S. Mofsky (1973) for references and a complete discussion.

[5]   See Lloyd E. Shefsky and Edward J. Schwartz (1973) for an analysis.

[6]   Private regulatory agencies, such as The (London) Stock Exchange, may be similarly averse to risks, as is discussed below.

[7]   Securities and Exchange Commission, Release 34-11079, effective as from 20 December 1974.

[8]   Annual rates of budget growth in constant dollars over the period 1955 to 1972 are as follows for the agencies that published the data: Food and Drug Administration, 15·6 per cent; National Labor Relations Board, 8·7 per cent; Federal Trade Commission, 8·3 per cent; Securities and Exchange Commission, 7·2 per cent.

[9]   The SEC does not publish staffing or cost data broken down by its 'lines of business'. Nor are figures for The Stock Exchange's Quotations Department's expenses available.

[10] Evidence on the extent to which many of these benefits are achieved by administration of the US Securities Acts is reviewed in chapter 4. This evidence does not support the contention that the Securities Acts have significantly increased the reliability or usefulness of published financial statements. There is little evidence that financial statements published before the passage of the Acts were more fraudulent or misleading than they are today or that, as a consequence of required disclosure, they are more useful to investors. But since one can never be certain that some unmeasurable (or unmeasured) benefit does not flow from the SEC's administration of the Acts, it is necessary to analyse the arguments for an SEC-type agency.

[11] Statutory Instruments are occasionally issued by the DT which clarify or extend (to a small degree) the Companies Acts.

[12] A survey of fifty companies that included a notice in their 1973 annual reports advising shareholders that they could obtain a copy of form 10-K on request revealed the following: (a) 0·16 per cent of the

companies' total number of investors requested the material; (b) in most cases, inclusion of the notice of availability of form 10-K did not appear to have elicited favourable comment from shareholders or others; (c) there was no correlation between the percentage of shareholder requests and the size of the company or number of shareholders of a particular company. ('Shareholders exhibit lack of interest in 10-K data', 1974.)

[13] Among the important instances that could be described are the failure of the SEC to prevent brokers from mishandling transfers and from maintaining inadequate capital and the SEC's support, until recently, of the stock exchanges' minimum commission schedules.

[14] Recent (1974) reports of Ponzi-type frauds of hundreds of millions of dollars would seem to support this possibility.

[15] See also Guzzardi (1974) for additional material.

[16] See section 2.4 for some additional material.

[17] See Bruce G. Picking (1973) for a concise comparison of auditing standards in the US and the UK.

[18] See Benston (1975a) for an elaboration of the differences, causes and consequences of explicit versus implicit accounting standards in the US and the UK.

[19] The much larger size and diversity of the US and historical accident are also important factors.

[20] See Rappaport (1972, chapter 5) for a review of the most important cases.

[21] See Rappaport (1972, chapter 4) for a review of the more important SEC opinions.

[22] See Lee J. Siedler (1969), whose survey leads him to conclude that: 'Whether they deserve it or not, accountants enjoy much higher status in the eyes of the British capital market than do their counterparts in the United States.' (p. 489, italics omitted.)

Bibliography

Archibald, T. Ross, 'Stock Market Reaction to the Depreciation Switch-Back', *Accounting Review,* vol. 47 (January 1972), pp. 22–30.

Arden, Mary, 'A Legal View of Current UK Practice', *Negligence and the Public Accountant,* Accountancy Age, Haymarket Publishing (London 1972), pp. 24–7.

Ball, Ray, 'Changes in Accounting Techniques and Stock Prices', *Empirical Research in Accounting: Selected Studies, 1972,* supplement to *Journal of Accounting Research,* vol. 10 (1974), pp. 1–44.

Ball, Ray and Brown, Phillip, 'An Empirical Evaluation of Accounting Income Numbers', *Journal of Accounting Research,* vol. 6 (Autumn 1968), pp. 159–77.

Barefield, Russell M. and Comiskey, Eugene E., 'Segmental Financial Disclosure by Diversified Firms and Security Prices: A Comment', *Accounting Review,* vol. 50 (October 1975), pp. 818–21.

Beaver, William, 'The Information Content of Annual Earnings Announcements', *Empirical Research in Accounting: Selected Studies, 1968,* supplement to *Journal of Accounting Research,* vol. 6 (1968), pp. 67–92.

Beaver, William, 'The Behaviour of Security Prices and Its Implications for Accounting Research (Methods)', supplement to *Accounting Review,* vol. 47 (1972), pp. 407–36.

Beaver, William, Kettler, Paul, and Scholes, Myron, 'The Association Between Market Determined and Accounting Determined Risk Measures', *Accounting Review,* vol. 45 (October 1970), pp. 654–62.

Beaver, William and Dukes, Roland, 'Interperiod Tax Allocation, Earnings Expectations, and the Behaviour of Security Prices', *Accounting Review,* vol. 47 (April 1972), pp. 320–32.

Beaver, William and Manegold, James, 'The Association Between Market Determined and Accounting Determined Measures of Systematic Risk: Some Further Evidence', *The Journal of Financial and Quantitative Analysis,* vol. 10 (June 1975), pp. 231–84.

Benston, George J., 'Published Corporate Accounting Data and Stock Prices', *Empirical Research in Accounting: Selected Studies, 1967,* supplement to *Journal of Accounting Research,* vol. 5 (1967), pp. 1–54.

Benston, George J., 'The Effectiveness and Effects of the SEC's

Accounting Disclosure Requirements', in Henry G. Manne (ed.), *Economic Policy and the Regulation of Corporate Securities,* American Enterprise Institute for Public Policy Research (Washington 1969a), pp. 23–79.

Benston, George J., 'The Value of the SEC's Accounting Disclosure Requirements', *Accounting Review,* vol. 44 (July 1969b), pp. 515–32.

Benston, George J., 'Required Disclosure and the Stock Market: An Evaluation of the Securities Exchange Act of 1934', American Economic Review, vol. 42 (March 1973a), pp. 132–55.

Benston, George J., 'Review of Unaccountable Accounting by Abraham J. Briloff', *The Wall Street Review of Books,* vol. 1 (December 1973b), pp. 465–70 (also published in the *Journal of Accounting Research,* vol. 13, (Spring 1975).

Benston, George J., 'Accounting Standards in the US and the UK: Their Nature, Causes and Consequences', *Vanderbilt Law Review,* vol. 28 (January 1975a), pp. 235–68.

Benston, George J., 'Accountants' Integrity and Financial Reporting', *The Financial Executive,* vol. 43 (August 1975b), pp. 10–14.

Boyle, A.J., 'The Derivative Action in Company Law', *The Journal of Business Law* (April 1969), pp. 120–27.

Briloff, Abraham, *Unaccountable Accounting,* Harper and Row, (New York 1972).

Brown, F.E., and Vickers, Douglas, chapter 5 in Friend, Irwin, Brown, F.E., Herman, Edward S., and Vickers, Douglas, *A Study of Mutual Funds,* prepared for the SEC by the Securities Research Unit, Wharton School of Finance and Commerce, University of Pennsylvania (US Government Printing Office 1962), pp. 289–358.

Brown, Phillip, 'The Impact of the Annual Net Profit Report on the Stock Market', *The Australian Accountant* (July 1970), pp. 277–83.

Cale, Edward G., 'A Study of Ineffective Investment Trust and Precious Metal Mining Issues', *Law and Contemporary Problems,* vol. 4 (January 1937), pp. 32–43.

Cohan, Avery D., *Yields on Corporate Debt Directly Placed,* National Bureau of Economic Research (New York 1967).

Collins, Daniel W., 'SEC Product-Line Reporting and Market Efficiency', *Journal of Financial Economics,* vol. 2 (June 1975), pp. 125–64.

Comiskey, Eugene E., 'Market Response to Changes in Depreciation Accounting', *Accounting Review,* vol. 46 (April 1971), pp. 279–85.

Cooke, A.F.B., 'New Issues', in *The Stock Exchange; Spring Lectures 1954,* The Institute of Bankers (London 1954), pp. 16–36.

Council of the Institute of Chartered Accountants in England and Wales,

'Accountants' liability to third parties – the Hedley Byrne Decision' (August 1965).

de Bedts, Ralph F., *The New Deal's SEC,* Columbia University Press (New York 1964).

Dewing, Arthur S., *The Financial Policy of Corporations,* 3rd revised edition, Ronald Press (New York 1934).

Diefenback, R.E., 'How Good is Institutional Research?', *Financial Analysts Journal,* vol. 28 (January–February 1972), pp. 54–60.

Dryden, Myles M., 'A Statistical Study of UK Share Prices', *Scottish Journal of Political Economy,* vol. 17 (November 1970), pp.369–89.

Edey, H.C., 'Company Accounting in the Nineteenth and Twentieth Centuries', *The Accountants Journal* (April–May 1956).

Edey, H.C., and Panitpakdi, Prot, 'British Company Accounting and the Law, 1844–1900', in Littleton, A.C. and Yamey, B.S. (eds), *Studies in the History of Accounting,* Sweet and Maxwell (London 1956), pp. 356–79.

Escott v. BarChris Construction Corp., 283 F. Supp. 643 S.D.N.Y. [1968].

Fama, Eugene, 'Efficient Capital Markets: A Review of Theory and Empirical Work', *The Journal of Finance,* vol. 25 (May 1970), pp. 383–417.

Foster, George, 'Accounting Earnings and Stock Prices of Insurance Companies', *Accounting Review,* vol. 50 (October 1975), pp. 686–98.

Freedman, Monroe H., 'A Civil Libertarian Looks at Securities Regulation', *Ohio State Law Journal,* vol. 35 (2 November 1974), pp. 280–89.

Friend, Irwin, and Herman, Edward S., 'The SEC Through a Glass Darkly', *The Journal of Business,* vol. 27 (October 1964), pp. 382–405.

Friend, Irwin, Blume, Marshall, and Crockett, Jean, *Mutual Funds and Other Institutional Investors,* McGraw-Hill (New York 1970).

Garrett, Ray, Jr, 'New Directions in Professional Responsibility', *The Business Lawyer,* vol. 29 (March 1974), pp. 7–13.

General Education Trust of the Institute of Chartered Accountants in England and Wales, *Guide to the Accounting Requirements of the Companies Acts 1948–1967,* Gee and Co. (London 1969).

Gonedes, Nicholas J., 'Some Evidence on Investor Actions and Accounting Messages – Part I', *Accounting Review,* vol. 46 (April 1971a), pp. 320–28.

Gonedes, Nicholas J., 'Some Evidence on Investor Actions and Accounting Messages – Part II', *Accounting Review,* vol. 46 (July 1971b), pp. 535–51.

Gonedes, Nicholas J., 'Evidence on the Information Content of

Accounting numbers: Accounting-Based and Market-Based Estimates of Systematic Risk', *Journal of Financial and Quantitative Analysis,* vol. 7 (June 1973a), pp. 407–43.

Gonedes, Nicholas J., 'Capital Market Equilibrium and Annual Accounting Numbers: Empirical Evidence', *Journal of Accounting Research,* vol. 12 (Spring 1974), pp. 26–62.

Gonedes, Nicholas J., 'A Note on Accounting-Based and Market-Based Estimates of Systematic Risk', *The Journal of Financial and Quantitative Analysis,* vol. 10 (June 1975), pp. 355–66.

Gormley, R. James, 'Accountants' Professional Liability – A Ten Year Review', *The Business Lawyer,* 20 (July 1974), pp. 1205–24.

Gourrich, Paul P., 'Investment Banking Methods Prior to and Since the Securities Act of 1933', *Law and Contemporary Problems,* vol. 4 (January 1937), pp. 44–71.

Guy, James R.F., *The International Diversification of Investment Portfolios: An Empirical Study from the British Point of View,* unpublished Ph.D. thesis, University of Pennsylvania 1974.

Guzzardi, Walter, Jr, 'Those Zealous Cops on the Securities Beat', *Fortune,* vol. 90 (December 1974), pp. 144–47, 192 *et seq.*

Hadden, Tom, 'The Control of Company Fraud', *Planning,* vol. 34 (September 1968), pp. 273–333.

Hagerman, Robert L., 'The Value of Regulation F: An Empirical test', *Journal of Bank Research,* vol. 3 (Autumn 1972), pp. 178–85.

Hagerman, Robert L., 'The Efficiency of the Market for Bank Stocks: An Empirical Appraisal', *Journal of Money, Credit and Banking,* vol. 5 (August 1973), pp. 846–55.

Hagerman, Robert L., and Richmond, Richard, 'Random Walks, Martingales, and the OTC', *Journal of Finance,* vol. 28 (September 1973), pp. 897–909.

Hammel, John, and Hodes, Daniel, 'Factors Influencing Price-Earnings Multiples', *Financial Analysts Journal,* vol. 23 (January–February 1967), pp. 90–2.

Hedley Byrne and Co. Ltd v. Heller and Partners Ltd, 2 All E.R.575 [1963].

Hill, Tom, Jr, 'The Liabilities of International Practice', in *Negligence and the Public Accountant,* Accounting Age, Haymarket Publishing (London 1972), pp. 3–10.

Hubbard, Thomas D., *Required Financial Statement Disclosure: A Quick Reference Guide,* American Institute of Certified Public Accountants, Continuing Education Division (New York 1973).

Institute of Chartered Accountants in England and Wales, *Explanatory*

Foreword, Statements of Standard Accounting Practice, revised edition, Gee and Co., (London 1975).

Interstate Hosiery Mills, Inc., 4 SEC 721 (1939).

Jaffe, Jeffrey F., 'Special Information and Insider Trading', *Journal of Business,* vol. 47 (July 1974), pp. 410–28.

Jenkins, Lord (Chairman), Report of the Company Law Committee, Board of Trade (HMSO 1962).

Jensen, Michael C., 'The Performance of Mutual Funds in the Period 1945–64', *The Journal of Finance,* vol. 23 (May 1968), pp. 389–416.

Jensen, Michael C., 'Capital Markets: Theory and Evidence', *The Bell Journal of Economics and Management Science,* vol. 3, (Autumn 1972) pp. 357–98.

Jones, C.P., and Litzenberger, R.H., 'Quarterly Earnings Reports and Intermediate Stock Price Trends', *Journal of Finance,* vol. 25 (March 1970) pp. 143–48.

Kaplan, Robert S., and Roll, Richard, 'Investor Evaluation of Accounting Information: Some Empirical Evidence', *Journal of Business,* vol. 45 (April 1972) pp. 225–57.

Kapnick, Harvey, 'Concern or Crisis? The Deteriorating Relationship Between the SEC and the Accounting Profession is Not in The Public Interest', *Executive New Briefs,* Arthur Andersen and Co., vol. 2, (April 1974).

Kellogg, Howard L., and Poloway, Morton, *Accountants' SEC Practice Manual,* Commerce Clearing House (Chicago 1971).

Kemp, Alexander G., and Reid, Gavin C., 'The Random Walk Hypothesis and the Recent Behaviour of Equity Prices in Britain', *Economica,* vol. 38 (February 1971), pp. 28–51.

Kochanek, Richard F., 'Segmental Financial Disclosure by Diversified Firms and Security Prices', *The Accounting Review,* (April 1974), pp. 245–58.

Kochanek, Richard F., 'Segmental Financial Disclosure by Diversified Firms and Security Prices: A Reply', *The Accounting Review,* (October 1975), pp. 822–5.

Krauss, Robert L., 'Securities Regulation in the United Kingdom: A Comparison with United States Practice', *Vanderbilt Journal of Transnational Law,* vol. 5 (Winter 1971), pp. 49–132.

Kripke, Homer, 'The SEC, The Accountants, Some Myths and Some Realities', *New York University Law Review,* vol. 45 (December 1970), pp. 1151–1205.

Kripke, Homer, 'The Myth of the Informed Layman', *The Business Lawyer,* vol. 28 (January 1973), pp. 631–38.

Latane, Henry, et al., 'Quarterly Data, Sort Bank Routines, and Security Evaluation', *Journal of Business,* vol. 43 (October 1970), pp. 427–38.

Latane, Henry, and Tuttle, Donald, 'An Analysis of Common Stock Price Ratios', *Southern Economic Journal,* vol. 33 (January 1967), pp. 343–7.

Levenson, Alan B., 'New Approaches to Disclosure in Registered Security Offerings: A Panel Discussion', *The Business Lawyer,* vol. 28 (January 1973), pp. 505–35.

MacMillan Committee, *Report of the Committee on Finance and Industry* (HMSO 1931).

Manne, Henry G., *Insider Trading and the Stock Market,* The Free Press (Glencoe, Illinois 1966).

Manne, Henry G., 'Insider Trading and the Law Professors', *Vanderbilt Law Review,* vol. 23 (1970), pp. 547–90.

Manne, Henry G., 'Economic Aspects of Required Disclosure Under Federal Securities Laws', in *Wall Street in Transition: The Emerging System and Its Impact on the Economy: The Charles C. Moskowitz Lectures,* New York University Press (New York 1974), pp. 21–110.

May, Robert, 'The Influence of Quarterly Earnings Announcements on Investor Decisions as Reflected in Common Stock Price Changes', *Empirical Research in Accounting, Selected Studies 1971,* supplement to *Journal of Accounting Research,* vol. 9 (1971), pp. 119–63.

McEnally, R., 'Information Effect and P/E Ratios', *Mississippi Valley Journal of Business and Economics,* vol. 5 (Spring 1970), pp. 24–38.

Mlynarczyk, Francis A., Jr, 'An Empirical Study of Accounting Methods and Stock Prices', *Empirical Studies in Accounting, Selected Studies, 1969,* supplement to *Journal of Accounting Research,* vol. 7 (1969), pp. 63–81.

Mofsky, James S., *Blue Sky Restrictions On New Business Promotions,* Mathew Bender (New York 1971).

Mofsky, James S., 'Some Comments on the Expanding Definition of "Security"', *University of Miami Law Review,* vol. 27 (Spring and Summer 1973), pp. 395–406.

Morris, R.C., 'Evidence of the Impact of Inflation Accounting on Share Prices', *Accounting and Business Research,* vol. 18 (Spring 1975) pp. 82–90.

Morris, R.C. and Breakwell, G.H., 'Manipulation of Earnings Figures in the United Kingdom', *Accounting and Business Research,* vol. 19 (Summer 1975), pp. 177–84.

Moyle, John, *The Pattern of Ordinary Share Ownership, 1957–1970,* Cambridge University Press (London 1971).

Niederhoffer, Victor, and Regan, P.J., 'Earnings Changes, Analysts' Forecasts and Stock Prices', *Financial Analysts Journal,* vol. 28 (May–June 1972), pp. 65–71.

O'Donnell, John L., 'Relationships Between Reported Earnings and Stock Prices in the Electric Utility Industry', *Accounting Review,* vol. 40 (January 1965), pp. 135–43.

O'Donnell, John L., 'Further Observations on Reported Earnings and Stock Prices', *Accounting Review,* vol. 43, (July 1968), pp. 549–53.

Officer, R.R., 'The Variability of the Market Factor of the New York Stock Exchange', *Journal of Business,* vol. 46 (July 1973), pp. 434–53.

Pankoff, Lyn P., and Virgil Robert, 'Some Preliminary Findings from a Laboratory Experiment on the Usefulness of Financial Accounting Information to Security Analysts', *Empirical Research in Accounting, Selected Studies 1970,* supplement to *Journal of Accounting Research,* vol. 8, pp. 1–61.

Panel on Take-overs and Mergers, *The City Code on Take-overs and Mergers,* revised edition (London, February 1972).

Parrish, Michael E., *Securities Regulations and the New Deal,* Yale University Press (New Haven 1970).

Patz, Dennis H. and Boatsman, James R., 'Accounting Principle Formation in an Efficient Market Environment', *Journal of Accounting Research,* vol. 10 (Autumn 1972), pp. 392–403.

Pettit, R. Richardson, and Westerfield, Randolph, 'A Model of Capital Asset Risk', *Journal of Financial and Quantitative Analysis,* vol. 7 (March 1972), pp. 1649–88.

Picking, Bruce G., 'Auditing Standards', *Accounting and Business Research,* vol. 13 (Winter 1973), pp. 60–70.

Rappaport, Louis H., *SEC Accounting Practice and Procedures,* 3rd edition, Ronald Press (New York 1972).

Reiling, Henry B., and Taussig, Russell A., 'Recent Liability Cases – Implications for Accountants', *The Journal of Accountancy,* vol. 130 (September 1970), pp. 39–53.

Rich, Wiley D., *Legal Responsibility and Rights of Public Accountants,* American Institute Publishing Co. (New York 1935).

Ripley, William Z., (ed.), *Trusts, Pools and Corporations,* new edition, Ginn and Co. (New York 1916).

Ripley, William Z., *Main Street and Wall Street,* Little Brown and Co. (Boston 1927).

Rose, Harold, *Disclosure in Company Accounts,* 2nd edition, The Institute of Economic Affairs (London 1965).

Samuelson, Paul 'Proof that Properly Discounted Present Values of

Assets Vibrate Randomly', *The Bell Journal of Economics and Management Science,* vol. 4 (Autumn 1973), pp. 369–74.

Schiff, Michael, 'Accounting Tactics and the Theory of the Firm', *Journal of Accounting Research,* vol. 4 (Spring 1966), pp. 62–7.

Schneider, Carl W., 'Nits, Grits, and Soft Information in SEC Filings', *University of Pennsylvania Law Review,* vol. 121 (1972), pp. 254–305.

Schneider, Carl W., 'New Approaches to Disclosure in Registered Security Offerings: A Panel Discussion', *The Business Lawyer,* vol. 28 (January 1973), pp. 505–35.

Schotland, Roy A., 'Unsafe at Any Price: A Reply to Manne, Insiders Trading and the Stock Market', *Virginia Law Review,* vol. 53 (1967), pp. 1425–78.

Securities and Exchange Commission, *A 25-Year Summary of the Activities of the Securities and Exchange Commission* (Washington 1959).

Securities and Exchange Commission, *The Work of the Securities and Exchange Commission* (Washington, May 1967).

Securities and Exchange Commission, *Cost of Flotation of Registered Equity Issues, 1963–1965* (US Government Printing Office, Washington 1970).

Securities and Exchange Commission, *Annual Report, 1972* (38th Annual Report for the Fiscal Year Ended June 30th) (US Government Printing Office, Washington, published in 1973).

Securities and Exchange Commission, *SEC 1973* (39th Annual Report of the Securities and Exchange Commission for the Fiscal Year Ended June 30th) (US Government Printing Office, Washington 1974).

'Shareholders exhibit lack of interest in 10-K data', *The Journal of Accountancy,* vol. 138 (November 1974), pp. 20, 22, 24.

Sharpe, William F., 'Mutual Fund Performance', *Journal of Business,* vol. 39 (January 1966), pp. 119–38.

Shefsky, Lloyd E., and Schwartz, Edward J., 'Disclosure and Reporting Under SEC's ASR No. 115', *Journal of Accountancy,* vol. 136 (September 1973), pp. 53–61.

Siedler, Lee J., 'Improving Accountants and Accounting: Lessons from the British', *The Accountant's Magazine* (September 1969), pp. 489 *et seq.*

Sloan, L.H., *Everyman and His Common Stocks,* McGraw-Hill (New York 1931), Whittlesey House (London 1931).

Sommer, A.A., Jr, 'New Approaches to Disclosure in Registered Security Offerings: A Panel Discussion,' *The Business Lawyer,* vol. 28 (January 1973), pp. 505–35.

Stamp, Edward, and Marley, Christopher, *Accounting Principles and the City Code: The Case for Reform,* Butterworth (London, 1970).

Stigler, George J., 'Public Regulation of the Securities Markets', *The Journal of Business,* vol. 37 (April 1964), pp. 117–42.

Stock Exchange, *The Admission of Securities to Listing,* Offices of the Council of the Stock Exchange (London, May 1975).

Sunder, Shyam, 'Stock Price and Risk Related to Accounting Changes in Inventory Valuation', *Accounting Review,* vol. 50 (April 1975), pp. 305–15.

Ultramares Corp. v. Touche, 255 N.Y. 170, 179–80, 174 N.E. 441, 444[1931].

Zeff, Stephen A., *Forging Accounting Principles in Five Countries: A History and Analysis of Trends,* Stipes Publishing Co. (Champaign, Illinois 1972).

Index

Some references are to note indices; where the reader cannot find the subject on the page given, he should turn to the notes at the end of the chapter for the necessary lead.

The author

Professor George J. Benston studied at Queens College (NYC), New York University and the University of Chicago for his BA, MBA and Ph.D. respectively, and became a Certified Public Accountant in 1955. From 1962 to 1966 he lectured at the University of Chicago, then took up his present position as Professor of Finance and Accounting at the Graduate School of Management in the University of Rochester. He was Visiting Professor at the London Graduate School of Business Studies and London School of Economics in 1973.